The True Origins of World War II
The Missing Pieces of the Puzzle

By Tigran Khalatyan, PhD

Editor: Dan Crissman

Tigran Hobbies / IngramSpark

New Jersey, USA

Copyright © 2021 by **Tigran Khalatyan**

Rebuffing Anglo-American stereotypes about good democracies and evil dictatorships *The True Origins of World War II* analyzes the period between the two World Wars from the perspective of geopolitics. From the link between anti-Semitism and anti-Communism to the unveiling the dirty secrets of appeasement *The True Origins of World War II* helps to find the missing pieces of the puzzle!

Tigran Khalatyan / Tigran Hobbies / IngramSpark

Editor: Dan Crissman
Cover: SelfPubBookCovers.com/Island
Book Layout © 2017 BookDesignTemplates.com

The True Origins of World War II / Tigran Khalatyan. -- 1st ed.
Paperback ISBN 978-0-578-81245-8
eBook ISBN 978-0-578-81246-5

To the memory of my grandfather who won World War II

"There never was a war in history easier to prevent by timely action than the one which has just desolated such great areas of the globe."

—WINSTON CHURCHILL

Contents

Author's Preface 1
   15 Steps towards World War II 4
   Key Leaders of World War II 6
Prologue: A Clash of Perspectives 7
   The Anglo-American Perspective 10
   Understanding World War II 14
   Double Standards 17
   Conclusion 20
Part I The War to End All Wars 1900-1919 21
Chapter 1: The Age of Empires 23
   Democracies or Empires? 25
   The Great Game in Asia 32
   The Great Game in Europe 35
   Conclusion 39
Chapter 2: World War I 41
   The July Crisis 44
   The Great War 53
   The February Revolution 55
   For Democracy or For Money? 57
   The Bolshevik Revolution 64
   The German Revolution 67
   "War is Peace" 68
   Conclusion 72
Chapter 3: The Victory of Democracy 73

    The Treaty of Versailles 75
    The Victory of the Bolsheviks 79
    Separatism versus Self Determination......................... 84
    The Nazi Response to Bolshevism 86
    The Secret of Isolationism 90
    Conclusion 96

Part II A Twenty-Year Armistice 1920-1937 99

Chapter 4: The Invisible Hand.. 101
    The Great Depression 103
    Communism vs. Capitalism 107
    The Rise of Fascism 112
    The Jewish Question 115
    Conclusion 121

Chapter 5: The Glory of Adolf Hitler 123
    The Rise of Hitler 125
    Why the West Supported Hitler 132
    Covert Support for Hitler 144
    Funding the German War Machine 148
    Conclusion 154

Chapter 6: Countdown to War 155
    The Start of Japanese Expansion 158
    A Period of Change 162
    The Ethiopian Precedent, ... 166
    The Spanish Civil War 168
    Conclusion 171

Part III Peace in Our Time 1937-1939 173

Chapter 7: The Second Sino-Japanese War 175
    A Century of Humiliation 177
    The Limit of Endurance 179

    The Battle of Shanghai 181
    The Failure of Collective Security 183
    The Rape of Nanking 187
    Stalemate 188
    Foreign Intervention 189
    The Aftermath 191
    Conclusion 192

Chapter 8: The Munich Pact 193
    Appeasement 196
    Halifax - Hitler Deal 199
    Anschluss 202
    The Sudeten Crisis 206
    Hitler Raises the Stakes 211
    The Munich Conference 216
    Conclusion 222

Chapter 9: The Sudden End of Appeasement 223
    Kristallnacht 225
    The Birmingham Speech 227
    Carpatho-Ukraine 237
    Conclusion 244

Chapter 10: The Non-Aggression Treaty 247
    The 18th Congress of the Communist Party 249
    The Polish Question 258
    The Leningrad Conference 262
    The Whaling Conference 264
    The Molotov-Ribbentrop Pact 266
    Conclusion 270

Conclusion to The True Origins of World War II 273

References 277

Author's Preface

World War II, the most destructive conflict in human history, still influences our lives and fascinates our imagination. At multiple points during the war, the fate of all nations hung in precarious balance. Winston Churchill worried about the possibility of "the abyss of a new Dark Age made more sinister, and perhaps more protracted, by the lights of perverted science." In Western cultures, World War II has long been cast as a necessary struggle of good versus evil. In reality, the story is far more complicated, and the terrible cost need never have been borne in the first place.

World War I, billed as "the war to end all wars" by its proponents, came to a conclusion in November 1918. Appalled by the scale of the senseless destruction, the victors pledged to make every effort to support lasting peace. The primary aggressor, Germany, was disarmed, forbidden to have an air force and submarines; its army could not exceed 100,000 men. The Austro-Hungarian, Ottoman and Russian empires collapsed and the greatest democracies—the United States, Great Britain and France—became the dominate world powers. The League of Nations was formed to peacefully negotiate disputes between sovereign states, supposedly eliminating any cause for war.

However just a decade later, in 1929, the Great Depression that began on Wall Street sent shockwaves around the world, and the forces of the imperialist conquest were reactivated. Japan invaded China, Italy invaded Ethiopia, and in Germany, a wicked man rose to power.

Adolf Hitler's goals were well known and openly stated: with the force of arms, Germany was going to not only avenge her defeat, but also conquer more territory to gain Lebensraum ("living space") for the Aryan race. Given the fact that Nazi Germany was under the watchful eye of the great democracies, as well as the reality that her army was smaller and weaker than even the armies of Czechoslovakia or Poland, one could only laugh at Hitler's ambitions. Yet in just six years from his ascent to power in 1933, Hitler managed to build a modern army, air force and navy to rival the greatest military powers in the world.

> *"How could it be, Soviet leader Josef Stalin wondered in 1939, "that non aggressive countries with vast opportunities, so easily and without resistance abandoned their positions and their obligations in favor of the aggressors?"*

Echoing his wartime comrade Churchill confessed in 1945:

> *"There never was a war in history easier to prevent by timely action than the one which has just desolated such great areas of the globe. It could have been prevented, in my belief, without the firing of a single shot, and Germany might be powerful, prosperous and honored today; but no one would listen and one by one we were all sucked into the awful whirlpool."*

Why?

That is the question this book seeks to answer. In the pages that follow, we will explore the origins and the course of World War II free from dominant Anglo-American stereotypes, like the absurd idea that the democracies let Hitler rearm because they wanted to save peace. We will prove beyond the reasonable doubt that World War II was not an ideological conflict between the great democracies and fascist dictatorships; it was the same old geopolitical struggle for global domination, a war of imperialist conquest for some and a war for national liberation for the others.

This book will not hide in the dreamland of good democracies and evil dictatorships. Instead it will expose all the facts that remain hidden from most of the population of in Western countries. The result will be a truly global picture of World War II that not only explains the past but also predicts the future.

I consider this book to be my own modest contribution in keeping the memory of those who sacrificed their lives to save the world from the great evil. We owe them an everlasting debt.

Tigran Khalatyan

15 Steps towards World War II

June 28, 1919
Treaty of Versailles, the official end of World War I

October 29, 1929
Great Depression starts in the United States

January 30, 1933
Hitler comes to power

January 26, 1934
German-Polish non-aggression pact

June 18, 1935
Anglo-German naval treaty

March 7, 1936
Germany is allowed to re-occupy Rhineland

July 17, 1936
Start of Spanish Civil War, "a dress rehearsal of World War II"

The True Origins of World War II

July 7, 1937
Japan attacks China, beginning the war in Pacific

March 12, 1938
Germany is allowed to annex Austria

September 29, 1938
England and France appease Nazi Germany
at the Munich conference

November 9, 1938
Kristallnacht, a pogrom against Jews in Nazi Germany

December 6, 1938
French-German pact

March 15, 1939
Germany is allowed to occupy Czechoslovakia

June 7, 1939
German-Latvian and German-Estonian non-aggression pacts

August 23, 1939
Soviet-German non-aggression pact

Tigran Khalatyan

Key Leaders of World War II

ALLIES

Joseph Stalin (1878-1953)
Leader of the Soviet Union

Franklin D. Roosevelt (1882-1945)
President of the United States

Neville Chamberlain (1869-1940)
Prime Ministers of Great Britain in 1937-1940

Winston Churchill (1874-1965)
Prime Ministers of Great Britain in 1940-1945

Chiang Kai-Shek (1896-1974)
Leader of China

AXIS

Adolf Hitler (1889-1945)
Fuhrer of Germany

Emperor Hirohito (1901-1989)
Demi-God Emperor of Japan

Benito Mussolini (1883-1945)
Duce of Italy

Prologue:
A Clash of Perspectives

Elbe Day, 25 April 1945

2nd Lt. William Robertson (U.S. Army) and Lt. Alexander Silvashko (Red Army) celebrate the meeting of Soviet and American armies in the middle of Germany in Torgau at the Elbe River.

The forgotten truth. In World War II, Russians and Americans were allies, even friends. Together, they defeated Nazi Germany.

Pop Quiz

Which two countries were the main antagonists of World War II?

    a) The United States and Nazi Germany

    b) Great Britain and Nazi Germany

    c) The Soviet Union and Nazi Germany

> *"The Red Army celebrates its twenty-seventh anniversary amid triumphs which have won the unstinted applause of their allies and have sealed the doom of German militarism. Future generations will acknowledge their debt to the Red Army as unreservedly as do we who have lived to witness these proud achievements. I ask you, the great leader of a great army, to salute them from me today, on the threshold of final victory."*
>
> Personal message for Marshall Stalin from Mr. Churchill. Received on February 23, 1945.

Let me ask you a question: Which countries fought in World War II? Who won? Who lost?

Most Americans would probably say that the United States and Great Britain "saved democracy" by "defeating dictators" in Germany and Japan. Those who are more educated might say that the Axis powers—Germany, Italy and Japan—lost the war to the Allied forces of the United States, Great Britain, France, Australia, Canada and others.

Neither of those answers come close to the truth. Until recently, in Western democracies you would almost have to be a trained historian to know that the central conflict of the war, with the key battles and by far the most casualties, was between Nazi Germany and Communist Russia. As a matter of fact, Russians killed four out of the five German soldiers who died in the battle.

In the modern world, it takes only seconds to find information on the internet; all sorts of data are freely available. Since World War II is the pivotal event of modern history, it would seem that everyone should know the basic facts about it. Yet, surprisingly, this is not the case. Indeed, whenever the complicated history of World War II is summarized for public use, it's

Tigran Khalatyan

truncated to fit the Anglo-American point of view and Western ideological dogmas. Mass media, popular books, school textbooks, movies, and museums each take their part in this revisionism. This book is a direct challenge to those efforts.

The Anglo-American Perspective

It's understandable that Americans and Britons are more interested in their side of the story, but the consistent Anglocentrism displayed in conventional narratives of World War II often destroys any sense of proportion. In American classrooms, Patton's slapping incident (or when he peed in the Rhine) may be described in greater detail than some of the most pivotal battles fought in Russia or China. Consider this paragraph from a U.S. school textbook History of Our World, published by Prentice Hall, that my daughters used to study, devoted to the end of the war in Europe:

> *"Victory in Europe. Following campaigns in North Africa and Italy, the Allies opened a western front against the weakened Germans. On June 6, 1944, Allied warships carrying 156,000 troops landed at Normandy, on the northern coast of France. Known as D-Day, the Normandy landing was the start of a massive Allied campaign eastward. Within six months, the Allied armies had reached Germany. After one last attempt for success in December 1944, known as the Battle of the Bulge, the German army collapsed. The Allies declared victory in Europe on May 8, 1945."*

If you see nothing wrong with the above paragraph, you are like most Americans. In fact, the German army collapsed not after the Battle of the Bulge, but after the Russians took Berlin, which prompted Hitler's suicide. If we wrote about the 2003 Invasion

The True Origins of World War II

of Iraq in the same fashion, it would look like this: "British troops invaded Iraq in 2003. After they took Basra, Iraqi resistance collapsed," without a word about American fighting or how they took Baghdad.

If you still think that I am exaggerating the problem, you might be surprised to learn that the above paragraph was actually improved in the next edition of the textbook. It now reads like this:

> "Victory in Europe. Following campaigns in North Africa and Italy, the Allies opened a western front against the weakened Germans. On June 6, 1944, Allied warships carrying 156,000 troops landed at Normandy, on the northern coast of France. Known as D-Day, the Normandy landing was the start of a massive Allied campaign from the west. Meanwhile, Russian troops continued their push from the east. Within six months, the Allied armies had reached Germany from both directions. The Germans made one last push back against the Allies in the west in December 1944, known as the Battle of the Bulge. The Germans then desperately tried to defend Germany. In late April, Russian troops entered Berlin, the German capital. The Allies declared victory in Europe on May 8, 1945."

This version is much more accurate, although it still presents mostly the American side of the story. (I'd like to think that the improvement was made because I reported the problem to the publisher.)

The above example is by no means an isolated incident. Here is how World War II is described in the government brochure given to those who apply for US citizenship:

> "World War II began in 1939 when Germany invaded Poland. France and Great Britain then declared war on Germany. Germany had alliances with Italy and Japan,

> *and together they formed the Axis powers. The United States entered World War II in 1941, after the Japanese attacked Pearl Harbor, Hawaii. The United States joined France and Great Britain as the Allied powers and led the 1944 invasion of France known as D-Day. The liberation of Europe from German power was completed by May 1945. World War II did not end until Japan surrendered in August 1945."*

This paragraph actually reflects pretty well how World War II is usually presented for an average American. As we can see, the two key participants—Russia and China—are not even mentioned.

Accounts leaving out these two nations are utterly ahistorical. The first four Allied powers that signed the Declaration by United Nations on January 1, 1942, were the United States, Great Britain, the Soviet Union, and China. Likewise, two of the seven famous *Why We Fight* documentaries commissioned by the U.S. government during the war were specifically dedicated to the fighting in Russia and China.

However, after the war, history was rewritten to diminish the contribution of the powers on the other side of the new Cold War ideological divide. The basic premise of postwar Anglo-American propaganda could be rephrased in the form of the motto of sheep from George Orwell's *Animal Farm*: "Democracy is good, dictatorship is bad." The origins of World War II were also squeezed into democracy-dictatorship paradigm, as shown in the following excerpt from another U.S. school textbook:

> *"After World War I, Americans were threatened by yet another war as dictators in Europe and Asia threatened democracy. The United States would defeat the threat by winning World War II."*

The True Origins of World War II

Here, the United States plays the role of the hero who saves damsel of the democracy from the clutches of evil dictators. Never mind that the key U.S. ally, the Soviet Union, was an "evil empire" that also expanded the sphere of its influence after Germany's surrender, spoiling the alleged victory of democracy.

Many of the common narratives of World War II in the West present this sort of distorted view of the reality. Ignoring Russia is the obvious problem; the key role Russia played in the war is impossible to ignore. When Russia is mentioned in the Anglo-American perspective, it's usually classified as a totalitarian dictatorship, standing in the same row as Nazi Germany and Fascist Italy. Stalin's purges of the 1930s are compared to the Holocaust. Vilifying 1939 German-Soviet Non-Aggression pact, Soviet Union is often labeled an ally of Nazi Germany and another instigator of World War II that later switched to the democratic camp only because of Hitler's betrayal.

Here is an example from "a good basic book on World War II" by Alan Axelrod that explicitly ties Communist Russia with the Axis:

> *"The second World War began with conflicts of nationality and ideology in central-eastern Europe. Fueled by the imperialist, expansionist ambitions of dictators – above all, those of Adolf Hitler, but also of Joseph Stalin and Benito Mussolini (soon to be augmented by the militarists of Japan) – the outbreak of war was enabled by what must be described as the collective exhaustion of the democratic powers, which could not summon the strength of will to oppose the Axis."*

From this perspective, the presence of Russia among the democratic winners of World War II looks as an anomaly that should be somehow fixed. The competing tactics of ignoring Russia on the one hand and vilifying Russia on the other happily coexist, each serving its purpose in the ideological battle to rewrite the war's history.

What is wrong with grouping Communist Russia and Nazi Germany together as the fellow totalitarian dictatorships? When asked this question, Dr. Nataliya Narotchnitskaya usually answers that one can also relate koala bear and caterpillar because they both eat eucalyptus leaves. We could also relate Hitler and Stalin because both of them had mustache.

Jokes aside, it boils down to the question: can the democracy-dictatorship paradigm explain the origins, the course, or the outcome of World War II?

Understanding World War II

Stepping outside the conventional Anglo-American perspective, one can distinguish three stages of World War II. In the first preliminary stage before 1939, Nazi Germany, being supported and appeased by Western democracies, was preparing for the war with Russia. In the second unexpected stage, 1939-1941, Nazi Germany went to the war with the West, while temporarily having good relations with Russia. In the third and final stage, 1941-1945, Russia and the great Western democracies fought together against Nazi Germany and other Axis powers.

The democracy-dictatorship paradigm can hardly explain even the second stage. Numerous distortions are required to make it fit the actual history of World War II more generally. In the first stage of the war, the democracies supported Hitler. In the second stage, they were defeated by him. In the third stage, they passed leadership of the war effort to the "bloody tyrant" Stalin. It is hard to see any argument for the supremacy of democracy in that telling.

The True Origins of World War II

Moreover, if everybody agrees that Adolf Hitler headed the forces of evil in World War II, than his main adversary should be the leader of the forces of good. That would cast Joseph Stalin in a heroic role, however shocking it sounds. Indeed, announcing Hitler's death his successor Admiral Doenitz was very clear about who the main enemy of the Nazis was:

> *"German men and women, soldiers of the armed forces: Our Fuehrer, Adolf Hitler, has fallen. In the deepest sorrow and respect the German people bow. At an early date he had recognized the frightful danger of Bolshevism and dedicated his existence to this struggle. At the end of his struggle, of his unswerving straight road of life, stands his hero's death in the capital of the German Reich. His life has been one single service for Germany. His activity in the fight against the Bolshevik storm flood concerned not only Europe but the entire civilized world. Der Fuehrer has appointed me to be his successor. Fully conscious of the responsibility, I take over the leadership of the German people at this fateful hour. It is my first task to save Germany from destruction by the advancing Bolshevist enemy. For this aim alone the military struggle continues. As far and for so long as achievement of this aim is impeded by the British and the Americans, we shall be forced to carry on our defensive fight against them as well. Under such conditions, however, the Anglo-Americans will continue the war not for their own peoples but solely for the spreading of Bolshevism in Europe."*

If you don't know, Bolshevism is how Russian Communism used to be called. As we can see, the only real enemy of Nazi Germany was Communist Russia, and not the British or Americans. According to Nazi logic, the democracies would "continue the war" against the Russian communist threat. And indeed, Doenitz was right; the Cold War repeated much of the Nazi anti-communist rhetoric and even employed former Nazis for the covert actions against Soviet Union.

The anti-Russian rhetoric went as far as to suggest that countries liberated by Russia "exchanged one tyranny for another" or "[Polish] citizens who survived went on to endure a lifetime of occupation, five years under Nazis, and more than forty under the Soviets". Defying common-sense the democracy-dictatorship paradigm cannot distinguish between Warsaw bombed to rubble by Nazis, and the Warsaw restored in her prewar beauty by the communist government. While watching movie "the Pianist" about the Holocaust survivor in Poland, the proponents of the paradigm can see no difference between the horrors of Nazi occupation and the happy end under "Soviet occupation".

In this book, we will examine the real history of World War II. Geopolitics can actually tie all three stages of World War II together. Cold-blooded national self-interests and the ongoing struggle for the world domination can explain more about the history of World War II than any ideology.

While geopolitics helps us to understand the real forces behind the historical events, it cannot explain the moral dilemmas of humanity. Despite all the fruits of the civilization and the lessons supposedly learned from history, suffering and violence are constant features of human society. Everybody agrees that Hitler was evil, but unfortunately, the covert operations, wars of aggression, racism, genocide and concentration camps are still used in the world—by democracies and dictatorships alike.

Woodrow Wilson's idea that supremacy of democracy means no wars turned out to be very far from reality. World War I was won by the democracies, yet just in 20 years they allowed the unfolding of World War II. The Cold War was also won by the democracy only a quarter of century ago, yet as the tensions in the world grow again, we can only wonder if we are heading to Cold War II—or straight to World War III.

Double Standards

Sometimes it's difficult to comprehend how much ideology exist in the everyday lives of the citizens of so-called democratic countries and how many ideologically motivated lies they get from the news or history books. World War II history is no exception.

On the daily basis, it is falsely assumed that the democracies want to save peace, while dictators enjoy waging wars. In what we call the double standards, the similar actions either condemned or excused depending on who is responsible. The heated TV debates about secondary matters hide the imposed opinions.

For example, when American media debates should the military force or sanctions and diplomacy be used against "Assad's regime" it actually hides from the public the alternative opinion that the United States should support Assad as the fighter of Radical Islamists and protector of Christians in Syria. The "different point of views" debated on "free" media are not so different after all.

In regard to "double standards" we should consider the question of balance between the freedom and security. There is famous quote of Benjamin Franklin "Those who surrender freedom for security will not have, nor do they deserve, either one." Nicely said. However real life is always the compromise between the extremes. There cannot be neither absolute freedom nor absolute security.

The infamous Guantanamo Bay detention center where people were held indefinitely without the trial was long criticized for being a blatant violation of human rights; it was even called "Gulag of our times". Still it's open for more than a decade because of American national security interests. As a matter of fact, in the United States the principles of democracy and freedom are often sacrificed when national security is threatened.

Yet when Americans talk about "human rights violations" in other countries, they are never concerned about national security of those countries. The reason for the double standards is very simple in this case. While Americans do care about the United States national security, at the same time they want to *undermine* the national security of their opponents. As a result, there can be violent armed coup in some country, which American media and politicians call "peaceful protest". This is exactly what happened when in 2014 President Obama supported extremists in Kiev, many of them openly fascist, who shot and threw Molotov cocktails on riot police, with the hypocritical statement "Respect for the right of peaceful protest –- including on the Maidan –- is essential."

Indeed, the principle of double standards often applies when the democracy raises voice against an autocratic or dictatorial power. There can be great cry about need for the democracy in some country behind which we see the selfish interests to undermine the country and grab its resources. "Spreading of democracy" in Iraq, Libya and Syria may suddenly lead to the rise of Islamic State.

Beware of foreigners who want only good for your country by liberating it from autocracy, dictatorship or communism. Like Wilson who wanted to "liberate" Germans from their autocracy in World War I or Hitler who tried to "liberate" Russians from communism in World War II.

It's also important to understand that propaganda content can change over time, while propaganda goals remain the same. For example, at the beginning of XX century, prominent Jewish American banker and businessman Jacob Schiff (1847-1920) had started anti-Russian campaign blaming Tsar for the discrimination of Jews and provided critical funds for Japan's military, the enemy of Russia in Russo-Japanese war. For his efforts, Schiff was awarded the Japanese Orders in 1905 and 1907. There is a curious historical parallel between Schiff and another even more prominent American industrialist and carmaker Henry Ford (1863-1947). While Schiff was Jewish activist, Ford on the other hand was the vehement anti-Semite. In 1920-s Ford published anti-Semitic newspaper in which he accused Jews in power grab in Communist Russia. Ford was one of the sources of inspiration and support for Hitler and his followers who used alleged Jewish conspiracy as an excuse to attack Russia. Like Schiff, Ford was decorated for his efforts. In 1938 he was awarded Grand Cross of the German Eagle, the highest medal Nazi Germany could give to a foreigner. Despite having opposite views about Jews, both Schiff and Ford represented American business that funded Russian enemies. Curiously one day Russia was attacked for discriminating Jews and another for having too many Jews in the government.

Ronald Reagan called the Soviet Union "an evil empire" on the grounds that communists don't believe in God. Well, after collapse of the Soviet Union religion revived its status as one of the pillars of the Russian state. Did Russia stop to be an "evil empire"? No. Instead western media praised Pussy Riot punks as the fighters against anti-liberal Russian Orthodox Church.

We have to understand this. There are always some human rights issues in any country, real or exaggerated. And there are important geopolitical threats such as growing Russian might. No matter Russia discriminates Jews or not, Russia is godless or too orthodox, if Russian power is growing Russian enemies has to be funded and western propaganda has to present Russia as a legitimate target.

Tigran Khalatyan

Conclusion

Ideology, double standards and narrow national perspectives may greatly distort history of World War II.

To unveil the real history of the war we are going to analyze it from the point of view of geopolitics and common sense, rebuffing some common western myths in the process.

Part I

The War to End All Wars

1900-1919

At the dawn of 20th century, the world reached the stage of Imperialism when a few European powers plus the United States had divided the world between them. Almost all third world countries were either colonized or belonged to someone's sphere of influence; there were no markets and resources left for grab. The struggle to redraw the world map on the global scale by major imperialist powers would lead to the First World War.

After four years of the bloody carnage the great democracies, England, France, and the United States won the First World War. Since the world now supposed to be "safe for democracy" everybody anticipated the lasting peace. However, the seeds of the Second World War have been already sown...

Chapter 1:
The Age of Empires

"Let's sit by the sea and wait for the weather!"
Russian propaganda poster at the beginning
of Russo-Japanese war. February 28, 1904

Mighty Russia, represented by a Cossack (left), is ready for an attack by Japan, shown here as a diminutive officer holding a sword. It would be understood by the intended audience that Japan was backed by England (John Bull) and the United States (Uncle Sam). While overestimating Russian strength, the poster correctly describes the geopolitical situation and the favorite Anglo-American tactic of the waging a war by proxy.

Pop Quiz

What is the most peaceful form of government?

    a) Democracy

    b) Dictatorship

    c) There is no peaceful form of government

> *"Strange as it may seem, England, being to the core monarchical and conservative at home, in her foreign relations always acted as the patroness of the most demagogic aspirations, always indulging in all popular movements aimed at weakening the monarchical principle."*
>
> Peter Durnovo. Report to the Czar, 1914.

Most Americans are taught that democracies seek peace, while dictators wage wars. As U.S. President Woodrow Wilson observed, "A steadfast concert for peace can never be maintained except by a partnership of democratic nations. No autocratic government could be trusted to keep faith within it or observe its covenants."

The truth, however, is that both democratic and authoritarian regimes may have expansionist and aggressive ambitions. After all, the most successful and powerful imperialists of the modern history were the great democracies—Great Britain, France, and the United States. Autocratic empires such as Russia and Japan operated in essentially the same manner as their democratic counterparts.

Democracies or Empires?

At the dawn of 20th century, there were only five major power centers in the world. *Great Britain* had the most colonies around the world and the most powerful navy. *France* was also a great colonial power, second only to Britain in terms of wealth and reach. Continental *Russia* spread across vast areas of northern Eurasia and had fast-growing population. The *United States*, another huge continental country, had the whole South American continent as its sphere of influence, while the recently annexed Hawaii and Philippines were its outposts in the Pacific. The fifth main power, *Germany,* lacked colonies but had the best army, great science, and fast-developing industry.

Of these five major powers, who would you say were the "good guys"? Who were the "bad guys"? The answer is not that simple as some may think. Dominant opinion always held that the "democratic" England, France, and the United States were morally superior to the "oppressive" and even "barbarian" Russia, while "civilized" but "autocratic" Germany fell somewhere in between.

We may expect the "good guys" to have respected human rights and wanted to save peace, while the "bad guys" were racist aggressors. Yet in that respect, we can see that so-called "civilized democracies" were actually the leading world racists and the most successful aggressors. While British or Americans like to think of themselves as the people of civilization and democracy, others around the world often see them as imperialists and aggressors. How else do you think they got their empires? Imperialists at the time believed strongly in white supremacy and saw their colonial expansions as a mission to bring "civilization" to "third world" countries. This thin justification allowed Western democracies to consistently suck resources out of less developed nations for their own use.

The British Empire was the best at subjugating and ruthlessly exploiting peoples around the world. India, for example, was run by a corporation called British East India Company for more than a century. The huge nation with rich ancient culture was reduced to the status of an English business. Another great example of Britain bringing "civilization" was the Opium Wars with China. When the Chinese emperor forbade the sale of British opium—which had turned millions of Chinese into drug addicts—British forces invaded. With Chinese cities in flames,

The True Origins of World War II

Chinese government acquiesced to the opium trade and was forced to pay a huge restitution and cede control of Hong Kong.

Americans also had long history of waging the wars of aggression. In 1899 while the British were plotting a war for control of gold mines in South Africa, the Americans were busy trying to subdue a local resistance in the Philippines. U.S. Senator Albert J. Beveridge captured the national mood well in a speech on the Senate floor in 1900, which he addressed to President William McKinley:

> "Mr. President, the times call for candor. The Philippines are ours forever, 'territory belonging to the United States,' as the Constitution calls them. And just beyond the Philippines are China's illimitable markets. We will not retreat from either. We will not repudiate our duty in the archipelago. We will not abandon our opportunity in the Orient. We will not renounce our part in the mission of our race, trustee, under God, of the civilization of the world. And we will move forward to our work, not howling out regrets like slaves whipped to their burdens but with gratitude for a task worthy of our strength and Thanksgiving to Almighty God that He has marked us as His chosen people, henceforth to lead in the regeneration of the world."

The Philippine-American War would end two years later, though the U.S. would retain a strong military presence in the region for the next four decades.

Apart from direct occupation, the United States also routinely installed puppet governments in the countries of Latin America and the South Pacific. The humiliating term "Banana Republic" could have been applied to quite a few governments that were controlled and, if needed, forcefully overthrown by the U.S. government to profit corporations like the infamous United Fruit Company.

Tigran Khalatyan

For example, in 1893, in one of so many similar acts, Americans overthrew the Hawaiian monarchy. Five years later, they annexed the country. In 1903, when the Colombian government refused to give up the rights to area surrounding the recently completed Panama Canal, Americans gave support to the local separatists. Following a coup, the newly independent state of Panama and gave the United States the rights to build and indefinitely administer the Panama Canal Zone and its defenses. The American Naval Base at Guantanamo Bay, Cuba—as well as its infamous prison—have been in active service since 1903 because the United States "leased" it indefinitely in the wake an invasion of the island during the Spanish-American War. The Cuban government has long demanded that the U.S. vacate the territory, but instead the Treasury simply sends a yearly "rent check" for the never-prorated funny sum of $4,085 to the Cuban government. Americans may not realize how much respect communist Cuba gained in Latin America because it could successfully defy the might of the United States.

In contrast to Britain and America, turn-of-the-century Russia seems rather tame. While Russia was also expanding by conquering its neighbors, she did not exterminate native populations, nor did she not treat those countries like inferior colonies to exploit. Newly acquired provinces and their peoples were simply absorbed into the Russian Empire. Christian Georgia, suffering from persecution by its powerful Muslim neighbors, actually begged the Russian Czar for protection. What is today modern Armenia was actually a small part of the ancient Armenia that was saved by incorporation into Russian Empire; elsewhere Armenians were either dispersed or outright exterminated. The sharp contrast between white "master race" and subjugated people of color in the democratic empires, was not so sharp in the multi-ethnic and multi-sectarian society of

Russian empire, although of course Ethnic Russians still clearly held much more power and prestige than the newly absorbed peoples.

Indeed, even before the modern era, the "civilized" West was not superior to Russia on the question of human rights. For example, unlike in Europe, the death penalty was relatively rare in Russian Empire, and there were long periods of time when it was banned. Even so, stories about the cruel and barbarous Russians circulated in the West for centuries. Perhaps those rumors started in the 16th century, when Russian Czar Ivan the Terrible (1530-1584) executed many members of his opposition while expanding his country. It is odd, though, that English King Henry VIII (1491-1547) did not acquire a similar "terrible" moniker despite the fact that his executions were no less cruel or widespread—including two of his six wives. The French were no better, as the brutal St. Bartholomew's Day massacre on August 24, 1572 shows. In one day, the French government slaughtered more people, including wedding guests, than Ivan the Terrible executed during his entire reign.

Despite this, unjustified attitudes about "Russian barbarity" have continued ever since, even while "civilized" Europeans were burning women as witches and hanging citizens for pickpocketing. Up until the beginning of the 19th century, under the so-called "Bloody Code," 220 crimes in England were punishable by death.

Americans could be proud that they established democracy and had a constitution while Russia was still an absolute monarchy. However, the celebrated U.S. democracy allowed both slavery and the extermination of Native Americans. Many of the vaunted Founding Fathers were in fact slave-owners. What kind of democracy is that?

Americans in general tend to always be proud of themselves. They are proud of Abraham Lincoln for liberating slaves and of Rosa Parks for refusing to give up her sit in the bus. They forget that by having slavery in the second half of 19th century and segregation in the second half of 20th century, they looked barbarians in the eyes of the rest of the world. As a matter of fact, Russian serfdom was abolished in 1861, four years before slavery was abolished in the United States in 1865, and there never were segregated buses in Russia.

By the way, there are curious historical parallels between Russian Czar Alexander II (1818-1881) who abolished serfdom and U.S President Lincoln (1809-1865) who abolished slavery. During American Civil War (1861-1865) Alexander II send Russian fleet to American shores thus preventing British intervention into the civil war on the side of Confederation. Alexander II also sold Alaska to the United States in 1867. And sadly enough both great statesmen were assassinated.

At the dawn of the 20th century, democratic countries could not claim moral superiority, but they still used liberal ideas to undermine their autocratic rivals. Many of the powerful Western states actually sponsored revolutionary movements in Russia and other countries. The first big success of Russian revolutionaries was the assassination of Alexander II, the Czar who actually started democratic reforms, in 1881. Just before his assassination, Alexander II proposed the establishment of a parliament in Russia. After the Czar's gruesome death in a carriage bombing, his outraged son Alexander III cracked down on revolutionaries and ended democratic reforms.

Who could support and fund Russian revolutionaries at the time? Well, the number one geopolitical rival of Russia was England, the great organizer of revolutions. Other great powers could have been involved too. Although democratic countries

The True Origins of World War II

always used wars as a tool of foreign politics, wars are costly, and covert operations present the great alternative. Assassinations, coups, or even revolutions are so much cheaper than wars, but bring similar results.

Starting with the first communist Karl Marx (1818-1883), revolutionaries always found safe haven in London. Karl Marx's idea to destroy capitalism was supposed to hit the most advanced industrial countries like England and the United States, but somehow it detonated in Russia instead. In fact, the Russian Communist Party was actually founded in London in 1903. London gave refuge to criminal revolutionaries too. One classic example was Maxim Litvinov (1876-1951, born Meir Wallach), the future famous diplomat of Communist Russia. In 1907, Litvinov was involved in a daring bank robbery in Russia, designed to finance arms trading from the West. Unfortunately for the revolutionaries, the captured bank notes had such a large denomination that it was not easy to cash them. In 1908, when Litvinov tried to cash some of the notes in France, he was arrested. Instead of being deported back to Russia, however, he ended up in London, where he lived in safety and continued his struggle against Russian autocracy.

The exporting of revolutions has continued until today. Remember when, in 2005, U.S. Secretary of State Condoleezza Rice stated, "it is time to abandon the excuses that are made to avoid the hard work of democracy," signaling the start of the Arab Spring? As I write these lines, Americans are busy sponsoring yet another revolution in the Ukraine. Then and now, powerful nations have not needed any excuses to support terrorists, nationalists, communists, fascists, radical Islamists—you name it—in the glorious task of toppling "regimes." A bloodbath is sure to follow in most cases, but it is easy to make sacrifices for "the hard work of democracy" when it is not your people who are going to suffer. Of course, any given revolution in any given country has to be caused not only by external but by internal factors as well, and it can bring not only destruction, but the progress as well. However, failing to analyze a revolution in the context of the global geopolitical struggle means failing to see the big picture. Selfish interests often lie behind the ideals of peace and freedom.

The titanic struggle that culminated into World War II started at the beginning of the 20th century as casual international rivalries. Germany and Russia had conflict of interests in Eastern Europe, while France wanted revenge over Germany for their humiliating defeat in 1871. As a result, France and Russia entered a military alliance aimed against Germany. Meanwhile, Germany challenged Great Britain by building a powerful navy, and Russia challenged Great Britain by expanding in Central Asia. True to her spirit, Great Britain would try to avoid direct confrontation with Russia or Germany, but instead would play a complex game to weaken both of them. The United States, another Anglo-Saxon power, supported their efforts behind the scenes.

The Great Game in Asia

In both World Wars, there were Pacific fault lines as well as European ones. The declining Chinese Empire, "the sick man of Far East", became easy prey for the Great Powers and the arena of their rivalry. A recently modernized Japan was eager to join the fray.

In the First Sino–Japanese War (1894–1895), Japan won the island of Taiwan, the Liaodong Peninsula, and control over Korea. However, after the peace treaty between China and Japan had been signed, Russia, Germany, and France forced Japan to withdraw from the Liaodong Peninsula. Shortly thereafter, the Russians moved into the peninsula and built their Port Arthur fortress, thus gaining a year-round operational base for the Russian Pacific Fleet. The Germans, in turn, moved into Jiaozuo Bay and turned into as the base of the German East Asia Squadron. Despite those setbacks, Japan became the major regional power.

For a while, the Great Powers were able to exploit China together, and everybody seemed more or less happy about it—except the Chinese. The Boxer Rebellion, a nationalist and religious movement against foreigners and their agents, rocked China. Boxer fighters believed that they were invulnerable to foreign weapons and plotted to exterminate all foreigners and Christians in China. In June 1900, Boxers marched on Beijing, where they received support from the imperial government. Diplomats, foreign nationals, and Chinese Christians were besieged in the Legation Quarter by the Imperial Army and the Boxers for 55 days. In response, an eight-nation alliance of Great Britain, Russia, Japan, France, United States, Germany, Italy, and Austria-Hungary sent troops to China and defeated the rebellion. The Boxer Protocol of September 7, 1901, mandated the execution of officials who had supported the Boxers, provisions for foreign troops to be stationed in Beijing, and a huge indemnity. It was perhaps the only truly international action of the modern era, and it showed once again that, when it comes to imperialism, democracies and autocracies behave the same way.

Even in this moment of unity, Great Britain and the United States were already starting to move against Russia and its growing presence in Pacific, employing dissatisfied Japan as their fighting dog. In 1902, Great Britain signed an alliance with Japan that promised British support in case of war with Russia.

Feeling secure with Anglo-American backing and receiving practical help from British intelligence, on 8 February 1904 the Japanese fleet suddenly attacked Port Arthur to push the Russian giant out of Pacific. History would repeat itself almost four decades later when during the Second World War Japan would suddenly attack Pearl Harbor, the Pacific base of another giant, The United States...

The ensuing Russo-Japanese War (1904-1905) was disastrous for the Russians, who met considerable difficulties in reinforcing their forces over extended supply routes. In addition to military problems, the war was unpopular in Russia, and a revolution broke out on the homefront. Since the revolutionaries are often financed by foreign powers, one may rightly be very suspicious of this coincidence.

The war came to a climax in the battle of Tsushima (May 27-28, 1905), when Russia's entire Baltic fleet, which had sailed halfway around the world, was almost completely wiped out. Although Japan was victorious, her economy was exhausted and both sides sued for peace.

The Americans were willing to mediate peace talks, but first they divided the spheres of influence with Japan. The Japanese promised to maintain an "open door" policy in China, which meant that they would not grab exclusive rights or annex territory there. On July 27, 1905, during a meeting in Tokyo between Japanese Prime Minister Kasturba and American Secretary of War Taft, the United States also recognized Japan's sphere of influence in Korea; in exchange, Japan recognized the United States' sphere of influence in the Philippines. In 1910, Japan would officially annex Korea, with no protest from the "civilized world."

American President Theodore Roosevelt (1858-1919) mediated the peace treaty between Russia and Japan signed in

Portsmouth on September 5, 1905, earning a Nobel Peace Prize for his efforts. Russia lost South Sakhalin, the base in Port Arthur, although the humiliating demand for reparations was categorically rejected. Americans, who were actually the major financers of Japan, now restrained Japanese ambitions, showing that they had lasting interests in Asia. Great Britain and the United States were using Japan to keep the Russian giant in check in the Pacific, but it did not mean that the Japanese would be allowed to break loose.

Then all of a sudden, the master of diplomatic intrigue, Imperial England, settled her differences with Russia. In the Anglo-Russian treaty of 1907, the spheres of influence had been divided in Central Asia: Afghanistan, Persia and Tibet. The similar Entente Cordiale agreement, signed in 1904, divided spheres of influence in Africa and Asia between England and France. By resolving the differences with her long-time rivals Russia and France, England became an informal member of the Russian-French alliance concluded in 1892-94 to oppose the coalition of the Central Powers: Germany, Austria-Hungary, and Italy.

Russia was sufficiently weakened by the war and revolutionary unrest. Her fleet was decimated, Port Arthur was lost, and prestige was low. Under those dire circumstances Great Britain offered "friendship" to her Russian enemy.

The Great Game in Europe

While China was "sick man of Far East", Ottoman Empire (modern-day Turkey) was the "sick man of Europe." When the Turks were pushed out of Balkans in the 19th century, the region became a point of contention between Russians and Germans. In particular, Russian ally Serbia had conflicting interests over Bosnia with German ally Austria-Hungary. In 1908,

Bosnia was annexed by Austria-Hungary, which checked Serbian hopes to create a large state. This conflict would ignite World War I.

Indeed, the main fault line laid in Europe, where the booming German economy and her increasing military and naval might had upset the existing balance of power. However, a strong alliance against Germany had yet to fully coalesce. Only France felt strong anti-German resentment, after the humiliating defeat in Franco-Prussian war (1870-1871) that brought the loss of Alsace-Lorraine provinces. Germany and Russia, on the other hand, were fellow monarchies that could cooperate for mutual benefit. The famous founder of German Empire and the winner of Franco-Prussian war, Otto von Bismarck (1815-1898), had actually warned not to invade Russia. However, after Bismarck left the office, German policy towards Russia became more aggressive. As for Great Britain, she had formal military agreement with no one, and while she was nervous about the German naval build up that was challenging her supremacy on high seas, she would not want the strengthening of the Russia either. Moreover, British King George V (1865-1936), German Kaiser Wilhelm II (1859-1941), and Russian Czar Nicholas II (1868-1918) were cousins, each having the famous Queen Victoria (1819-1901) as their common grandmother.

In the end, only intensive diplomatic maneuvering helped to form the opposing alliances. The main intrigue was the position of Great Britain, who may or may not stay neutral in the coming war and thus decide its outcome. As for the United States, nobody expected it to participate in a European conflict, but if she did she could shift the balance of power to either side.

In early 1914, when tensions in Europe reached the boiling point, Edward M. House (1858-1938), the intimate adviser of U.S. President Woodrow Wilson (1856-1924), nicknamed

The True Origins of World War II

"Colonel" arrived on a diplomatic tour of Europe, visiting Berlin, Paris, and London. The stated purpose of House's trip was "to persuade Germany and Britain to join with the United States in a diplomatic alliance in order to preserve peace, not only in Europe but in the world." Note that House did not visit Russia, and neither Russia nor France was included in the proposed alliance.

House's meeting with Kaiser Wilhelm II on June 1 is very telling in that regard. According to House's diary record, they discussed "the European situation as it affected the Anglo-Saxon race," i.e., Great Britain and the United States. The Kaiser expressed an opinion that Britain, Germany, and the United States, as the best representatives of Christian civilization, were natural allies against the semi-barbarous Latin and Slavic nations (France and Russia), but that all the Europeans should ally in defense of Western civilization. House tried to persuade Wilhelm that Britain would not seek to ally with Russia if Germany would cease the challenge to its naval power. In his report sent to President Wilson, House wrote:

"The situation is extraordinary. It is militarism run stark mad. Unless someone acting for you can bring about a different understanding, there is some day to be an awful cataclysm. No one in Europe can do it. There is too much hatred, too many jealousies. Whenever England consents, France and Russia will close in on Germany and Austria. England does not want Germany wholly crushed, for she would then have to reckon alone with her ancient enemy, Russia; but if Germany insists upon an ever increasing navy, then England will have no choice. The best chance for peace is an understanding between England and Germany in regard to naval armaments and yet there is some disadvantage to us by these two getting too close."

House's trip in Europe gives us a great insight into the geopolitics of both World Wars, as well as into the coded language that politicians use to hide their true intentions. Let's start with the stated purpose of the trip: "to persuade Germany and Britain to join with the United States in a diplomatic alliance in order to preserve peace." Given the fact that France and Russia were not included in the proposed alliance, Germany actually could have been encouraged to start the war instead of being deterred from it.

The Kaiser stated that Germany, Britain and the United States "should ally in defense" against "semi-barbarous" France and Russia. "Defense" is a common code word for wars of aggression. Likewise, "barbarous" is a code word for the victims of aggression, since nobody is going to attack good guys. If Wilson's advisor really wanted peace, he could have explained to Wilhelm II that France and Russia are not "semi-barbarous" nations. Instead, he told the Kaiser that Britain would not seek to ally itself with Russia if Germany would cease the challenge to its naval power. In plain English, that meant that if Germany gave up naval rivalry with Britain, it should be free to attack Russia.

So why did Wilhelm not accept such a good offer? Because by giving up its strong navy, Germany would voluntarily lose the status of a great power, equal to England. Perhaps Wilhelm had higher ambitions than being a British fighting dog against Russia. Throughout this period, Anglo-Saxons said much about "peace," both publicly and privately. But if they really wanted peace, they wanted it only for themselves. The best way to wage war is to make others fight for your interests.

On June 27, House met with British Foreign Secretary Sir Edward Grey (1862-1933), in London. They discussed how to "save peace" in the midst of rising tensions and agreed that "neither England, Germany, Russia, nor France desire war." Less than 24 hours later, history changed its course.

Conclusion

At the dawn of 20th century, the world was divided between great empires that were destined to clash in the global war. There were large strong empires with established spheres of influences, Great Britain, France, Russia and the United States, weakening empires China and Turkey, and new aggressive empires Germany and Japan eager to join the fray.

The geopolitical struggle for the world domination also began to take on a significant ideological dimension, and not only wars but also propaganda and revolutions were going to be used to destroy the enemy. The democracies were able to use liberal ideas to undermine their autocratic opponents, despite the fact that they themselves were the most successful racist aggressors. The Anglo-Americans also mastered backstage diplomacy and were able to use Japan against Russia and then Russia against Germany for their own benefit.

Chapter 2:
World War I

Cousins and World War I allies
Russian Czar Nicholas II and British King George V
Berlin, 1913

Guess which one is which, who betrayed who, who was shot together with his wife and children, and whose descendants are on the throne to this day..

Pop Quiz

Why did the United States join World War I?

    a) To make the world safe for democracy

    b) To protect massive loans made to Great Britain and France

    c) To dominate the world

> "We are glad, now that we see the facts with no veil of false pretense about them, to fight thus for the ultimate peace of the world and for the liberation of its peoples, the German peoples included: for the rights of nations great and small and the privilege of men everywhere to choose their way of life and of obedience. The world must be made safe for democracy. Its peace must be planted upon the tested foundations of political liberty. We have no selfish ends to serve. We desire no conquest, no dominion. We seek no indemnities for ourselves, no material compensation for the sacrifices we shall freely make. We are but one of the champions of the rights of mankind."
>
> Woodrow Wilson
> Address of Congress, April 2, 1917

US President Woodrow Wilson may well have believed what he said when he asked Congress for authority to enter World War I on the Allied side, but there were far more practical reasons as well. The United States could not tolerate the resumption of the unrestricted submarine warfare by Germany, which had led to the sinking of American merchant ships crossing the Atlantic. Americans had also made large loans to England and France, so they had a vested interest in an Allied victory.

Joining the war also gave United States the opportunity to increase its own global influence and prevent German victory that would change balance of the power in the world. The decision was triggered by the revolution in Russia in March 1917, which allowed Western leaders to redefine the imperialist war as the war of democracy against autocracy. Couched in this way, the victors could strike Germany down without sharing the spoils of victory with the collapsed Russian Empire.

If the justification for war was redefined three years into the fighting, why did the war actually start? In August 1914, nations plunged into the First World War without a second thought. As a rule, enthusiastic masses cheered on the troops going to the front in patriotic fervor. The public in almost every country was sure that the war would be short and with little casualties. Nothing could have been farther from the truth...

The July Crisis

On June 28, 1914, the heir to the Austro-Hungarian throne, Archduke Franz Ferdinand (1863-1914) and his wife Sophie were shot dead in the streets of Sarajevo, Bosnia. The assassin, Bosnian Serb student Gavrilo Princip (1894-1918), was a member of a separatist organization with alleged ties in Serbia. In the heart-breaking scene, Franz and Sophie died after a short agony. "For God's sake, what has happened to you?" asked Sophie before losing consciousness. Franz implored "Sophie dear, Sophie dear, don't die! Stay alive for our children!"

The assassination was probably directed by the infamous Serbian colonel Dragutin Dimitrijević (1876–1917), also known as Apis, who in 1903 organized a military coup that resulted in the brutal murder of the previous Serbian King and Queen. The intended aim was to further the cause of Serbian nationalism, but the Archduke and his wife ended up being the first casualties in a global conflict.

However, wars do not start because brutal terrorists provoke them. It's the other way around. "Civilized" governments routinely use the acts of terror as an excuse to start wars that had been long planned. The United States used the terrorist attacks

The True Origins of World War II

on September 11, 2001 as justification for the 2003 war in Iraq, even though Iraq played no role in the attacks.

The start of the First World War that followed the assassination in Sarajevo was also confusing, as the governments tried to hide their true motives. It went like this: Instead of an immediate action, outraged Austria waited a month to declare war on Serbia. The next day, July 29, Russia started general mobilization, but cancelled it few hours later. They reversed course yet again on July 30, and general mobilization commenced. On August 1, Germany declared war on Russia and then ... moved its troops in opposite direction towards the French border. France, a Russian ally, started to mobilize as well, but did not declare war on Germany outright. On August 3, Germany declared war on France and invaded Belgium. On August 4, England declared war on Germany for violating Belgium neutrality, which England had promised to protect in a treaty dating back to 1839. Finally, on August 6, Austria declared war on Russia, as if to remind everyone that the war actually started because of already forgotten Austro-Serbian conflict. More declarations of war would follow later as various countries around the world tried to benefit from the quarrel.

This confusing complexity is often presented as a series of unfortunate events that brought a war that no one seem to be wanted. Some blame Germany for declaring war on Russia; others blame Russia for provoking Germany. Still others blame Austria-Hungary for declaring war on Serbia, or Serbia for provoking Austria-Hungary.

Indeed, there is plenty of blame to go around. The Austro-Hungarian government wanted to punish Serbia and teach Slav separatists a lesson, but hesitated at first. They knew that Serbia's ally, Russia, could come to her aid. However, Austria was encouraged by Germany; German Kaiser Wilhelm II contested his support for whatever action Austria-Hungary would consider necessary, which remained in history as "a blank check". (Twenty-five years later, Hitler would call British and French guarantee to the Polish independence "a blank check to act as Poland pleases".) Apparently, Germany was ready for "preventive war"; at the moment, it was militarily superior to both Russia and France.

After much delay of the behind-the-scenes politics, Austria-Hungary presented a ten-point ultimatum to Serbia that demanded crackdown on terrorist organizations. When Serbia denied only the most humiliating point, that Austrian police should be allowed to operate on Serbian soil, Austria-Hungary refused to compromise and declared war on Serbia. Since the Austrian ambassador had already left Belgrade, the declaration of war was delivered by ... telegram.

Russia, couldn't stay idle while a fellow Slavic nation was about be massacred by its big neighbor. However, trying to avert a wider war, Czar Nicholas II sent a telegram to his cousin Kaiser Wilhelm II, who was also a cousin of the German-born Czarina.

> "In this serious moment, I appeal to you to help me. An ignoble war has been declared to a weak country. The indignation in Russia shared fully by me is enormous. I foresee that very soon I shall be overwhelmed by the pressure forced upon me and be forced to take extreme measures which will lead to war. To try and avoid such a calamity as a European war I beg you in the name of our old friendship to do what you can to stop your allies from going too far."

The telegram was signed "Nicky", the nickname the relatives and friends use addressing each other. The Kaiser's response was similarly friendly in tone, and he signed it "Willy":

> *"It is with the gravest concern that I hear of the impression which the action of Austria against Serbia is creating in your country. The unscrupulous agitation that has been going on in Serbia for years has resulted in the outrageous crime, to which Archduke Francis Ferdinand fell a victim. The spirit that led Serbians to murder their own king and his wife still dominates the country. You will doubtless agree with me that we both, you and me, have a common interest as well as all Sovereigns to insist that all the persons morally responsible for the dastardly murder should receive their deserved punishment. In this case politics plays no part at all.*
>
> *On the other hand, I fully understand how difficult it is for you and your Government to face the drift of your public opinion. Therefore, with regard to the hearty and tender friendship which binds us both from long ago with firm ties, I am exerting my utmost influence to induce the Austrians to deal straightly to arrive to a satisfactory understanding with you. I confidently hope that you will help me in my efforts to smooth over difficulties that may still arise.*
>
> *Your very sincere and devoted friend and cousin"*

Nicky-Willy telegrams would go back and forth over the next day, giving the hope that the war could be averted. Late in the day on July 29, Czar canceled general mobilization that he had ordered several hours earlier. However, on July 30, Russian Foreign Minister Sergey Sazonov (1860-1927) pressured Czar to go ahead with the mobilization. He argued that German actions—and especially its failure to bring Austria to "reason"—indicated that Germany wanted war. Delaying mobilization further would only put Russia at a disadvantage.

Amazingly, at this faithful moment of history the only person who could prevent World War I was peasant Grigory Rasputin (1869-1916). Rasputin, the faith healer of Czar's son and a saint in Czarina's eyes, was much hated by the Russian elite for his influence with the Czar's family. While most of those around the royal family were caught up in patriotic fervor, Rasputin begged the Czar to do everything in his power to avoid war, rightly predicting the disastrous consequences for the monarchy and the country. However, at the time of the decision, Rasputin was out in the hospital recovering from a suspiciously timed assassination attempt. Rasputin could not escape his fate and was assassinated three years later in 1917. Famous British Intelligence officer Oswald Raymond (1988-1961) is believed to be the one who delivered the final shot into Rasputin's head.

Nicholas II gave in to the pressure and ordered general mobilization, fully aware that it could be considered an act of aggression. Still, he sent yet another telegram to his cousin Willy, explaining that "these measures do not mean war and that we shall continue negotiating." On August 1, however, Germany declared war on Russia. In a telling misstep, the German Ambassador accidentally presented both copies of the declaration of war, one which claimed that Russia refused to reply to Germany and the other that said Russia's replies were unacceptable.

But there is a missing piece to the puzzle of how the war unfolded: England. While crises was unfolding in Europe, England positioned itself as a neutral power that mediated peace between Austria-Hungary and Serbia and between Germany and Russia. The Anglo-German naval rivalry and the common perception of the Triple Entente of England, France and Russia were suddenly forgotten. British public opinion and the majority of British Cabinet members were against the intervention into a European war and on July 29, The Daily News asserted:

The True Origins of World War II

"The most effective work for peace that we can do is to make clear that not a British life shall be sacrificed for the sake of Russian hegemony of the Slav world."

The opinion of England, the most powerful country in the world, was decisive. In fact, already twice in recent history in 1911 and 1912 when there was a danger that Germany might start a big European war, England's unambiguous stance that she is not going to stay neutral forced Germans to back up.

However, British Foreign Secretary and "peacemaker" Sir Edward Grey had his own ideas about war and peace. Being in close contact with German, Russian, French and Austrian ambassadors, he was the most informed and influential person in Europe. On July 6, Grey met with his friend German ambassador Prince Lichnowsky (1860-1928) and was told about Austrian plans to attack Serbia and about German plans to support Austria in the case Russia decided to intervene. Lichnowsky frankly explained that the Germans were concerned about Russia's growing military strength, so "trouble now would be better than trouble later." Lichnowsky wanted to know British position in the upcoming conflict. Instead of warning Germans to back up their dangerous game, Grey was optimistic and "believed that a peaceful solution would be reached". He even promised to assist in taming Russia.

Two days later on July 8, Sir Grey met Russian ambassador Count Benckendorff (1849-1917) and was suddenly no longer optimistic. Grey warned him about the danger coming from Austria and Germany. Russians in turn told Grey that they are going to back up Serbia, so Grey knew in advance that a "Serbian war meant a general European war." To emphasize the seriousness of the situation, Grey later said that his meeting with Benckendorff "made his hair stand on edge." Being informed about danger coming from Germany, Russians still proceeded to mobilize, and thus giving Germany an excuse for attack.

The next day, on July 9, Grey again met Lichnowsky. Once again, the optimistic Grey confirmed that "Britain was not working in concord with France and Russia" and explained that if Austria starts war with Serbia, Russia will become involved. It was like telling the Germans: go ahead start war with Russia if you wish, England won't restrain you. The German "blank check" given to Austria was now endorsed by England. The encouraged Germans and Austrians proceeded with the ultimatum to Serbia.

Some history books characterize this situation as Grey failing to realize the urgency of the situation. Assuming the good intentions of British and American politicians is a trick that often used by Western propaganda. An honest historian analyzing the actions or inactions of such experienced diplomat as Grey should assume that they were intentional, or at the very least just state the facts and say: "Grey did not act despite the urgency of situation". Instead, most Anglo-American historians seemingly cannot admit that a British or American politician might intentionally provoke war.

Contemporary quotes from the time, however, show that Grey was likely executing England's game plan. As we saw in the previous chapter, Edward M. House predicted this very outcome in a report to U.S. President Woodrow Wilson in May 1914:

> "Whenever England consents, France and Russia will close in on Germany and Austria. England does not want Germany wholly crushed, for she would then have to reckon alone with her ancient enemy, Russia; but if Germany insists upon an ever increasing navy, then England will have no choice."

The True Origins of World War II

Grey also ignored Russian and French pleas to publicly condemn Austrian ultimatum. On July 24, Grey hinted to the German ambassador that if European war did indeed happen, England was going to stay neutral. British desire to stay neutral in the coming war was confirmed on July 26 in a discussion between British King George V (1865-1936) and the brother of German Kaiser.

At the same time, Russian ambassador Benckendorff wrote to foreign minister Sazonov on July 25 that Grey and other British officials left him with the impression that England was not going to stay neutral. Thus, England encouraged both sides to be bold; the Germans hoped that the British would not intervene, while the Russians hoped to receive British support.

Not surprisingly, German Chancellor Bethmann Hollweg (1856-1921), in a message to the German ambassadors, stated that the principal aim of German foreign policy was to make it appear that Russia had forced Germany into a war, in order to keep Britain neutral and ensure that German public opinion would back the war effort. On the eve of the war, Grey went so far as to tell his friend Prince Lichnowsky, the German Ambassador, that not only would Britain stay neutral if Germany refrained from attacking France, but France would likely remain neutral as well. The German-Russian war could go ahead; Grey would not care.

Upon receiving this news, the elated Kaiser exclaimed, "Now we can go to war against Russia only." The Kaiser's proposal lead to fierce protests from his chief of staff von Moltke, however, who explained that German forces were already advancing towards France. According to Schlieffen Plan, a wartime strategy that the meticulous Germans had been preparing for many years, German army had to quickly defeat France in the West and then move all its forces to the East to deal with Russia. To change the plan and redeploy the troops against Russia would require time, and the opportunity to quickly destroy French power would be lost. At the end, Moltke persuaded Kaiser to continue movement of German troops in the west for "technical reasons". Germany quickly delivered an ultimatum to France to renounce its alliance with Russia or face a German attack.

With the German invasion expected soon, France suddenly found out that there was no commitment of support from still neutral England. The disappointed French Ambassador in London complained to the press on August 2,

> *"I do not know whether this evening the word 'honor' will not have to be struck out of the English vocabulary."*

Indeed, only few British politicians were openly pro-war at this point. Among them was charismatic First Lord of the Admiralty Winston Churchill (1874-1965), the son of the British aristocrat and the daughter of American millionaire, who was already famous for his daring escape from captivity in the Anglo-Boer War, as well as for his journalism. Churchill was also vivid whisky drinker and cigar smoker who took daily naps, even during the war.

On August 3, sticking to its original plan, Germany declared war on France. For military reasons, the Germans attacked France through Belgium, thus violating Belgium neutrality, which at first may have looked like a trivial matter. It was not. On August 4, Great Britain suddenly declared war on Germany, using an excuse from the very old 1839 treaty that guaranteed Belgian neutrality. Receiving the devastating news, German Chancellor von Bethmann-Hollweg called the treaty "a scrap of paper". During the war, British propaganda capitalized on "scrap of paper" remark, issuing numerous posters and postcards that explained that for England it was a question of honor to support Belgium. Of course, geopolitically, Belgium's neutrality was not only a question of "honor"; it was also an important buffer zone that protected British coast as well.

Knowing in advance about German plans to invade Belgium, Sir Grey used the Belgium card to turn around British public opinion in favor of war only when it was too late for Germany to back out. Thus, apart from German "arrogance" and Russian "foolishness," the war was also the fault of England's dubious diplomacy. If England had at once declared her solidarity with Russia and France and her intention to fight if necessary, Germany and Austria almost certainly would have hesitated to start the war.

The next generation of British politicians would continue this sort of British "peace seeking" effort. Twenty-five years later, on the eve of World War II, Neville Chamberlain would write to Hitler not to ignore the British guarantee to Poland, as the British guarantee to Belgium was ignored. Once again, Britain's uncompromising stance would come too late to prevent another World War.

The Great War

A detailed history of World War I is beyond the scope of this book, but the seeds of the next great war were planted almost from the beginning of the conflict.

For example, Italy, a member of the Central Powers, double crossed her allies and joined the Entente in the war against Austria-Hungary and Germany in 1914. Interestingly enough, one of the Italian pro-war activists was Benito Mussolini (1883-1945), the former socialist and the future fascist dictator, who received money from British Intelligence for his pro-war newspaper. In World War II, Mussolini would turn against his British supporters.

Like Italy, Japan also fought against Germany in the First World War to grab German possessions in China. Also like Italy, she would turn against her British supporters in the next war.

The Ottoman Empire (modern-day Turkey) joined the Central Powers and during the war solved the problem of Armenian separatism by the first genocide of 20th Century. "Who, after all, speaks today of the annihilation of the Armenians?" would assert Hitler in 1939 in preparation of his own Holocaust.

Along with Hitler, quite a few Nazi leaders were decorated veterans of World War I. During that war, future Nazi second-in-command Hermann Goering (1893-1946) was an ace pilot. Future Deputy Fuhrer Rudolf Hess (1894-1987) was a brave frontline soldier. Future Nazi Minister of Foreign Affairs Joachim von Ribbentrop (1893-1946) was an officer.

These soldiers and many others faced unspeakable conditions on the front lines that would shape their worldview for decades. World War I is most remembered for its trench warfare. It became very costly to break through well-fortified defenses of the enemy, but even if a breakthrough was achieved, it was equally difficult to sustain an offensive and maintain the supply lines. The rule of thumb was that the offensive party loses many more men than the defender. As a result, combatants would often sit in the same trenches for many months, killing each other without achieving anything.

The doom of the senseless sacrifice and destruction hung upon the nations. It felt like the fighting dragged on for no apparent reason. Antiwar revolutionary movements, including communist ones, gained strength with each year of war. There were antiwar labor strikes in France, Russia, and Germany. Propaganda and intelligence services would not stay idle either, making every effort to demoralize the enemy. The key to victory, it seemed, lay on the homefront.

The February Revolution

Russia cracked first. In March (February by old style calendar) 1917, riots erupted in the capital, Petrograd. Instead of suppressing the rebellion, Russian troops began to mutiny. On March 15, army leadership forced Czar Nicholas II to abdicate and a liberal provisional government assumed power. As usual, a people's revolution in the streets and a murky palace coup went hand-in-hand.

The February Revolution in Russia was enthusiastically cheered in the West as the great victory of democracy over autocracy. On April 2, U.S. President Woodrow Wilson stated:

> *"Does not every American feel that assurance has been added to our hope for the future peace of the world by the wonderful and heartening things that have been happening within the last few weeks in Russia?"*

In the same speech, Wilson proposed war on Germany, which Congress declared on April 6. The timing of these events is very telling. The February Revolution allowed American hawks promote the war as the fight of the democracy against autocracy, although it was in fact still an imperialist quarrel.

The allies did more than cheer on the revolution in Russia. They actively fomented it. Rumors abounded that on hearing the news of Russian revolution British Prime Minister David Lloyd George exclaimed, "One of England's goals has been achieved!" The Grand Duke Alexander Mikhailovich, a cousin of the Czar, remembered:

Tigran Khalatyan

> *"The saddest thing was that I learned how conspirators were encouraged by the British ambassador at the imperial court, Sir George Buchanan. He imagined that his behavior was best to protect the interests of the allies and that the future liberal Russian government would lead Russia from victory to victory."*

It was a real paradox: Germans fomented revolution to take Russia out of the war, while the Allies did the same in an effort to redouble Russian war effort. Of course, the Allies' real goal was much simpler. Both the German and Russian Empires represented a threat to Western interests, so why would they want a Pyrrhic victory over the German Empire only to face the even stronger Russian Empire in return? Remember Edward M. House's statement: "England does not want Germany wholly crushed, for she would then have to reckon alone with her ancient enemy, Russia." The forces of democracy, a.k.a. Anglo-Saxon civilization, now received the great opportunity "to kill two birds with one stone" and strike down both Germany and Russia. In fact, the American effort would not turn the tide of the war in the Allied favor until the chaos to Russia led to her exclusion from the victor's list.

This may sound like the conspiracy theory, but actually it is a very basic geopolitical reality. Russia was considered the threat not because it was an autocracy, but because it was big, strong, and independent. Thus, promoting democracy in Russia always had the hidden goal of weakening it. Concerns about human rights violations or unfair elections in Russia always go hand-in-hand with the strong desire of reducing the sphere of Russian influence. Indeed, democracy for Russia always assumes weak state that preferably is broken into pieces. Both times in modern history, in 1917 and 1991, when the victory of democracy in Russia was cheered in the West, the collapse of the big Russian state followed.

Likewise, the stronger Russia becomes, the more despotic is her public image. This is how double standards in ideology serve the needs of the struggle for world domination.

For Democracy or For Money?

The Russian Revolution was not the only reason that the United States entered the war against Germany, although it definitely became the breaking point. Among other reasons was the necessity to guarantee American private loans to England and France. Over the course of the war, US loaned England 100 times more money than it did to Germany. The war also allowed producers of munitions to make huge profits. The scandals about "war profiteers" would rock American politics in the coming decades. For example, in 1935:

> "The Nye [Senate] Committee investigations showed that Wilson had in effect, lied country into war. He had undermined neutrality by allowing loans and other support to the Allies, deliberately exaggerated claims of German atrocities, and covered up the fact of his knowledge of the secret treaties. Far from being a war to further democracy, it had been a war to redivide the spoils of empire."

You'll recognize that last line as a cutting allusion to Wilson's famous speech, in which he rallied the nation with a shiny goal: "The world must be made safe for democracy". The basic idea of Wilson's rhetoric was that peace-loving democracies are morally superior to aggressive autocracies, and in a world ruled by democracies there should be no wars. It implied that countries that are "not good for the democracy" should be defeated.

In the era of colonization, a country was a legitimate target because it was "barbarian" and needed to be "civilized," according to American standards.

The important part of the Wilson's Deceit, as we are going to call his famous speech, is to convince the people of a targeted country that they will be better under foreign occupation, happily exchanging their independence for the democracy. We pay special attention to the Wilson's Deceit not only because it influenced the history, but also because it defined the core of the "democracy-dictatorship" paradigm so crucial to the Western historical curriculum. In fact, Wilson implied that Americans were going to kill Germans for their own benefit, and in order to drive a wedge between the people and their rulers in Germany he pretended that the German nation did not enthusiastically support the start of the war:

> *"We have no quarrel with the German people. We have no feeling toward them but one of sympathy and friendship. It was not upon their impulse that their government acted in entering this war. It was not with their previous knowledge or approval. It was a war determined upon as wars used to be determined upon in the old, unhappy days when peoples were nowhere consulted by their rulers and wars were provoked and waged in the interest of dynasties or of little groups of ambitious men who were accustomed to use their fellowmen as pawns and tools."*

Wilson's next deceit was about never existed moral superiority of the democratic countries in the questions of war and peace:

> *"Self-governed nations do not fill their neighbor states with spies or set the course of intrigue to bring about some critical posture of affairs which will give them an opportunity to strike and make conquest. Such designs*

can be successfully worked out only under cover and where no one has the right to ask questions. Cunningly contrived plans of deception or aggression, carried, it may be, from generation to generation, can be worked out and kept from the light only within the privacy of courts or behind the carefully guarded confidences of a narrow and privileged class. They are happily impossible where public opinion commands and insists upon full information concerning all the nation's affairs. A steadfast concert for peace can never be maintained except by a partnership of democratic nations. No autocratic government could be trusted to keep faith within it or observe its covenants..."

Wilson went as far in his lies as to assert that people in the democratic countries are unselfish:

"Only free peoples can hold their purpose and their honor steady to a common end and prefer the interests of mankind to any narrow interest of their own."

It was a new kind of racism. It did not preach moral superiority of one race over another, but gave moral superiority to the person who could vote over the person who could not, as if people in the democratic countries never lie, cheat, or steal. Democratic propaganda such as this in some sense is the worst type of propaganda, since it's the most cynical. In democratic countries, the propaganda lies can be unmasked thousand times over. Yet a hundred years later, American politicians would repeat the same lies to justify another imperialist war.

Such bold and inspiring lies should teach us never underestimate the power of ideals and propaganda. We also should not seek simplistic explanations such us "greed of the war profiteers." We should look deeper.

This is how George Friedman, the modern guru of geopolitics and the founder of Stratfor, described the reasons for US entry into First World War:

> "The United States intervened in the war a few weeks after the Russian czar abdicated and after the Germans began fighting the neutral countries. The United States could not to lose access to the Atlantic, and if Russia withdrew from the war, then Germany could concentrate on its west. A victory there would have left Germany in control of both Russian resources and French industry. That would have created a threat to the United States. It tried to stay neutral, then was forced to make a decision of how much risk it could bear. The United States opted for war."

Let's compare Wilson's speech with the above paragraph. Where Wilson is appalled by the alleged German barbarity, Friedman is concerned by the growing German might. Wilson says that abdication of Russian Czar is "wonderful"; Friedman is afraid that Russia may withdraw from the war. Feel the difference between propaganda and reason, the difference between ideology and geopolitics.

The single most important reason for the entrance of the United States into World War II was that Germany tipped the balance of power. As the possibility of Germany winning the war became real, the United States was confronted with the challenge of a new European superpower and related risks to her own domination. The alleged German war crimes were only an excuse.

The Russian factor in the United States decision to enter the war was twisted as well. It could be argued that Wilson might have been little naïve and could not anticipate that the revolution was not going to bring democracy to Russia. How many times, though, have we heard about naïve but good-intentioned

The True Origins of World War II

American and British leaders? Wouldn't it be reasonable to suggest that their idealist naivety was just a cover-up?

Fear of Russian autocratic power may have been the real reason for America's delayed entry. Indeed, regarding the attitude of the democracies towards autocratic Russia, we can see that it was in direct correlation with its distance from Germany, which instills doubts about their objectivity. France, Germany's neighbor, was by far the least concerned about Russian autocracy. Britain, protected by the English Channel, had more concerns but still allied with Russian Czar. However, Americans, being an ocean away, fretted openly about how the Russian Czar discriminated against Jews, although at the time many US hotels accepted neither Jews nor Negros.

No matter what politicians say, the struggle for domination is always the main motivator in global politics. The trigger for action is a change in the status quo, while ideology serves as a cover-up. After all, when Germany presented bigger danger in World War II, America did not hesitate to ally with Communist Russia, supposedly a far more brutal regime than Russian monarchy. Indeed, if Wilson had lived long enough, he might have even become a supporter of Hitler, although as we know Hitler politics had nothing to do with democracy.

Nonsense? Well, Wilson's speech about making the world safe for democracy was mirrored by the speech of another famous liberal, British Prime Minister David Lloyd George, which he made on April 12, 1917. In the speech, Lloyd George praised America's entry into the war and went on exploring the now popular democracy against tyranny theme:

> *"I am glad; I am proud. I am glad not merely because of the stupendous resources which this great nation will bring to the success of the alliance, but I rejoice as a democrat that the advent of the United States into this*

war gives the final stamp and seal to the character of the conflict as a struggle against military autocracy throughout the world.

That was the note that ran through the great deliverance of President Wilson. It was echoed, Sir, in your resounding words today. The United States of America have the noble tradition, never broken, of having never engaged in war except for liberty. And this is the greatest struggle for liberty that they have ever embarked upon...

Prussia was not a democracy. The Kaiser promises that it will be a democracy after the war. I think he is right. But Prussia not merely was not a democracy. Prussia was not a State - Prussia was an army. It had great industries that had been highly developed; a great educational system; it had its universities, it had developed its science.

All these were subordinate to the one great predominant purpose, the purpose of all - a conquering army which was to intimidate the world. The army was the spear-point of Prussia; the rest was merely the shaft...

I can see peace coming now - not a peace which will be the beginning of war; not a peace which will be an endless preparation for strife and bloodshed; but a real peace. The world is an old world. It has never had peace. It has been rocking and swaying like an ocean, and Europe - poor Europe! - has always lived under the menace of the sword.

When this war began two-thirds of Europe were under autocratic rule. It is the other way about now, and democracy means peace. The democracy of France did not want war; the democracy of Italy hesitated long before they entered the war; the democracy of this country shrank from it - shrank and shuddered - and never would have entered the cauldron had it not been for the invasion of Belgium.

The True Origins of World War II

> *The democracies sought peace; strove for peace. If Prussia had been a democracy there would have been no war...*
>
> *The breaking up of the dark rule of the Turk, which for centuries has clouded the sunniest land in the world, the freeing of Russia from an oppression which has covered it like a shroud for so long, the great declaration of President Wilson coming with the might of the great nation which he represents into the struggle for liberty are heralds of the dawn.*
>
> *"They attacked with the dawn," and these men are marching forward in the full radiance of that dawn, and soon Frenchmen and Americans, British, Italians, Russians, yea, and Serbians, Belgians, Montenegrins, will march into the full light of a perfect day."*

Notice how Lloyd George conveniently forgets to mention the imperialist goals of the supposedly virtuous democracies, Great Britain included? Would it surprise you to learn that, in less than two decades, proud democrat Lloyd George would become a staunch supporter of Adolf Hitler, calling for friendship between Great Britain and Nazi Germany?

In 1936, Lloyd George referred to Hitler as the "George Washington of Germany — the man who won for his country independence from all her oppressors." If we are to take Lloyd George's 1917 pronouncements at face value, why it did not bother Lloyd George that Nazi Germany had less democracy than the Kaiser's Germany? Why it did not bother him that Nazi Germany was more militarized than the Kaiser's Germany?

Lloyd George's words were as false as those of Wilson and numerous other Anglo-American politicians, who still use big words about democracy and tyranny to cover up their own aggressive international politics.

Tigran Khalatyan

The Bolshevik Revolution

The high-minded rhetoric deployed in the West would eventually be undermined by a small group of radicals called Bolsheviks (from the Russian word for majority, the name of Russian communists at the time). The Bolsheviks missed the February Revolution; their leaders were mostly in exile or abroad. Now, sensing new opportunities, they all headed to the capital, Petrograd, warmly invited by the new liberal government they would soon overthrow.

Liberated by amnesty, future leader of the Soviet Union Joseph Stalin (1878-1953, born Jugashvili) returned from a harsh exile in Siberia. At this point, though, Stalin was an underling of the charismatic Bolshevik leader Vladimir Lenin (1870-1924, born Ulyanov). While Stalin came from a family of Georgian cobblers, Lenin was born into middle class family with a diverse ethnic background that included not only Russian but also Jewish, Kalmyk, Swedish and German blood.

In an unprecedented action, Lenin, who had been living in luxurious exile in Switzerland, received permission from the German government to travel with a group of his mostly Jewish comrades through German territory in a sealed train. The Germans reasoned that Bolshevik revolutionaries would sow discord in the capital and knock Russia out of the war. There were reports that Bolsheviks also secretly received huge sums of money from German sources. Arriving at the train station in Petrograd, Lenin immediately held a rally and proclaimed the need for a socialist revolution.

The third key Bolshevik and future head of Red Army was Leon Trotsky (1879-1940, born Lev Bronshtein). At the time of the revolution Trotsky was in New York, where he apparently found wealthy sponsors. He also headed to Russia with another group of Jewish activists. There were reports that in New York before his departure, Trotsky had given a speech in which he said: "I am going back to Russia to overthrow the provisional government and stop the war with Germany." For such an important task, an American passport to allow his travel was allegedly granted to Trotsky by the personal intervention of President Wilson. There were also reports that Trotsky left New York with $10,000 cash in his pocket (around $200,000 in today's money).

The above claims can be reasonably disputed, but the following is a fact. Trotsky's ship was intercepted in Nova Scotia, Canada, where Trotsky was interned by British officials as a dangerous revolutionary and German agent who could sabotage the Russian war effort. However, very important people intervened on Trotsky's behalf, and he was released within a month.

As amazing as it may seem, powerful forces in Russia, Germany, England and America worked in unison to support the Bolshevik Revolution and finish off the Russian Empire. We can understand that Germany was the enemy of Russia, and that's why Germans helped Lenin. But Trotsky arrived from the United States, with British permission.

The new Russian government welcomed all Bolsheviks, no matter whose agents they were, with the open arms. Still, Russia had to be prepared for the new revolution first. The liberal provisional government was up to the task and worked hard to discredit the ideas of democracy in Russia for decades to come. In the midst of the world war, elections were allowed in the army, and soldier's representatives could now overrule their officers. Coupled with the abandonment of the death penalty on the front, this insured the disintegration of the army and high rates of desertion.

Dissolving police combined with general amnesty spurred high crime rates. The governors of all provinces were fired, and as a result control over the huge country pretty much disintegrated. Meanwhile, liberated labor was going from one strike to another to hasten the economic collapse of the country. High inflation followed and the new Russian notes nicknamed "Kerenky", in honor of lawyer Alexander Kerensky (1881-1970), the last head of the provisional government, became cheaper than the paper they were printed on. The bills were often used as wallpaper or burned in stoves.

As the support for the provisional government waned, the country became ripe for a communist takeover. On November 7, 1917, Bolsheviks headed by Lenin and Trotsky seized power in Petrograd and arrested the provisional government. Kerensky escaped in the car of the American ambassador and left the country, ending his days in the United States. Only few days before the Bolshevik Revolution, on November 3, the first American soldiers died in combat on the Western Front in France. American involvement in World War I and the chaotization of Russia were well coordinated.

After taking power, the very first decree signed by Lenin was a proposal for an immediate peace with Germany without annexations and reparations. Bolsheviks then launched a vast propaganda campaign against the "corrupt world of capitalism." Two months later on 8 January 1918, President Wilson countered with his "Fourteen Points" postwar peace plan, a policy of open seas, free trade, disarmament, and self-determination. In a more practical sense, the Fourteen Points prescribed the dissolution of the Austrian and Ottoman empires, the creation of a new Polish nation, and territorial gains for France, Italy, and Serbia.

The most ambiguous was the lengthy sixth point, which concerned Russia:

> *"The evacuation of all Russian territory and such a settlement of all questions affecting Russia as will secure the best and freest cooperation of the other nations of the world in obtaining for her an unhampered and unembarrassed opportunity for the independent determination of her own political development and national policy and assure her of a sincere welcome into the society of free nations under institutions of her own choosing; and, more than a welcome, assistance also of every kind that she may need and may herself desire.*
>
> *The treatment accorded Russia by her sister nations in the months to come will be the acid test of their good will, of their comprehension of her needs as distinguished from their own interests, and of their intelligent and unselfish sympathy."*

A few days before the above was published, the Bolsheviks had dissolved democratically elected Russian Constituent Assembly, and it is telling that Wilson did not insist on preservation of the democracy in Russia as part of his new world order. Emboldened, the Bolsheviks could now tighten their hold on power, which was apparently fine with Wilson.

The German Revolution

Meanwhile, with desertions now rampant, the Russian army rapidly disintegrated, and the Bolsheviks had no choice but end the war with Germany. On March 3, 1918, the Treaty of Brest-Litovsk was signed, under which large territories were annexed by Germany including Ukraine and the Baltic states. Germany was now free to move all her forces to the Western Front for the final push.

The new spring offensive in France started off well, but by the summer it ran out of steam. Large numbers of American troops were arriving every day, and all of a sudden the Germans realized that they were losing the war. The German high command requested an armistice, but President Wilson demanded the abdication of the Kaiser as a precondition, hinting that only a democratic German government can expect a just peace. The Kaiser refused.

The German Revolution started with a mutiny of the German navy in the port city of Kiel on November 3, 1918. German sailors refused to go into battle with the British Navy, and then following Russia's example created a Worker's and Soldier's Council that took power. Revolution quickly spread all over Germany, and on November 9 the Kaiser was forced into exile. Two days later on November 11, German delegation of the new republican government signed an armistice whose terms resembled an outright surrender. The German army was obligated to evacuate all occupied territories, give up all heavy weapons and wait defenseless at victor's mercy.

At the time of the German surrender, a former homeless artist, but now bearer of an Iron Cross for bravery, Corporal Adolf Hitler (1889-1945) was recovering from a British gas attack that had almost blinded him. On hearing the news of surrender and realizing that all German sacrifice was in vain, he cried. Twenty years later, he would make millions of people cry, too.

"War is Peace"

The history of mankind is the history of wars. We do not analyze wars of the distant past, such as the wars between Rome

The True Origins of World War II

and Carthage, in dramatic terms. Historians generally do not talk about aggressors and liberators, good and evil. Instead, we see ancient wars, rightly, as conflicts of selfish interests, fights for power and resources.

In studying more recent history, ideology and emotional sentiment tend to cloud our vision. It is certainly true that ideology plays a particularly important role in the history of World War II, not only because the war is relatively recent historical event, but also because it actually presented a clash of the communist, fascist, and democratic ideologies. However, as we compare World War II to the other conflicts of the past, we can see so many striking similarities in completely different ideological backgrounds. World War I is the one obvious example: it started when there were neither communist nor fascist powers. Napoleon's wars a century earlier are another example. We can even tell the Napoleon/Hitler stories together, which may go as follows:

Charismatic leader [Napoleon/Hitler] of [France/Germany], with his great army easily conquered almost all of Europe except the Island of Britain, which had a superior naval fleet. War with Russia was avoided through a peace treaty signed in [Tilsit/Moscow].

Unable to blockade and starve the British, [Napoleon/Hitler] invaded Russia. His armies reached Moscow, where his vaunted war machine suffered its first major defeat during the cold Russian winter. Later, Russians and their allies reach [Paris/Berlin] ending the rule of [Napoleon/Hitler].

Let's put aside for a while the deception about great democracies fighting totalitarian dictatorships and analyze what actually causes wars. First, the most obvious motivation behind a country's actions is national self-interest. A great power and its rulers always want control over resources and trade routes, more territory to annex or influence. The obvious instrument of imperialist expansion is war, and quick and victorious wars are enthusiastically supported by society, the democratic or autocratic alike.

On the other hand, the senseless carnage of World War I clearly showed that, without cooperation, mankind is headed towards self-destruction. Thus, to justify the costly and destructive wars of the 20th century and beyond, world leaders have adopted peace-loving rhetoric to mask their true interests, making all major warmongers look like peace warriors on paper.

For example, when the Kaiser gave Austria the "blank check" for the war with Serbia that ignited World War I, he had to mention his "love of peace". The famous report of the Austrian ambassador in Berlin stated:

> *"The Kaiser said he understood full well that it would be difficult for His Imperial and Royal Apostolic Majesty to march into Serbia, given his well-known love of peace; however, if we really deemed a military operation against Serbia necessary, he (Kaiser Wilhelm) would find it regrettable if we did not seize the present moment, which was so favorable for us."*

On the onset of World War II politicians also competed to show their "love of peace".

"Our love of peace perhaps is greater than in the case of others, for we have suffered most from war," said Hitler in 1935 while starting his rearmament program.

"For the people of East Asia, there can be no happiness without a just peace in this part of the world," retorted Japanese Prime-Minister Konoe in 1937, just before starting the war with China.

"America hates war. America hopes for peace. Therefore, America actively engages in the search for peace," replied

The True Origins of World War II

President F. D. Roosevelt that same year, while doing nothing to deter aggressors in Europe and Asia.

"I believe it is peace for our time," stated British Prime-Minister Chamberlain after signing the Munich Pact with Hitler in 1938, just one year before his country declared war on Germany.

"As always, I sought to bring about a change by peaceful means," asserted Hitler in 1939, as the war in Europe began.

World War II leaders' "love of peace" continued ceaselessly until October 16, 1946, when the noose was placed over Nazi Foreign Minister Ribbentrop's neck. His last words were, "I wish peace to the world."

Who were the deceivers in the above quotes—the dictators or the democratic leaders? The answer is both. By the word "peace," some actually meant a war of aggression. Others meant peace at home; they did not mind the war away from their shores that weakened their opponents. Nobody cared for peace for everyone. If they truly did, war could have been easily averted.

As we have seen, there are different types of war. The Spanish-American War was clearly a war of aggression. So was the Boer War. When Japan attacked Russia in 1904, they had support of Great Britain and United States, which is an example of the war by proxy. Encouraging the war between your opponents is less obvious. Why on the onset of World War I did the British hint to Germany that they can go to war with Russia, but not with France? Why did the United States stay away from the war in Europe and then suddenly get involved at the end? Among other reasons, they wanted to knock down both Germany and Russia. If you don't agree, consider how miraculously the war between Germany and Russia made them both lose.

71

This may seem incredible, but the outcome of the war was predicted by some even before it had started. At a meeting in Paris in January 1914, six months before the assassination of Fraz Ferdinand in Sarajevo, Jozef Pilsudski (1867-1935), the future dictator of Poland, predicted that the war was imminent and that:

> "the problem of the independence of Poland will be definitely solved only if Russia is beaten by Austria-Hungary and Germany, and Germany vanquished by France, Great Britain and the United States; it is our duty to bring that about."

That was precisely what happened on the day of the German surrender, November 11, 1918. Was Pilsudski that smart, or was he just more attuned than others to grand geopolitical designs?

Conclusion

World War I did not just happen, it was deliberately caused by the great powers, autocratic and democratic alike. In particular, England wanted a war between Germany and Russia to weaken both nations and strengthen their own position.

The democracies won the war and promised to support a just, lasting peace. However, the peace was based on a false assumption that wars are caused by autocratic governments. The desire of Anglo-Saxon powers to provoke wars between their opponents was not unmasked and condemned. Yet in the blueprint for the Second World War, Germany and Russia were again supposed to "destroy each other".

Chapter 3:
The Victory of Democracy

"Comrade Lenin cleans the earth of evil
Soviet Propaganda Poster, 1920.

The Western democracies allowed communists win the civil war in Russia, then imposed a punitive peace treaty on Germany which led to the creation of Nazi movement, the communist antipode.

Pop Quiz

Did foreign powers help the Bolsheviks win the Russian Civil War?

    a) America and other great nations do not get involved in other nations internal affairs, Russia included.

    b) Tired of World War I, the great world powers were reluctant to be involved in any foreign conflicts.

    c) Communists were covertly supported by the great powers as the force that can destroy Russian Empire.

> *"We have no quarrel with the German people. We have no feeling toward them but one of sympathy and friendship"*
>
> Woodrow Wilson, declaring war on Germany,
> April 2, 1917

After the end of World War I, the world was waiting for the just peace that had been promised by the great democracies that won the war. Under Allied pressure Germany was proclaimed a Republic, gave up all heavy weapons and pulled back their forces from the occupied territories, expecting more favorable terms in return. The reality turned out to be somewhat different.

Instead of a just peace, Germany received the retribution of the angry victors. The naval blockade of Germany continued after the armistice for eight months to insure German obedience in negotiations. As a result, around 100,000 Germans died from hunger after the end of the war. Internal disorder followed. In January 1919, German communists tried to seize power, but the coup failed. With no clear leadership at the top and a devastated economy, Germany had little leverage in the coming peace talks.

The Treaty of Versailles

This was how President Wilson spoke about a potential peace with Germany during the war:

> *"There shall be no annexations, no contributions, no punitive damage ... All the parties to this war must join in the settlement of every issue anywhere involved in it; be-*

> *cause what we are seeing is a peace that we can all unite to guarantee and maintain and every item of it must be submitted to the common judgment whether it be right and fair, an act of justice, rather than a bargain between sovereigns."*

After the war was over, though, his tone became very different:

> *"[The Versailles treaty] seeks to punish one of the greatest wrongs ever done in history, the wrong which Germany sought to do to the world and to civilization; and there ought to be no weak purpose with regard to the application of the punishment. She attempted an intolerable thing, and she must be made to pay for the attempt."*

The Paris Peace Conference opened on January 18, 1919 and concluded five months later with a treaty signed in Versailles on June 28, 1919. The leaders of the victorious powers imposed their will on the defeated. All key questions were decided by the leaders of France, Great Britain and the United States. Italy did not get the spoils it felt it deserved. Russia was excluded from the conference altogether, allegedly for signing the separate peace with Germany. The catch was that the Bolsheviks who signed the peace were not considered the legitimate government of Russia, but the anti-Bolshevik Russian leaders were not invited either.

The Austro-Hungarian Empire was split up into Austria, Hungary and Czechoslovakia, with some of its territories also going to other states. The Kingdom of Yugoslavia, dominated by Serbs, was created nearby. In a bitter irony, the terrorists from Sarajevo had achieved their goal of creating the greater Serbia, although quarter of Serbian population was sacrificed in the process.

The Ottoman Empire was also dismembered under the separate treaty. What was left of it became modern Turkey, and the rest, the oil-rich Arab countries of the Middle East, were divided between the British and French. German colonies in Africa were similarly redistributed among the great powers. German possessions in China were not returned back to Chinese, but were given to Japan instead. Outraged Chinese would not soon forget this insult.

Back in Europe, France got back the Alsace-Lorraine region it had lost in 1870 and the coal-rich Saarland. The westernmost province of Germany, the Rhineland, was demilitarized to prevent sudden attack on France. In the East, a chunk of German territory was lost to the newly created Polish state. This carving of land violated Wilson's principle of self-determination, as German populated territories went to France, Czechoslovakia, and Poland. Moreover, German-speaking Austria was forbidden to reunite with Germany.

Finishing with carving a new map of the world, the victors turned their attention to retribution. They blamed Germany for being the sole instigator of the war and demanded that she pay an enormous sum in reparations. As the final humiliation, Germany was denied a seat in the newly created League of Nations.

Starved and disarmed Germany had no choice but to accept the peace treaty, but the "Versailles Diktat" would be deeply resented. Germans also started question the worthiness of a democratic revolution that did not help to bring a just peace and almost ended with German communists taking power. More importantly the fact that the German army was still on enemy territory in France, Belgium, and Russia when the armistice was signed gave rise to the "stabbed in the back" theory that the German army didn't actually lose the war but was betrayed by socialists, communists, and Jews on the homefront. The large labor strikes that broke out in Germany in January 1918 with the socialist slogan for "peace without annexations" added more credence to this theory.

Those controversies would enormously help future Nazi propaganda. For example, Hitler said in 1941:

> *"Only through its internal dissensions Germany has failed in 1918. The consequences were terrible. After hypocritical claim that they fought only against the Kaiser and his regime, and after the German Army laid down its weapons, the scheduled destruction of the German Reich has begun".*

The main proponents of the harshest treatment of Germany were the French, who were not interested in Wilson's idealism and wanted compensation for their very large losses in lives and property, as well as the security against future attacks. The French wanted to permanently weaken Germany by moving their border over the Rhine, the mighty river that could protect either France or Germany from the sudden attack. However, British and Americans would not allow French power to go beyond a certain limit and vetoed the idea.

As a result, Germany was neither pacified nor permanently weakened. Upon hearing the outcome of Versailles treaty, Allied supreme commander Marshal Ferdinand Foch (1851-1929) predicted with frightening accuracy:

> *"This is not peace. It's an armistice for twenty years."*

The Victory of the Bolsheviks

Back in Russia, Bolsheviks had started building a communist society by nationalizing factories and redistributing land among peasants when they seized power in 1917. The "progressive classes" of workers and peasants took power and property from the "oppressive classes" of capitalists, landlords, aristocracy and clergy. With the elimination of the oppressive classes, true equality was supposed to be achieved.

The main Bolshevik slogan was the famous "Workers of the world, unite!" from Karl Marx's Communist Manifesto. Nationalism was condemned in favor of internationalism, and the much-anticipated "world revolution" was supposed to bring the era of imperialist wars to the end. Bolshevik slogans such as "land to peasants, factories to workers, peace to peoples" were simple, clear and popular among common people. The Bolsheviks also declared that there is no God, and the Church was attacked as the institution that brainwashed common people to insure their obedience to their masters.

However, there was no democratic way of bringing in such radical changes, and a "dictatorship of workers" was instituted by design. In January 1918, the Bolsheviks dissolved the newly elected Constituent Assembly after only one day of work.

Bolshevik rule was met with wide opposition. Given the fact that there were many Jews among the Bolshevik leaders, they were accused of not respecting core Russian values and traditions, abusing the beloved Russian Orthodox Church, and killing Russian patriots. At the same time, Bolsheviks were transforming from the small conspiracy group into a mass movement and were getting more and more support in progressive areas of Russian society.

A bloody civil war soon erupted. To fight the war, the Bolsheviks created the Red Army, called just "the Reds" colloquially. Anti-Bolshevik forces were called "the Whites." Thus, the Russian Civil War became known as the fight between the Reds and the Whites. The respective Red Terror and White Terror were carried out with utmost brutality. In addition, bands of local warlords roamed the countryside taking advantage of the power vacuum.

Amid the chaos, Czar Nicholas II and his family soon met their terrible fate. There was an attempt to exile them to England, but the British government refused to let them in. The Anglo-Saxons were not interested in saving the Russian monarch, betraying their ally to whom they had just recently given all possible honors, including the title of British field marshal. While Nicholas repeatedly rejected the idea of the separate peace treaty with Germany because that would be dishonorable towards his allies, his British cousin King George V forgot about honor. On July 16, 1918 the Czar, his wife, teenage son and daughters, as well as his loyal servants faced the Bolshevik firing squad. Lenin finally got his revenge for his elder brother, who was executed for revolutionary activities back in 1887.

British, French, Japanese and Americans supported the Whites in their fight against "Godless Bolsheviks" and even invaded parts of Russian territory. Not many people actually believed that the Bolsheviks were going to win. It looked like that Russia is just going to disintegrate into pieces.

Then a miracle happened. Bolsheviks prevailed, and in 1922 in the place of the Russian Empire they created the Union of Soviet Socialist Republics. There were some losses of territory. Former Russian provinces Finland, Poland and newly created Baltic States became independent, Western Ukraine and Western Belorussia were annexed by Poland, and Bessarabia was

The True Origins of World War II

annexed by Romania. However, Bolsheviks retook Eastern Ukraine, Transcaucasia, Central Asia, Siberia and the Far East. The Russian state was mostly preserved.

So how did the victory of Bolsheviks happen? They certainly offered fresh ideas and new hope after both monarchists and liberals had discredited themselves. Still, the Bolshevik victory was hardly possible if the Allies had not let them win. Despite their stated alliance the opposition, the Whites received very little support and only when it suited the Allies' interests.

For example, White leader General Denikin received some supplies from the British, but only to enable him to tighten the blockade against the Germans. However, when in summer 1919 Denikin started his march on Moscow, British support waned. Another prominent White leader Admiral Kolchak happened to take hold of major portion of Russian gold reserves. In January 1920, Kolchak was betrayed by the French and Czech, who let him to be captured and executed by Bolsheviks while they hijacked the train with the gold. Indeed, though the British, French and Americans publicly recognized all new states that declared their independence from Russia, they never recognized either Denikin or Kolchak as the lawful Russian leaders.

Moreover, Allied troops almost never met Reds in the battle. Only Churchill, who always saw one step ahead, wanted active British involvement in the fight against Bolsheviks, urging the Allies to "strangle Bolshevism in its cradle." The secret to such Allied behavior was simple; they did not want reunited Russia. Bolshevik or not Bolshevik, they did not care so long as Russia was weak and no threat to their global interests.

In summer 1919, British Prime Minister Lloyd George told Churchill explicitly that he did not want Denikin to win, since a reunited Russia may become big threat to Great Britain. In November 1919, Lloyd Gorge publicly confessed about it in the

Tigran Khalatyan

House of Commons. His very revealing speech is full of historical parallels:

> "Let us really face the difficulties. What is the other difficulty? Here you have got the Baltic States on one side. There is Finland, there is Poland, there is the Caucasus, Georgia, Daghestan, Azerbaijan, the Russian Armenians; then you have Koltchak and Petlura, all those forces anti-Bolshevist. Why are they not united, why cannot you get them united? Because their objects in one fundamental respect are incompatible. Denikin and Koltchak are fighting for two great main objects. The first is the destruction of Bolshevism and the restoration of good government in Russia. Upon that he could get complete unanimity amongst all the forces, but the second is that **he is fighting for a reunited Russia**. Well, it is not for me to say whether that is a policy which suits the British Empire. There was a very great Statesman, a man of great imagination, who certainly did not belong to the party to which I belong, Lord Beaconsfield, who regarded **a great, gigantic, colossal, growing Russia rolling onwards like a glacier towards Persia and the borders of Afghanistan and India as the greatest menace the British Empire could be confronted with.** ... The Esthonians do not want a reunited Russia; to the Latvians and Lithuanians, it is poison. The Ukrainians I am not quite so sure of. They are divided, and I would not dogmatise about them. I met a Ukrainian the other day. He was the late Russian Minister of Finance. He told me he was bred and born in the Ukraine, and he said, as far as he was concerned, he had never before the War heard of the Ukraine nationality. As far as he knew, there was no difference between that part of Russia and any other part. He said, "I am a Russian, and the mere fact that I was born in the South does not make any difference." Denikin and Petlura take different views. It shows how difficult it is for you to thread your way in this tangle when you get two honest Ukrainians like Mr. Bark and General Petlura who disagree about the country where they were born."

The True Origins of World War II

Likewise, colonel House wrote in 1918:

"the rest of the world will live more calmly if instead of a huge Russia there are four Russias in the world. One is Siberia, and the rest is the divided European part of the country."

The official map compiled by the US Department of State for the Paris Peace Conference also proposed Russia split up into pieces. The annex to this map said:

"All of Russia should be divided into large natural areas, each with its own economic life. Moreover, no region should be so independent as to form a strong state."

Indeed the biggest mistake the Whites made was that, being true Russian patriots, they openly stated that they were fighting for a reunited Russia. Clearly, this was a mortal sin in Allied eyes and ensures that fellow Whites in Poland, Finland and other breakaway provinces would never come to Russia's aid. The Bolsheviks, on the other hand, subscribed to Wilson's principle of self-determination and immediately recognized independence of the breakaway states. Later, when the opportunity presented itself, they conquered what they could back with the help of local comrades.

Remarkably, while the Whites of central Russia and the Whites in the breakaway provinces were the enemies, the Reds were friends and comrades everywhere. And so it happened that the "state of workers and peasants" became a reality, promoting the ideas of communism around the world. With the support from Moscow, communist movements would spring up in many countries—giving new hope to many oppressed peoples around the world and representing a "Red Scare" to everyone else.

Tigran Khalatyan

Separatism versus Self Determination

Separatism has negative meaning for patriotic nationalists who do not want the split up of their country. Self-determination, on the other hand, has a positive meaning for the proponents of national liberation. The world usually cheers when small nations declare their independence, as it did when Poland, Finland and the Baltic States broke away from Russia.

But aren't separatism and self-determination the sides of the same coin? They are, and in the world politics, the coin can be turned on either side depending on the player's goals. As recently as in 2008, Kosovo declared independence from Serbia with the military and political support of the United States and NATO, and over objections of Russia. Same year Abkhazia and South Ossetia declared independence from Georgia with the military and political support from Russia and over objections from the United States and NATO. So what takes precedent sovereignty or self-determination? It simply depends on which camp you are in. When the Serbian minority of Kosovo asked to join their mother country, a United States official responded that they were going to support "territorial integrity of Kosovo", although they had just completely disregarded the territorial integrity of Serbia.

During World War I, President Wilson was the champion of the self-determination, with the goal of splitting up of Austro-Hungarian, Ottoman and Russian empires. He then proclaimed:

> "National aspirations must be respected; people may now be dominated and governed only by their own consent. Self- determination is not a mere phrase; it is an imperative principle of action. . . . "

The True Origins of World War II

Understandably, Wilson's principle of self-determination at the time did not go as far as to give self-determination to British, French and American colonies. Moreover, under the cover of self-determination one could see the good old "divide and conquer" strategy beloved by imperialists. A great way to weaken or destroy a country is by splitting it up along ethnical or religious lines. This tool is often used by the great powers, who are always ready to exploit people aspirations for their own benefit.

At the onset of World War II, there was another champion of the self-determination: Adolf Hitler. Hitler's notorious aggression had started under the cover of protection of German minority in Czechoslovakia and Poland and its rights to the self-determination. In his infamous speech on January 30, 1939 Hitler specifically said:

"Among the 14 points which President Wilson promised Germany in the name of all the Allies as the basis on which a new world peace was to be established when Germany laid down her arms, was the fundamental principle of the self-determination of peoples."

Needless to say that to protect his blood brothers in those countries, he eventually invaded and occupied them. But Hitler "protected" not only the rights of Germans. Most notably, he supported Ukrainian nationalism with the goal of separating the "bread basket" of Ukraine from Soviet Russia. During World War II, many Ukrainian nationalists cooperated with Germany, providing Nazis with troops, killing teams and guards for the concentration camps. Today Ukrainian nationalists are again used in the geopolitical game against Russia. Russia responds by supporting Russian separatism a.k.a. self-determination in Ukraine. The game goes on.

We should point out that in regards to Russia so-called "world opinion" always supports the splitting up of Russia and never supports Russian expansion or pro-Russian self-determination in Russian breakaway provinces. If it breaks Russia, it will be cheered; if not, it will be condemned. Nothing has changed in that approach for hundreds of years.

The Nazi Response to Bolshevism

After the war, veteran and adherent nationalist Adolf Hitler watched with growing anxiety as communists spread their ideas among disappointed masses using simple slogans, while traditional parties lost support by boring common people with their high-falutin talk. Hitler would learn from the communist success to create the new type of party that would appeal to the masses. His new Nazi party would promote socialist ideas of equality and government regulation of the economy. It would not be the party of privileged, but the workers' party. It would use the propaganda techniques of simple slogans and mass rallies that had worked so well for the Bolsheviks.

It is often pointed out that the visible attributes of Nazis and Communists were similar. Both parties used red flag, while the melodies of some popular Nazi and Communist party songs were identical. It supposedly implies the similarity of "totalitarian ideologies", although in reality Nazis just deliberately copied some Communist brands to win over German workers. Modern liberal propaganda tries hard to equate Communism and Nazism as equally bad, yet any unbiased researcher could see that core ideas of Nazis and Communists were fundamentally different. If Communists were internationalists who wanted all people of all races to be equal, Nazis were adherent nationalists who planned to enslave other nations on the grounds of the alleged racial superiority of German nation. What could be more different than that?

The True Origins of World War II

Thus, the communist antipode and its sworn enemy was born by the name of National-Socialist German workers party—or in short the Nazi party. In the next decade, one of the main task of Nazis would be to fight communists on the streets of the German cities. The party was baptized by fire in 1923 when Hitler and his followers attempted to seize power in the German state of Bavaria. The coup, known to history as Munich Beer Hall Putsch, failed when police fired on marching Nazis, killing sixteen of them. Hitler escaped death by chance, while his comrade Goering was badly wounded in the stomach. Hitler was sentenced to five years in prison, of which he served only nine months. In prison, Hitler had started to dictate the core book of Nazi regime, Mein Kampf ("My struggle") that contained his autography, political manifesto and plans of conquest.

In Mein Kampf, Hitler articulated a racial theory of master and inferior races. According to Hitler, Germans belong to master Aryan race of creators, while Jews are the inferior race of parasites. Communism, invented by the Jew named Karl Marx, would allow Jews to conquer the world by undermining national states.

Hitler believed that Russians were inferior barbarians, and their land should be occupied by Germany to satisfy the need for Lebensraum ("living space"):

> *"If land was desired in Europe, it could be obtained by and large only at the expense of Russia, and this meant that the new Reich must again set itself on the march along the road of the Teutonic Knights of old, to obtain by the German sword sod for the German plow and daily bread for the nation."*

Moreover if in the past Russians were supported by German blood in the veins of their nobility, now they were ruled by Jewish Bolsheviks. Thus, occupying Russia would not only satisfy

Germany's need for land, it would also do a great service to mankind by destroying the Jewish base.

Hitler also argued that master and inferior races should not mix, offering the United States as an example of a country that kept its power and status thanks to segregation between Whites and Negros. Latin America on the other hand, according to Hitler, was on decline only because Latinos were mix of whites, blacks and native Indians.

The idea of white supremacy was widespread at the time. When the Japanese proposed a racial equality clause in the League of Nations covenant at the Versailles peace conference, it caused quite a stir among British, French and Americans, including the "great democrat" Wilson. Wilson had to make serious concessions to Japanese to make them withdraw the clause. Thus Hitler's racism was quite in line with Anglo-Saxon tradition that at the time.

Hitler wrote in Mein Kampf that by adopting National Socialism, Germany would avenge her defeat in World War I. But how could Germany rearm and start a new war under the watchful eyes of the Great Democracies who defeated her? Hitler's answer, which American and British children never learn in school, is right there in Mein Kampf:

"For such a policy there was but one ally in Europe: England.

With England alone was it possible, our rear protected, to begin the new Germanic march. Our right to do this would have been no less than the right of our forefathers. None of our pacifists refuses to eat the bread of the East, although the first plowshare in its day bore the name of 'sword'! Consequently, no sacrifice should have been too great for winning England's willingness. We should have renounced colonies and sea power, and spared English industry our competition. Only an absolutely clear orienta-

tion could lead to such a goal: renunciation of world trade and colonies; renunciation of a German war fleet; concentration of all the state's instruments of power on the land army. The result, to be sure, would have been a momentary limitation but a great and mighty future."

At the beginning of his political career, Hitler clearly chose the path of becoming the British proxy and as we will see later, it served him very well up until 1939. To appease the British, Hitler explicitly expressed regret in Mein Kampf that in 1904 Germany did not became the British proxy instead of Japan:

"... at the turn of the century London itself attempted to approach Germany. For the first time a thing became evident which in the last years we have had occasion to observe in a truly terrifying fashion. People were unpleasantly affected by the thought of having to pull England's chestnuts out of the fire; as though there ever could be an alliance on any other basis than a mutual business deal. And with England such a deal could very well have been made. British diplomacy was still clever enough to realize that no service can be expected without a return. Just suppose that an astute German foreign policy had taken over the role of Japan in 1904, and we can scarcely measure the consequences this would have had for Germany. There would never have been any 'World War.' The bloodshed in the year 1904 would have saved ten times as much in the years 1914 to 1918. And what a position Germany would occupy in the world today!"

The fantasy of the maniac? Perhaps. But wasn't there a possibility of an Anglo-German alliance if Germans stopped their naval build up, as Colonel House suggested?

An English gentleman who read Mein Kampf may have been satisfied that Hitler seemed to understand well how Germany should behave in regard to naval strength. Also after Germany was crushed in World War I, our English gentleman might start worrying about France or Russia gaining supremacy in Europe. A stronger Germany was needed as a counterbalance to their ambitions. And after all, who likes those aggressive Russian communists, who talk day and night about "world revolution" while building yet another powerful Russian state? The events of the next decade would show that many powerful English gentlemen did indeed share this view.

The Secret of Isolationism

The word "Geopolitics" has the prefix "geo" for a good reason. Geography does play an important role in world politics. For example, the popular U.S. policy of Isolationism is directly related to the geographical fact that America is isolated from the rest of the world by the Pacific and Atlantic oceans. In the past, we could also see that the closer a major democratic country was to Germany, the friendlier it was to Russia. Geography often defined politics.

According to geopolitical science theory, there are sea and land powers. Sea powers are islands such as Great Britain or the "Continental Island" of the United States. These nations project their power through high seas, search for colonies and zones of influence all around globe, and heavily rely on their fleet in trade, war, and for the protection of their borders. On the other hand, land powers such as Germany, China, or Russia expand around their core, use mostly land trade routes, and heavily rely on their army during war and for the protection of their borders.

In peacetime, a sea power may not maintain a big standing army, but it always has its navy ready. A Land power, on the other hand, always maintains a big standing army even if only for protection of its borders. Britain, as a sea power, was nerv-

The True Origins of World War II

ous about German naval build up, but she was okay with a large German army. On the other hand, the German idea of Lebensraum (the living space), that was so dear to Hitler, belonged to the expanding Land power.

Classic geopolitics theory posits that the Eurasian continent is the key to world domination. If one power dominates the whole continent, it becomes self-sustainable and cannot be defended by surrounding "islands". Thus, the task of sea powers is to incite conflict between land powers in Eurasia, and prevent alliances such as between Germany and Russia, or between Russia and China. Keeping in mind that geography naturally plays an important role in world politics, we should point out that the method of dividing and setting up of your opponents against each other is universal. In that regard, the alliance of two powers may raise a red flag in the eyes of the third power.

Let's illustrate the last point. There was this remarkable fellow, Ernst Hanfstaengl (1887-1975) who happened to be the friend of both Adolf Hitler and Franklin D. Roosevelt. One of Hanfstaengl's tasks, which he ultimately failed to accomplish, was to warn Hitler not to alienate the United States. What do you think he was telling Hitler in that regard? In fact, he warned Hitler not to ally with Japan. Indeed, when the Axis pact between Germany, Italy, and Japan was concluded in 1940, President Roosevelt condemned it in the strongest words:

> *"Never before since Jamestown and Plymouth Rock has our American civilization been in such danger as now. For, on September 27, 1940, by an agreement signed in Berlin, three powerful nations, two in Europe and one in Asia, joined themselves together in the threat that if the United States interfered with or blocked the expansion program of these three nations—a program aimed at world control—they would unite in ultimate action against the United States."*

Despite World War II being in full swing at that point in time, none of the aggressive actions of Germany, Italy, and Japan presented such an acute danger in the president's opinion as the formal pact signing. Potential threats that come from even formal unity of the opponents are taken very seriously in global politics. The history from both world wars showed us constant attempts by the great powers to divide their opponents, and Hitler's rise to power could be explained in large part by the fact that he initially seemed to guarantee the split between Germany and Russia.

It is now time to describe the pattern for the US game that we call "Isolationism-Involvement" that was played with some variations during both world wars. It goes as follows. A conflict is brewing overseas. The United States has financial and military means to intervene and preserve peace, but refuses to do so. It may even encourage the conflict behind the scenes. In the first "isolationism" stage of the game, American people say that the United States should not get involved as they could not care less if millions of people die overseas, and perhaps it's good to "let them kill, as many as possible," since those peoples are "not good for democracy" anyway.

I am not making it up. As a matter of fact, Senator Truman, future American President, commented on the Nazi Germany invasion of Russia in 1941:

> *"If we see that Germany is winning we ought to help Russia and if Russia is winning we ought to help Germany, and that way let them kill as many as possible"*

Contemporary historian Alan Axelrod did not disapprove of Truman with the following comment:

The True Origins of World War II

"As most Americans saw it, both Nazism and Communism were totalitarian tyrannies, and neither was good for democracy"

In the second, "involvement" stage of the game, one side of the conflict starts winning, thus threatening to change the balance of power in the world. The United States enters the war while the news of American ships which were sunk under suspicious circumstances or terrorist attacks turn around public opinion. Americans suddenly remember that they are actually enraged by the atrocities that were going for a while already, and hurry to make the world "safe for democracy."

Entering late, America ends the war with fewer casualties compared to other combatants, dictates peace terms, and greatly benefits economically, while its competitors lay devastated.

Despite great success of such tactics, American people suddenly realize that they were dragged into the war by the "imperialists" and "war profiteers." They become disillusioned and start the new round of isolationism until the next war. Curiously, the new war grows directly from the "world safe for democracy" as Nazi Germany grew from the Peace of Versailles. After all, policing the world and saving peace doesn't bring many benefits—engaging late does.

To this day, Americans keep arguing which is better—to be involved, or to stay away—from this or that conflict overseas, and choosing the right moment for the strike in the ever going "Isolationism-Involvement" game.

Here are examples of the famous sunken ships that became casus belli, the excuses for U.S. to start wars:

- 15 February 1998, USS Maine exploded in the Havana harbor under suspicious circumstances and became an excuse for the start of the Spanish-American war.

- 7 May 1915, the British ocean liner RMS Lusitania that sailed despite German warnings and was torpedoed, It was used to justify United States entrance into World War I. In fact, the Lusitania was engaged in a secret mission to supply British with weapons.

- 7 December 1941, provoked, but at least real, Japanese attack on Pearl Harbor, that sunk the battleship USS Arizona and other ships. This brought the United States into World War II.

- 2-4 August 1964, American ships USS Maddox and USS Turner Joy attacked under murky circumstances provoked United States entry into Vietnam War.

In the modern world, ship sinking is no longer popular. Instead there are plane crashes and other terrorist attacks that are used to manipulate public opinion. In the twenty-first century, America woke up from another stage of "isolationism" after the 9/11 terrorist attacks that were used to justify the invasion of Iraq. However after conquering Iraq, Americans once again became disillusioned and withdrew their troops, leaving a terrorist Islamic State behind—the great excuse for the next "Involvement."

Please note that I am not preaching a conspiracy theory about a secret society that rules America from generation to generation and designs those games. The real conspiracies may exist, but the games we talk about can be very well explained by geography, human nature, economics, and political culture.

The True Origins of World War II

What game was played by Great Britain—at the time a primary player in European affairs? The famous British politician Winston Churchill described the British game in one of his speeches:

> *"For 400 years the British policy has been to oppose the strongest power in Europe by uniting all the lesser powers against it. Sometimes it's Spain, sometimes it's Germany, sometimes France. I should have felt exactly the same about Napoleon that I now feel about Hitler"*

In World War I, Germany was the strongest power in Europe, so Great Britain naturally allied with other powers against it. However, after Germany was defeated and Russia collapsed, France became the strongest power in Europe. This gave rise to Franco-phobia in England. Churchill, who was a prophet, realized early the danger of Hitler and warned his fellow British citizens that the time had come to oppose Germany instead of France. However, as we know, Churchill was in the back seat of British politics until 1940. The British rule of supporting the lesser power against the strongest one initially collided with Hitler's alleged desire to become the British proxy. As a matter of fact, British press attacks against the Versailles treaty were second only to such attacks in the German press and while French wanted to receive full amount of reparations from Germany, England was the "voice of reason."

British, like Americans, also create a false impression that they were not going to be involved into the conflict, thus encouraging the aggressors. We already described how the British were hesitant on the onset of World War I. They repeated the hesitation game at the onset of the World War II as well. Once again, Winston Churchill gave insight to these British tactics when he warned Nazi Foreign Minister von Ribbentrop:

Tigran Khalatyan

"... you must not underrate England. She is a curious country, and few foreigners can understand her mind. Do not judge by the attitude of the present administration. Once a great cause is presented to the people all kinds of unexpected actions might be taken... Do not underrate England. She is very clever. If you plunge us all into another Great War she will bring the whole world against you, like last time."

We are going to unveil the mystery of those "curious" and "clever" Anglo-Americans who were hesitant and indecisive when they held all the cards, but later became defiant and uncompromising under much more difficult circumstances. Those games of Anglo-Americans have one goal, and that goal is not peace. The true goal of those games was always to push their opponents against each other, join late into the conflict, and win it with minimal casualties!

Conclusion

The 1919 Versailles treaty did not bring a just peace. The Wilson's promise "There shall be no annexations, no contributions, no punitive damage" was forgotten. History shows that well sounding principles of international politics, such as the principle of the self-determination, are applied only when they fit the selfish national interests of the great powers.

The surprising victory of Bolsheviks in Russia can be attributed in part to the desire of the great powers to avoid reunification of Russia. Meanwhile, Hitler could expect success in Germany because he positioned himself as the friend of England and the enemy of Communist Russia.

The True Origins of World War II

The history shows that the main geopolitical strategy of Anglo-Saxon powers is to divide their opponents, provoke war between them, and join late into the conflict to win it with the minimal casualties. The separation of England and the United States from the Eurasian continent fits well into this two-stage strategy, where first stage is "isolationism", and the second stage is "crusade" to make the world "safe for democracy".

Part II
A Twenty-Year Armistice
1920-1937

World War I was called "the war to end all wars". It was a terrible deadly conflict and people pledged to learn their lesson and avoid future wars at all cost. Or so it seemed. In reality, preparations for the next war started as soon as the First World War was over. Wilson and Lloyd George promised that after the democracies won the war they could maintain lasting peace, but it was a deceit. While talking about "peace," politicians actually thought that they could wage war smarter the second time around.

Chapter 4:
The Invisible Hand

Unemployed men lined up for free food outside a soup kitchen opened by Al Capone during Great Depression.
Chicago, the United States, 1931.

There were millions of unemployed, hungry and homeless in the United States during Great Depression of 193-s that began for no apparent reason in the peaceful, democratic, free-market economy. Guess what helped to end this economic calamity for the "peace loving" country? World War II.

Pop Quiz

What event marked the turning point towards the beginning of World War II?

    a) The Nazi-Soviet Non-Aggression Pact of 1939

    b) Hitler's ascent to power in 1933

    c) The American stock market crash of 1929.

> *"It is the jungle law of capitalism. You are backward, you are weak—therefore you are wrong; hence, you can be beaten and enslaved. You are mighty—therefore you are right; hence, we must be wary of you. ... We are fifty or a hundred years behind the advanced countries. We must make good this distance in ten years. Either we do it, or we shall be crushed"*
>
> Joseph Stalin. Moscow, February 4, 1931.

> *"Thus, both in Europe and in Asia, conditions were swiftly created by the victorious Allies which, in the name of peace, cleared the way for renewal of war."*
>
> Winston Churchill

Both World Wars were greased by ideologies. In World War I, liberal democracy prevailed against the monarchies of Russian, German, and the Austro-Hungarian and Ottoman empires; hundreds of years of well-established traditional rule were wiped out overnight without a trace. However, victory actually weakened liberal democracy on the ideological front. War torn, disillusioned and dissatisfied peoples all around globe felt that democracy was only for the benefit of the chosen few.

The Great Depression

The crisis of democracy became acute when the Great Depression started in the United States out of the blue in 1929, casting doubts about the free market economy and Adam Smith's "invisible hand" that supposedly improves the lives of men like magic.

For no apparent reason, banks and businesses began closing one after another. Unemployment skyrocketed and millions of people in the United States and around the world become hungry and homeless. Farmers could not sell their crops because of falling prices, and their farms went bankrupt. The U.S. government then set production quotas on farmers; the "excess" wheat was burnt in stoves; cotton was plowed under and piglets were slaughtered.

Serious doubts emerged about the sanity of the system that burns food while millions starve. Indeed, while there have been numerous famines in the world history caused by bad harvests, natural disasters, wars and food requisitions, only democracy introduced hunger marches while there was overproduction of food!

The extent of hanger and hardship of the Great Depression in the United States would be noticeable even in 1941 when the country entered the war and a massive draft began. Although

> *"the Army would accept anyone sane over 5 feet tall, 105 pounds in weight, possessing twelve or more of his own teeth, and free of flat feet, venereal disease and hernias, no fewer than 40 per cent of citizens failed these basic criteria."*

According to historian Arnold Toynbee,

> *"In 1931, men and women all over the world were seriously contemplating and frankly discussing the possibility that the Western system of society might break down and cease to work."*

The head of the Bank of England, Montagu Norman (1871-1950), stated the same year:

"Unless drastic measures are taken to save it, the capitalist system throughout the civilized world will be wrecked within a year."

When President Franklin D. Roosevelt (1882-1945) addressed the nation in his first inaugural speech on March 4, 1933 he sounded very much like communist:

"... Only a foolish optimist can deny the dark realities of the moment... The money changers have fled from their high seats in the temple of our civilization. We may now restore that temple to the ancient truths. The measure of the restoration lies in the extent to which we apply social values more noble than mere monetary profit.

Happiness lies not in the mere possession of money; it lies in the joy of achievement, in the thrill of creative effort. The joy and moral stimulation of work no longer must be forgotten in the mad chase of evanescent profits. These dark days will be worth all they cost us if they teach us that our true destiny is not to be ministered unto but to minister to ourselves and to our fellow men."

It was against this threatening background that peoples of the world looked for alternatives to the liberal democracy and free market economy. There were actually big doubts that "free market" really existed after all, as the world economy was already in the tight grip of few banks and corporations. Names like Morgan or Rockefeller projected more power than some emperors of the past, while their behind the scenes role in politics was giving an insidious double meaning to the idea of an "invisible hand". A free market economy stops being "free" when it is monopolized by the few.

Numerous banks, businesses and farms that went bankrupt during the Great Depression did not just disappear; they became the property of the few lucky ones. While so many people lost their money in the stock market, someone else bought all those stocks very cheap and rode the subsequent economic upswing to even greater wealth. Was the crisis of free market economy genuine, or it was orchestrated behind the scenes for the benefit of the few?

In either case, socialism in one form or another was the call of the day. The classical definition of socialism is the government regulation of the economy and the establishment of certain mandatory benefits for citizens. The most radical version of socialism is the communist approach of the nationalization of businesses and agriculture collectivization, as in the Soviet Union. Italy and Germany responded with another form of government, fascism, in which government regulations actually enforced the privileges of big business.

In the United States, Roosevelt's New Deal offered a series of social reforms and government backing for banks, but stopped short of a full-on socialist approach. Right after his inauguration speech, President Roosevelt temporarily closed all banks in the United States. Shortly thereafter he also forbade the use of monetary gold.

The financial revolution that eventually eliminated the gold standard is outside the scope of this book, but we should mention that the financial oligarchy plays an enormous role in the modern democracy. We learn in school that there are legislative, executive and judicial branches of a government, but in the modern world there is also financial branch of the government in the form of the independent central bank that prints money, provides credit to other banks, and in effect has the most power over the economy. The U.S. President can fire the heads of CIA or FBI at any time, but he cannot fire the Chairman of the Federal Reserve, the American central bank.

The True Origins of World War II

By the way, while U.S. constitution is outdated to reflect the reality of four branches of government, the independence of Central Bank is spelled out in the modern Russian Constitution, that was written in 1993 with the help of American advisers.

The "founding father of international finance" Mayer Amschel Rothschild (1744-1812) allegedly said, "Let me issue and control a nation's money and I care not who writes the laws." Well, the Bank of England, the Banque de France, and the Federal Reserve of the United States, all three key world central banks were privately owned and independently operated in the era of both World Wars. The conspiracy theories about bankers who rule the world behind the scenes do have some facts to back them up.

Apart from the economic changes, the Great Depression reactivated the forces of the imperialist conquest. War, as the fastest way to plunder resources and eliminate the competitors, was always one of the solutions for the crisis, although it was rarely stated openly. Great changes in the world economy had to bring not only social change, but new rearmament as well. Ideology served as the catalyst for this process.

Communism vs. Capitalism

The real alternative to the capitalist system was tried in Communist Russia, where as a rule all banks, businesses and land were owned by the state. Party elite, scientists, and skilled workers were sure to have more income and better living conditions than the rest of the population, but the income gap between rich and poor was very narrow. In fact, there was no real "rich" left, as even the most privileged citizens were rather poor compare to ordinary American millionaires. Also for the first time in world history, education and health care became free for everyone.

This new fair society was not easy to build. After death of Lenin in 1924, there was power struggle between Trotsky and Stalin for the leadership in the party and the country. Trotsky, the model for the Nazi caricature of "Jewish-Bolsheviks", was a gifted orator, a passionate writer and a popular leader of Red Army. As an orthodox Marxist, he supported the idea of Russia becoming "the firewood in the fire of World Revolution" a.k.a. the theory of the permanent revolution. In other worlds, Trotsky believed that building socialism in Russia without world revolution was meaningless.

Stalin, on the other hand, was neither a passionate speaker nor a good writer; in fact, he spoke slowly with the noticeable Georgian accent. He was not imposing public figure either; he was short, had a damaged left arm and a face permanently scarred by smallpox. But he was a smart politician and a great organizer. Defying orthodox communists, Stalin proclaimed that socialism can be built in one country, Soviet Russia, and that task should take priority.

By 1927, Stalin won political and ideological struggle with Trotsky and became the undisputed leader of the party and the country. Trotsky was exiled from Russia in 1929 and assassinated in Mexico on Stalin's orders in 1940. Upon winning the power struggle, Stalin set ambitious goals of rapid industrialization, sensing that new imperialist war may crash backward Russia.

"We are lagging behind the advanced countries in 50-100 years," Stalin said in 1931. "We must make good this distance in ten years. Either we do it, or they crush us." His words were prescient; in exactly ten years, Germany would invade Russia.

Thousands of new industrial enterprises sprang up in the Soviet Union in the following years. New huge hydro-electrical plants and new roads were built. As new plants and factories needed more engineers, the education and science were on the rise. Illiteracy that was as high as 70 percent before the revolution rapidly declined. During that time, while United States was still in the grip of the Great Depression, thousands American engineers found jobs in the Soviet Union. As a matter of fact, some American companies had significant impact in advancing Soviet technology. Wall Street didn't cooperate much with the Czar's Russia, but apparently it had no problem making deals with the Bolsheviks.

Russian industrialization was linked with the collectivization of agriculture, started in 1929. Peasants were forced to unite into collective farms where tractors could be used to plow the land and thus increase the productivity. Peasants left without work would move into the industrial workforce.

The dark side of collectivization aimed to extract crops from peasants to pay for the industrialization needs. Rich farmers a.k.a. kulaks, were purged as class enemies and exiled to Siberia, while their property was confiscated. Because of those disturbances and a bad harvest, there was widespread famine in rural areas in 1932-33.

Neither there was much democracy in Russia. The country became a one party dictatorship with total control of the society by the government. Anglo-American historians tend to view such governments unfavorably, but under Stalin the Soviet Union was successfully fighting an ideological war with the democracies. True, there were political persecutions of peasants in the Soviet Union, but at the time, there was hunger and hardship even in the United States. More importantly, intellectuals around the world viewed the Soviet Union as the most progressive nation. Indeed, apart from the successes in the economy, communists were also leading in the questions of women equality, anti-colonial and anti-racist movements. Jews and other minorities held many of the important positions in Communist Russia. The leader of the country Stalin was son of the cobbler, and it was by no means the only example of people from the former unprivileged classes raised to the top.

Russia was winning on the propaganda front as well. In the 1936 Soviet movie Circus, a white American circus artist becomes a victim of racism after giving birth to a black baby, but finds refuge, love and happiness in the Soviet Union. At the end of the movie, an evil manager shows the black baby to the public in the Soviet circus, thinking that Russians would be outraged by the American artist's "immorality". Instead, her black son is embraced by the friendly Soviets. The movie climaxes with a lullaby being sung to the baby by representatives of various Soviet ethnicities.

Despite all the ideological successes and alleged absolute unity of the communist party under Stalin's leadership, the power struggle in the Soviet Union was far from over. In 1937, on the 20th anniversary of the revolution, the first communist country was rocked by the Great Purge. The purge started as the familiar persecution of former kulaks and class enemies from the Civil War era; however, it soon widened to include leadership of the army and the communist party. In one year of the purge, hundreds of thousands people were shot or sent to labor camps.

Among the most notable victims of the purge were Mikhail Tukhachevsky (1893–1937), the leading military leader and the Chief of General staff, and Nikolay Bukharin (1888-1938), distinguished party leader and the principal framer of the Soviet Constitution of 1936. The closest Lenin's comrades Lev Kame-

The True Origins of World War II

nev (1883-1936) and Grigory Zinoviev (1883-1936) were executed a year earlier, in 1936.

The purge ended with the arrests and executions among security police that carried out the purge in the first place. The head of the security police Genrikh Yagoda (1891-1938) was shot. His successor Nikolai Yezhov (1895-1840), who was the main executor of the Great Purge, was also shot. Yezhov was replaced by Stalin's fellow Georgian Lavrentiy Beria (1899-1953), who brought the Great Purge to the end and freed most people arrested by Yezhov.

Western historians tend to talk about the bloodthirsty tyrant Stalin who killed many innocent people. However, there was some gloomy fairness in the purges; communist elite of the country actually suffered most. Supporters of the democracy-dictatorship paradigm miss the ironic paradox: if Stalin killed only good people, does it mean that communists were actually good?

The purge was complex event and thus cannot be blamed on Stalin alone. The responsibility is shared between Stalin and others like Yezhov who technically was also a "victim" of Stalin's purges. It was revolution from the top in which the old Bolshevik guard that used to rule the country and had connections with foreign powers was almost completely eliminated. There were real conspiracies against Stalin, and pretending that all accused did not do anything wrong is not an honest approach to history. While so many innocent people died, the purge also punished many guilty ones.

By the way Churchill in his memoirs called it "the merciless, but perhaps not needless, military and political purge in Soviet Russia". The old saying "the revolution devours its children" once again became true. Stalin consolidated his power, eliminated possibility of the coup, and liquidated the fifth column that might surrender the country in the coming war.

It's also anti-historical to increase number of the purge victims from hundreds of thousands to millions or even tens of millions, as is often done. If Stalin was so extraordinary bad, why do his opponents constantly need to stretch the facts?

The Rise of Fascism

To the threat of communism, the conservative "civilized world" responded with fascism, the idea of the strong state that could provide national unity against internal and external enemies, and especially against communists. In a fascist country, one party dictatorship and government regulations of economy could provide stability and shield big business, landlords and aristocracy from the devastating class struggle.

Fascists preferred brown or black shirts, saluted with outstretched right arm, and were extremely militarized and ready to wage wars of conquest. While in the democratic countries labor movement and intellectuals were sympathetic to communism, the trademark of all fascist countries was vehement anti-communism.

The first fascist state was Italy (word "fascist" comes from the Italian word for bundle), where Benito Mussolini seized power in 1922 by marching his militants on Rome. At the cost of silencing opposition and suppressing political freedoms, the Italian Fascist government allowed order and stability. Italians remember that during Mussolini trains started coming on time, and the Sicilian Mafia was decimated.

Even more importantly Fascism provided reliable defense against communism, of which the elites of the democratic coun-

The True Origins of World War II

tries could not disapprove. In 1927, Churchill visited Rome and proclaimed:

> *"If I had been an Italian I am sure that I should have been whole-heartedly with you from the start to finish in your triumphant struggle against the bestial appetite and passions of Leninism. I will, however, say a word on an international aspect of fascism. Externally your movement has rendered a service to the whole world. The great fear which has always beset every democratic leader or a working-class leader has been that of being undermined or overbid by something more extreme than he. Italy has shown that there is a way of fighting the subversive forces which can rally the masses of the people, properly led, to value and wish to defend the honour and stability of civilized society. She has provided the necessary antidote to the Russian poison. Hereafter no great nation will be unprovided with an ultimate means of protection against the cancerous growth of Bolshevism."*

Remember the fairy tale about how fascists and communists threatened democracy? In reality, the democracies had fascists as their allies against the communists. We quoted only Churchill, but there were many others prominent representatives of the democracies who supported Mussolini. Do you know how Kim Philby (1912-1988), the star Soviet spy in England, managed to receive work in British Intelligence MI6 apart from showing his abilities? He simply demonstrated his sympathy to fascists, and that proved his political trustworthiness for the democracy.

With the support of the democratic powers, fascism was on the rise. Throughout the 1920s and 1930s, many other countries abandoned democracy to become fascist or semi-fascist right-wing dictatorships. As a rule, new regimes were setup after violent coup and were often headed by generals. Poland, Portugal and Lithuania became dictatorships in 1926, Austria in

1933, Latvia and Estonia in 1934. Classic fascism won in Spain in 1939 and in Romania in 1940.

Another, not classic fascist, but certainly nationalist and militarist state was Japan. Japan was a constitutional monarchy with an elected parliament. God Emperor Hirohito (1901-1989) was the head of state; he appointed the government and approved its policy. In practice, Japan's politics was determined by violent power struggle between the nobility and military elites. Emperor's power was limited, but he was not just powerless figurehead as Americans presented it after the war.

Once an ally and the junior partner of Great Britain and the United States, Japan was hit hard by Great Depression. Lacking natural resources and even food, Japan heavily relied on international trade, but at the time of economic crisis United States and other countries protected their markets with high tariffs. Economic hardships fueled the rise of Japanese militarism; the country would try solving her problems with the force of arms.

The rising militarism came into conflict with moderates in Japanese government who did not dare to challenge the supremacy of the United States and Great Britain. The conflict came to a head when Japanese Prime Minister Inukai Tsuyoshi (1855-1932) ratified the London Naval Treaty, which limited the size of the Imperial Japanese Navy and asserted the naval supremacy of British and Americans. On May 15, 1932, a group of young officers assassinated the 77-year-old Tsuyoshi.

"If I could speak you would understand," said the old wise man before dying.

"Dialogue is useless," the assassins answered.

The assassination of Tsuyoshi was followed by an attempted military coup in 1936 that ended with murders and purges of

The True Origins of World War II

many high-ranking officials. Slowly but surely, the army was taking more and more power in the government.

Yet the main fascist power was Nazi Germany, where to militarism, nationalism and anti-communism Adolf Hitler added the most vehement anti-Semitism.

The Jewish Question

The conspiracy theory promoted by Henry Ford and Adolf Hitler stated that "international Finance-Jewry" organized First World War and sponsored Bolsheviks in the quest to rule the world. The theory was fueled by the fact of the strong position of Jews in the area of the international finance. At the time the famous Jewish banking firms included Rothschilds, Lazards, Warburgs and Kuhn-Loeb.

The influence of the Rothschilds, once the wealthiest family of the world, on European politics of the nineteenth century became legendary. Five Rothschild brothers headed banks in Frankfurt, Vienna, London, Naples and Paris and were known for financing wars, stopping wars, and trashing Austrian government bonds when the Austrian government attempted to introduce an anti-Semitic law. To many, it seemed as though the European governments did not matter and the real rulers of Europe were Rothschilds.

In the twentieth century as a demonstration that Jewish finance does not have national allegiance, there was a story of Warburg brothers, Paul and Max. Paul Warburg (1868-1932) advised the American government and was one of the founders of the American Federal Reserve, while his brother Max Warburg (1867-1946) was a leading German banker who advised the German government. Surprisingly, Max continued his service for Germany even during early years of Nazi rule, until Hitler's anti-Semitic policies forced him out in 1938.

While Jewish influence in international finance was significant, Anglo-Saxon financial influence was perhaps even more significant. Famous Anglo-Saxon banking firms included Morgan, Brown Brothers, and Barings. The influence of the Rockefeller and Vanderbilt families should not be overlooked either. Some modern conspiracy theories actually view the world wars as the struggle between the Rothschilds and the Rockefellers.

Anti-Semitic conspiracy theories have existed for centuries, but active participation of Jews in the communist movement brought them to the new level after 1917 as Jews apparently got not behind the scenes, but real power in Russia. The predominance of Jews among the communist leadership of Russia at the beginning of the twentieth century was readily apparent. For example, four out of the seven original communist politburo members—Trotsky, Zinoviev, Kamenev and Sokolnikov—were Jews. (The three others were Lenin, Stalin, and Bubnov.) The assassin of the Czar and his family was also a Jew.

The world got even more worried when communism started to spread beyond Russian borders. The revolutionary zeal of Russian Jews could have been explained by the discrimination of Jews in the Russian Empire; however, that explanation did not really work for Europe, where Jews were well integrated into society. The Hungarian Soviet Republic was the most striking example. In the turmoil followed World War I, Hungarian communists seized power in Budapest on March 21, 1919. Their leader, Bela Kun (1886-1938), was a Jew, and twenty-two of his twenty-five commissars were also Jews. The London Times called this regime "the Jewish Mafia".

The new Communist government decreed the abolition of aristocratic titles and privileges, separation of church and state, free education, and language and cultural rights to minorities. It nationalized industrial and commercial enterprises, socialized housing, transport, banking, medicine, cultural institutions, and all landholdings of more than 40 hectares. The communists also wanted to destroy Hungarian historical monuments, statues and national symbols, since they represented "reactionary" kings and heroes. The national anthem was banned, and the national flag was replaced by the red flag.

This short-lived Hungarian Soviet Republic collapsed when Romanian troops occupied Budapest on August 6, 1919. Bela Kun escaped to the Soviet Union, where he became one of the leaders of the Communist International. Like other prominent communists, he was arrested and shot during the Great Purge.

As in Russia, the progressive character of communist reforms in Hungary went hand in hand with the measures that deeply insulted people's sense of national identity. With so many Jews in the communist government, those actions were often seen as nothing more than the Jewish attempt to undermine the national state.

In the 1920s, "The Protocols of the Elders of Zion" that described alleged Jewish plan to achieve world domination, became very popular reading, despite being condemned as forgery. In February 1921, Henry Ford said in an interview: "The only statement I care to make about the Protocols is that they fit in with what is going on." Ford published the Protocols and other anti-Semitic materials in the weekly newspaper The Dearborn Independent that reached a circulation of 900,000 by 1925.

The idea of a worldwide Jewish conspiracy was shared even by respected politicians. Winston Churchill's article "Zionism versus Bolshevism: A Struggle for the Soul of the Jewish People," published in 1920, covers very well all aspects of the "Jewish Question" as it was seen at the time by the respectable circles in the democratic counties. In his article Churchill talked about "Good and Bad Jews". While praising "National Jews" and "Zionist Jews" Churchill strongly condemned so called "International Jews":

> *"In violent opposition to all this sphere of Jewish effort rise the schemes of the International Jews... This movement among the Jews is not new. From the days of Spartacus-Weishaupt to those of Karl Marx, and down to Trotsky (Russia), Bela Kun (Hungary), Rosa Luxembourg (Germany), and Emma Goldman (United States), this worldwide conspiracy for the overthrow of civilisation and for the reconstitution of society on the basis of arrested development, of envious malevolence, and impossible equality, has been steadily growing...*
>
> *It has been the mainspring of every subversive movement during the Nineteenth Century; and now at last this band of extraordinary personalities from the underworld of the great cities of Europe and America have gripped the Russian people by the hair of their heads and have become practically the undisputed masters of that enormous empire."*

As we can see, Churchill explicitly accused Jews of being the dominant force behind communism and revolutions. He was not referring to racist or religious theories, only to the undeniable fact of Jewish predominance in the early communist movement:

> *"There is no need to exaggerate the part played in the creation of Bolshevism and in the actual bringing about of the Russian Revolution by these international and for the most part atheistical Jews. It is certainly a very great one;*

it probably outweighs all others. With the notable exception of Lenin, the majority of the leading figures are Jews. Moreover, the principal inspiration and driving power comes from the Jewish leaders..."

Churchill also wrote about Jewish role in Bolshevik terror:

"In the Soviet institutions the predominance of Jews is even more astonishing. And the prominent, if not indeed the principal, part in the system of terrorism ... has been taken by Jews, and in some notable cases by Jewesses. The same evil prominence was obtained by Jews in the brief period of terror during which Bela Kun ruled in Hungary.

The same phenomenon has been presented in Germany (especially in Bavaria), so far as this madness has been allowed to prey upon the temporary prostration of the German people. Although in all these countries there are many non-Jews every whit as bad as the worst of the Jewish revolutionaries, the part played by the latter in proportion to their numbers in the population is astonishing."

Obviously, Adolf Hitler was far more radical in his views. Unlike Churchill who distinguished between "Good and Bad Jews," Hitler assumed that Jews were inherently bad. While Churchill talked about "A Struggle for the Soul of the Jewish People," Hitler simply wanted to exterminate all Jews. However, apart from this, conservatives like Churchill and racists like Hitler had very similar views about communism. For both of them, Bolshevik rhetoric about the equality of all peoples and international solidarity was nothing more than "a scheme to denationalize other races and undermine civilization".

European Jews became Hitler's first target, but the second and largest target was "Jewish" Russia with her vast resources. It was very convenient to hate Jews to grab their property in

Germany, then grab Russian land and property allegedly to free Russians from Jewish influence.

Using the Jewish Bolshevism bogeyman, Hitler and his followers succeeded in bringing a civilized and tolerant Germany into the grips of the most vehement anti-Semitism the world had ever seen. It would not be a stretch to say that Jews were simply made scapegoats for all German problems and all evils in the world. Conservatives in other countries might not have approved of such an approach, but many were somewhat sympathetic to Hitler's anti-communist ideas.

Today Jewish involvement in the communist movement is largely forgotten, as it does not fit the dominant paradigm about good Anglo-American democracies and evil German-Russian totalitarian dictatorships. It's easier to ignore inconvenient questions like "Why did the Nazis link Jews to communism?" or "Was communism really good if Nazis hated it so much?"

We hear neither apologies for Jewish participation in Bolshevik terror nor attempts to point out the progressive character of communist ideals. A research about Jewish participation in communist movement that is not labeled as anti-Semitic virtually cannot exist. Anti-Semitism in Nazi Germany is explained only in the terms of racial stereotypes and religious intolerance, while the significant anti-communist part of the story is hardly even mentioned. Democratic ideology manages to hate Hitler's anti-Semitism and at the same time share Hitler's anti-communism, although for Hitler "Jewish Bolshevism" was a singular notion. In January 1939, as Hitler made a self-fulfilling prophecy about the Holocaust, he once again stressed out his anti-Communism:

> *"If the international Finance-Jewry inside and outside of Europe should succeed in plunging the peoples of the earth once again into a world war, the result will be not*

*the **Bolshevization** of earth, and thus a Jewish victory, but the annihilation of the Jewish race in Europe."*

According to Hitler, the victory of the Jews would mean the victory of communism in the world.

Conclusion

Anglo-American propaganda states that in 1930s democracy was threatened by the two types of totalitarian sects—communists on the left and fascists on the right. In reality, democracy was mostly threatened by the crises of its own market economy. Moreover, the elites of the democratic countries were actually using fascism as the defense against communism.

It should be also noted that while anti-Semitism of the past was driven mostly by religious intolerance, after the Russian Revolution anti-Semitism became entwined with anti-communism on the grounds of the active participation of Jews in the communist movement. The concept of "Jewish Bolshevism" became widespread and fueled Nazi ideology. However the bond between Nazi anti-Semitism and anti-Communism is ignored by Anglo-American propaganda, since it does not fit its ideological paradigms.

Chapter 5:
The Glory of Adolf Hitler

Adolf Hitler, Fuhrer of Germany, 1937

Pop Quiz

After losing World War I, Germany was disarmed, forbidden to build an air force or submarines, and its army could not exceed 100,000 men. So how was Hitler able to start World War II?

a) He did it sneakily, tricking the naïve yet well-intentioned democracies—England, France, and the United States.

b) Trying to avoid war, the democracies wanted to satisfy reasonable demands of Nazi Germany, hoping to pacify it. But dictators cannot be appeased!

c) Hitler was actually supported by the democracies to counter the growing power of the Soviet Union.

> *"He is as immune from criticism as a king in a monarchical country. He is something more. He is the George Washington of Germany — the man who won for his country independence from all her oppressors. To those who have not actually seen and sensed the way Hitler reigns over the heart and mind of Germany this description may appear extravagant. All the same, it is the bare truth. This great people will work better, sacrifice more, and, if necessary, fight with greater resolution because Hitler asks them to do so."*
>
> David Lloyd George
> Prime Minister of Great Britain in 1916-1922
> Daily Express, London, 17 November 1936

Hitler's ascent was amazing in many respects. First, his totalitarian dictatorship grew within a democracy; Hitler came to power in the democratic Germany only after the Nazi party won elections. Second, the German economy and living conditions of Germans improved under Nazi rule. Third, the elites of the great democratic powers treated Hitler with distinct benevolence. In fact, initially the only true enemies of Hitler were not the democracies, but the communists. How does all of the above fit the fairy tale about good democracies and evil dictatorships?

The Rise of Hitler

After the First World War, Germany became a dysfunctional democracy. The new government dealt with both left and right political extremism, including the assassinations of two prominent politicians of Jewish origin, leader of the revolution in Bavaria Kurt Eisner (1867-1919) and German foreign minister

Walther Rathenau (1867–1922). Hyperinflation wiped out the savings of the middle class; working people were suffering from hunger, unemployment and poverty.

Communist influence was steadily growing through the 1920s, but the communists soon had to compete with Nazis who presented themselves as an alternative revolutionary movement. Apart from fighting each other on the streets, Communists and Nazis were also legally participating in elections and getting more and more votes. In the 1928 elections, communists got 10.6% of votes, while Nazis got only 2.6%. After the Great Depression, Nazi popularity suddenly soared, leaving their communist competitors behind. Economic problems were supposed to help communist propaganda, but Nazis received financial support from German industrialists and other wealthy sources, and, as we know, in elections money can play the decisive role.

In March 1932, Hitler participated in the German presidential elections. The other two main candidates were the aging World War I hero Paul von Hindenburg (1847-1934) and the leader of German communists Ernst Thalmann (1886-1944). The communist prophetic slogan was "A vote for Hindenburg is a vote for Hitler; a vote for Hitler is a vote for war", but Thalmann got only third place with 10.2% of votes in the second round. Hitler got 36.8% and second place, while Hindenburg won with 53%. In the following parliamentary elections, communists increased their share to 14.32%, while Nazis swept 37.27% of votes to become the largest party in Reichstag. Although the Nazis were short of an absolute majority, President Hindenburg, fulfilling the communists' prophecy, made Hitler the head of the government on January 30, 1933.

After Hitler became the Chancellor of Germany, he quickly established a dictatorship. On February 27, the suspicious

The True Origins of World War II

Reichstag fire was blamed on communists, and their party was banned. Communist leaders were subsequently arrested and sent to the newly created concentration camps. Former presidential candidate Thalmann would spend 11 years in prison without a trial before being murdered at the end of World War II.

With the communists out of the way, Hitler pushed through the Enabling Act, which made him de-facto dictator. From that moment on, the Reichstag ceased its legislative function and turned into an arena for Hitler to make his speeches.

In the summer 1934, Hitler ordered the assassination of his political opponents inside and outside Nazi party in what came to be known as "The Night of the Long Knives". The most important was the execution of Ernst Roehm (1887-1934) and other leaders of SA, the leftist Nazi party militia, which marked the end of the revolutionary era in Nazi movement to the satisfaction of the German army, landlords, and industrialists.

When President Hindenburg died from natural causes on August 2, 1934, Hitler combined the offices of Chancellor and President and became the Fuhrer of Germany. As the icing on the cake, the military oath was changed and the armed forces swore to be loyal not to the country or constitution, but personally to Hitler.

What happened next? Nothing short of a miracle. Germany suddenly saw economic growth, unemployment was diminished, autobahns were built; health care, sports and other aspects of social life were improving. Then Hitler began to re-arm the military in violation of the Versailles treaty, to which none of the great powers objected. The international prestige of Germany was steadily growing.

Conservative elites of the democratic countries publicly praised Hitler and ignored the existence of the concentration camps and the increased activity of the Gestapo, which was rounding up everyone who spoke out against Nazis. International prestige of Germany did not suffer much even after the adoption of the 1935 Nuremberg Laws, which deprived Jews of German citizenship and prohibited racially mixed sexual relations and marriages. (At the time, interracial marriages were prohibited in some U.S. states too.)

In 1936, Hitler hosted the Summer Olympic Games in Berlin that were attended by all major democratic countries. American historians like to mention that Afro-American athlete Jesse Owens won four gold medals during the Olympics and that cast a shadow on Hitler's racism. However, Owens later complained about his treatment by his own country, not Germany:

> *"Hitler didn't snub me – it was FDR who snubbed me. The president didn't even send me a telegram."*

Quite a few prominent figures from the democratic countries openly supported Hitler. We already mentioned Henry Ford from the United States, who published an anti-Semitic newspaper and had many business contacts with Nazi Germany. Hitler even had a portrait of Henry Ford on the wall of his office in Munich and had only kind words for him in Mein Kampf.

The British list of Hitler's admirers was even more impressive. It included Mortague Norman (1871-1950), the governor of Bank of England, British King Edward VIII (1894-1972) and Lloyd George, the famous British Prime Minister from the World War I era.

Norman's influence was enormous; he was the governor of Bank of England, the leading banking institution of the world, for twenty-four years.

> *"Norman had to be one of the keys to reestablishing Germany's credit abroad. No major bank, in either Lon-*

don or New York, would think of lending money to Germany without a nod from him".

Hjalmar Schacht (1877-1970), Hitler's minister of economics who helped bring Hitler to power and then successfully brought Germany out of the recession was close friend and protégé of Norman.

Norman's finest hour would come in March 1939, when after German occupation of Czechoslovakia, he transferred Czech gold reserve, which was in London for safekeeping, to a German account. Thus, Norman rewarded Hitler for the invasion that was officially condemned by his own government. Norman was not punished for this incident and kept his post until his retirement in 1944.

Edward VIII was King of the United Kingdom and the Dominions of the British Commonwealth, and Emperor of India, from January 20, 1936, until December 11 of the same year. Apart from having such an autocratic title for the head of a democratic state, Edward was also well-known Nazi supporter. Unfortunately for Hitler, Edward was forced to abdicate because he wanted to marry a divorced American woman. In October 1937, Edward and his wife visited Germany, where he met Hitler and gave full Nazi salutes. Relations between Edward and Hitler were so good that many historians have suggested that Hitler was prepared to reinstate Edward as king in the hope of establishing a fascist Britain.

Another Hitler admirer was the famous British Prime Minister from World War I era David Lloyd George. In 1936, Lloyd George visited Germany where he enjoyed Hitler's hospitality. Here few excerpts from the article that Lloyd George published upon returning from Germany:

> "The fact that Hitler has rescued his country from the fear of a repetition of that period of despair, penury and humiliation has given him unchallenged authority in modern Germany".
>
> "The establishment of a German hegemony in Europe which was the aim and dream of the old pre-war militarism, is not even on the horizon of Nazism."
>
> "He is the George Washington of Germany — the man who won for his country independence from all her oppressors."
>
> "Re-armament proceeds quite openly, and they vaunt it. It accounts for the outburst of defiance hurled against Russia. They feel safe now."
>
> "I found everywhere a fierce and uncompromising hostility to Russian Bolshevism, coupled with a genuine admiration for the British people with a profound desire for a better and friendlier understanding with them."
>
> "Germany is no more ready to invade Russia than she is for a military expedition to the moon."

Sweet, isn't it? Keep in mind that the article wasn't written by some marginal politician, but by one of the leaders of World War I who signed the Versailles Treaty. It was the same Lloyd George who in 1918 had commended militarized authoritarian Germany and stated "democracy means peace".

Remember how most histories tell you that everybody in the democratic world hated Hitler, but did not act because of indecisiveness, internal problems or naivety? In fact, as we can see, some "democrats" actually respected Hitler very much. The secret formula of Hitler's success was spelled out in the article. It was

> *"a fierce uncompromising hostility to Russian Bolshevism, coupled with a genuine admiration for the British people".*

Naivety was also certainly a factor, though. According to Lloyd George, Nazi hostility towards communists was not supposed to bring about war between Germany and Russia. Why this counterintuitive conclusion? Because in 1930s the democracies did not want to admit in public what they knew—and wanted—privately. Hitler played along. For example, to reassure his friends in the West, Hitler made the following speech during Nuremberg rally on September 12, 1936:

> *"How Germany has to work to wrest a few square kilometers from the ocean and from the swamps while others are swimming in a superfluity of land! If I had the Ural Mountains with their incalculable store of treasures in raw materials, Siberia with its vast forests, and the Ukraine with its tremendous wheat fields, Germany and the National Socialist leadership, would swim in plenty!"*

Two days later Hitler again confirmed his hate for Communist Russia, promising that he was never going to ally with it:

> *"I can come to no terms with a bolshevism which everywhere as its first act after gaining power is - not the liberation of the working people - but the liberation of the scum of humanity, the asocial creatures concentrated in the prisons - and then the letting loose of these wild beasts upon the terrified and helpless world about them".*

Not surprisingly, Lloyd George downplayed Hitler's intentions:

Tigran Khalatyan

> *"What then did the Führer mean when he contrasted the rich but under-cultivated lands of the Ukraine and Siberia and the inexhaustible mineral resources of the Urals with the poverty of German soil? It was simply a Nazi retort to the accusation hurled by the Soviets as to the miseries of the peasantry and workers of Germany under Nazi rule. ... It is only an interchange of abusive amenities between two authoritarian Governments. But it does not mean war between them."*

Why the West Supported Hitler

How could it happen that the peaceful democratic Germany was the pariah of the world, yet the rearming Nazi dictatorship received so much praise? We have to face reality and understand that the democracies—and especially Great Britain—deliberately supported Nazi regime.

There were a few reasons for that. The first obvious reason was that Hitler made Germany "the bulwark against communism". The democracies might not completely approve of Hitler's anti-Semitism, but it was OK since it had a distinctly anti-Communist flavor. The democracies might not completely approve of Hitler's concentration camps, but they were OK since the inmates were communists. The democracies might worry about Hitler's rearmament, but it seemed OK as long it was directed against Communist Russia.

When high level representative of British government Lord Halifax (1881-1959) met Hitler in November 1937, he congratulated Hitler for "the achievement of keeping Communism out of his country", despite the fact that the methods Hitler used to achieve this result were not the least bit democratic.

There were also geopolitical factors that played into Hitler's hands. Remember how Churchill said, "British policy has been

The True Origins of World War II

to oppose the strongest power in Europe by uniting all the lesser powers against it." From the moment of the German surrender in World War I that made France the strongest nation on the continent, we can see the stark difference between British and French approaches towards Germany. Whenever there was a disagreement about disarmament or reparations, the British were always proposing some sort of "reasonable" solution that suited Germany at the expense of France.

Those geopolitical realities have never been a secret and were openly discussed in the publications of respected historians. The truth was, of course, covered by the smokescreen of propaganda about democracy, but the smart reader always could add two and two.

For example, contemporary historian Margaret Macmillan wrote in Paris 1919 about Versailles Peace Conference:

> *"Illusion or not, the British were determined to disengage themselves from the Continent and its problems. A balance of power there had always served Britain well; interventions was needed only when a single nation threatened to dominate the whole. Germany had been that threat, but it would be foolish now to destroy it and leave France supreme. As passions cooled, the British remembered both their old rivalry with France and the potential for friendship between Germany and Britain. Britain wanted stability on the Continent, not the sort of chaos that could be clearly be seen farther east; a solid Germany at Europe's center could provide that".*

Can the above geopolitical considerations explain the support Hitler received from Great Britain? Of course they can—"balance of power", "chaos seen farther east", and other considerations could have applied to Hitler's case perfectly, as they had nothing to do with "democracy". With the British sabotage, the anti-German détente became ineffective and that sabotage did not end when Hitler came to power.

Neville Chamberlain (1869-1940), who became the prime minister of England in 1937, made telling two remarks a year earlier about French-German dispute over Rhineland:

> *"In the end we succeeded in bringing the French to reason"* and *"I don't know whether the French or the Germans are more impossible to deal with. They both appear to me to be utterly unreasonable".*

In 1936, Hitler was already firmly in control, but British officials were still calling their French counterparts "unreasonable", exactly as it happened in 1919 during the Versailles Peace Conference.

Moreover, unlike Hitler, the democratic Germany was not up to the dual task of keeping France in check and confronting Communist Russia. In April 1922, the western democracies were struck by the Rapallo agreement concluded between Russia and Germany that normalized the relations between them. The two pariah states needed each other to overcome the isolation they were thrown into after World War I. There was even secret military cooperation between Germany and Russia. Handicapped by the disarmament articles of the Versailles treaty, Germans opened military schools in Russia where experts of both countries could be trained away from the eyes of British and French inspectors. Some indecent historians present these facts as proof that Stalin made significant contributions to Hitler's rearmament. In reality, the military cooperation was rather limited; Russians benefited from it as much as Germans did, and it ended when Hitler came to power.

The idea that Germany and Russia can become allies was always the geopolitical nightmare for the Western powers.

The True Origins of World War II

Combining Russian resources and German industry would make the Eurasian continent impenetrable for Anglo-Saxon sea powers, and it would negate the power of France in Europe. If you don't believe me, ask the leading U.S. expert in Geopolitics George Friedman. On February 4, 2015 Mr. Friedman openly stated at the Chicago Council on Foreign Affairs:

> "The primordial interest of the United States, over which for centuries we have fought wars–the First, the Second and Cold Wars–has been the relationship between Germany and Russia, because united there, they're the only force that could threaten us. And to make sure that that doesn't happen."

From the point of view of the democracies, Germany required a leader ideologically incompatible with Communist Russia, and Hitler seemed like the perfect choice. The German foreign minister Rathenau was assassinated two months after he signed the Rapallo agreement, and this strike against German democracy suited not only right-wing nationalists like Hitler, but British, French and American democracies as well.

Apart from being the dedicated fighter against "Jewish Bolshevism," Hitler also pledged his loyalty to England. Thus, in the British view, Hitler could be safely used to wage the war against the Soviet Union without the danger of Germany turning west, as it had happened in World War I. The democracies always denied that they let Hitler rearm so he can attack Russia, but, as in Lloyd George article, there were numerous clumsy attempts to downplay Hitler's intentions. British politicians must have read Mein Kampf and assumed that Hitler had changed his plans, despite the numerous hints that he had not.

For example, there was this interview that Hitler gave to London Daily Express in 1931. In the interview, Hitler admitted that he had only two demands: the cancellation of the war reparations and a "free hand in the East." "While he was not interested in restoration of the old frontiers or even the return of lost colonies, he demanded that the surplus millions of Germans must be allowed to expand into the Soviet Union", making it crystal clear that his main goal was a war of aggression to colonize Russia.

The alleged "naivety" about Hitler's intentions reminds me of the children's play about the hunter and the wolf. In the play, the unsuspecting hunter walks through the forest where the wolf is hiding. "Wolf! Wolf!" shout the kids. The surprised hunter looks around, failing to see the wolf that "hides" next to him. The politicians lying with innocent looks on their faces always remind me of that hunter.

Moreover, if the democracies weren't sure that Hitler re-armed to confront Russia, they would have choked him at once. Here is yet another telling episode of how French ambassador Francois-Poncet was protesting Hitler's "flagrant violation of the Treaty of Versailles":

> *"Hitler confident, solemn retort was that his intentions were purely defensive. France had nothing to fear. His main enemy was Communism, he said, and launched into such a diatribe against the Russians that Francois-Poncet left feeling almost confident that Hitler had no desire to wage war against either France or Britain – only determination to destroy the Soviet regime."*

In world politics, nobody—not even such a "nice guy" as Adolf Hitler—is ever allowed to change the status quo without a valuable excuse. As we can see, Hitler's intent to attack Russia not only was a secret, it was in fact the proof of his "good" intentions!

We can also see that France was handicapped in her foreign politics. On the one hand, the French elite feared domestic and international communism. On the other hand, it pursued traditional security arrangements with Russia against growing German threat. However, to stop Hitler, France had to give up British friendship and she just could not do it, fearing international isolation and remembering the vital British help she received in World War I. Indeed, despite their anti-French policy, the British were not supposed to allow Germany to invade France, as it would tilt the European balance too much to Germany's favor. Under those circumstances, all France could do is to build its Maginot line fortifications on French-German border.

After some delay, the British also started to rebuild their air force. Hitler was allowed to rearm to attack Communist Russia, but he had to be deterred from ever turning his attention from the east to the west.

In early 1935, Hitler declared that Germany is going to rearm in defiance of her treaties. It was the moment when, as Churchill later put it, Hitler could be stopped "without firing of a single shot". In a speech on May 21, 1935, Hitler underlined his hostility towards Communist Russia, reassured England that he was going to respect her naval superiority, and said that "the military alliance concluded between France and Russia without doubt carries the element of legal insecurity". This kind of reasoning worked miracles for Hitler.

Hitler of course began his speech by underlining how much he loved peace:

> "It is said Germany is threatened by nobody; there is no reason why Germany should rearm at all. Why did not the others, then, disarm? ...Our love of peace perhaps is greater than in the case of others, for we have suffered most from war. None of us wants to threaten anybody, but we all are determined to obtain the security and equality

of our people. ... With equality, Germany will never refuse to do its share of every endeavor, which serves peace, progress and the general welfare. The World War should be a cry of warning here. Not for a second time can Europe survive such a catastrophe"

Then Hitler attacked communists and hinted that, despite his love for peace, war with Russia was still possible since Russia was the only state with which he was not going to conclude a non-aggression pact:

"National Socialists and Bolshevists both are convinced they are a world apart from each other and their differences can never be bridged... we are ready to negotiate non-aggression pacts with our neighbor States. We, however, are unable to supplement such pacts by the obligations of a system, which dogmatically, politically and factually is unbearable for us. National Socialism cannot call citizens, of Germany, that is, its adherents, to fight for the maintenance of a system, which in our own State, manifests itself as our great enemy. Obligations for peace – yes! Bellicose assistance for Bolshevism we do not desire, nor would we be in a position to offer it."

This was followed by one of many promises that Hitler broke later, and the essential promise not to challenge the superiority of the British naval fleet:

"Germany has neither the wish nor the intention to mix in internal Austrian affairs, or to annex or to unite with Austria."

"The limitation of the German Navy to 35 percent of the strength of the British Navy is still 15 percent lower than the total tonnage of the French fleet."

Chamberlain admitted that the speech made him "intensely relieved". Hitler was allowed to rearm, since he provided all the necessary excuses. His rearmament was aimed against Russia, and he specifically promised that Nazi Germany and Communist Russia could never be friends. Germany was also not going to challenge British naval supremacy as she did before the First World War.

What could be better than that? It was so good that Hitler's interpreter Schmidt noted:

> *"Only two years ago the skies would have fallen if German representatives had put forward such demands as Hitler was now doing as though they were the most natural thing in the world".*

There was a revealing reaction to the Hitler's rearmament in The Milwaukee Sentinel, an American newspaper. Uncovering what was really going on, U.S Rear Admiral Yates Stirling, Jr. published an article on June 8, 1935, suggesting that Germany should rearm to attack the Soviet Union and kill two birds with one stone: defeat communism and grab Russian resources. However, the title of Stirling's article did not mention Hitler. Instead, it read in big letters, "Europe, Ripe for Strife, Faces Menace of Russian Red Forces". The article was even illustrated with a large picture of Soviet Defense Minister Kliment Voroshilov (1881-1969).

In the article, Stirling analyzed "complicated and confusing" political situation in Europe. He noted that Germany and Japan left League of Nations and that they were hostile to Communist Russia. He also noted that France felt threatened by German rearmament and as a result negotiated a pact for mutual assistance with the Soviet Union. My favorite Stirling's note reads, "Great Britain once again is in her historical role of peace-maker." The "peace-maker" as we know, had already provoked

World War I, and was now working hard to provoke World War II.

Stirling went on to state that "world unrest today primarily is the result of the unequal division among the nations of the essentials of industry – raw materials". In that regard, Stirling pointed out that while Germany and Italy had deficit of raw materials,

> "Russia has, to all intents and purposes, withdrawn a fertile and populous land ... from the usual economic intercourse with the world. This has upset the delicate economic balance of Europe."

After listing in detail all the resources of Russia—which included 16 percent of world's iron, 12 percent of world's oil and 21 percent of world's wheat—Stirling complained that Russian trade was only 2 percent of the world's trade, which meant that greedy Bolsheviks kept most of the raw materials for themselves. Then Stirling remembered that Lenin's words were "Our task – world Revolution", that communists hated capitalism and assisted revolutionary movements in the colonies. It of course could not make happy

> "nations of the world whose economic security is built upon capitalistic principles and the bourgeoisie, nor to those nations whose resources of raw materials and man-power are locked up in their dependencies and colonial possessions."

The conclusion that Stirling reached seemed obvious:

> "Europe today seems ripe for strife. Can these great armies, fully panoplied, be effaced without war? Will the full force of this universal desire for conflict be expended in a

The True Origins of World War II

fratricidal war in Europe? Or may we not look for a united front against Communism?

Germany in sum an alliance must become the great organizer and industrial producer. In her factories the instruments of war on a colossal scale could be turned out.

The resources of the world can be assured to such an alliance only through the command of the seas. This would be obtained should Great Britain throw in her sword on that side. With the seas open for trade, the American markets could not be expected to remain closed.

In the guise of such a great crusade, maybe yet inarticulate in men's thoughts, cannot one see the outlines of a daring plan, not only forever laying the ghost of Bolshevism but for opening up the fertile lands of Russia to a crowed and industrially hungry Europe?"

"A great crusade" against Bolshevism—this is what it was all about. Stirling's frankness helps us to understand what many politicians in the democratic countries actually thought, but dare not say aloud.

Was Russia really such a threat that the democracies had no other choice but to support Hitler as a counterbalance? American and British kids are not discussing it in school, since they first would have to admit that the democracies intentionally supported Hitler. The only allowed argument is that the democracies wanted bad Communists and equally bad Nazis to "destroy each other", but they presumably did not do anything to expedite that mutual destruction.

In the brutal logic of the geopolitical struggle for world domination, the bet on Hitler by the democracies made much sense. However, it showed that the President Wilson's idea that the western democracies do not use "cunningly contrived plans of deception or aggression" was a blatant lie. In reality, the democracies first let the Bolsheviks win to break up the Russian Empire, and then they supported the Nazis as an anti-Communist counterbalance, paving the way to World War II.

Apart from public rhetoric, there was another important aspect in the risky game that the democracies played with Nazi Germany. Hitler was allowed to rearm to attack Communist Russia, but he had to be deterred from ever turning his attention from the east to the west. Seeing this danger Churchill criticized his government for slow rearming with his fancy oratory:

> "The Government simply cannot make up their minds, or they cannot get the Prime Minister to make up his mind. So they go on in strange paradox, decided only to be undecided, resolved to be irresolute, adamant for drift, solid for fluidity, all-powerful to be impotent."

However, Churchill did not explain that British government indecision was coming not from weakness, naivety or stupidity, but from the conflicting objectives. Was it really necessary to spend money on rearmament if Nazi Germany was going to be friendly to England? If the British really wanted to prevent Hitler from starting a war with Russia, they had to prevent his rearmament or try to remove him from power. Instead, the whole debate was about should or should not Great Britain to rearm to insure that Hitler attacks only in the East and never in the West.

This indecisiveness was on display when British prime minister Stanley Baldwin (1867-1947) rejected a French plea to punish Hitler for his reoccupation of the Rhineland in March 1936. As popular historian Andrew Roberts wrote in The Storm of War: A New History of the Second World War:

> *"Had the German Army been opposed by the French and British forces stationed near by, it had orders to retire back to base and such a reverse would almost certainly have cost Hitler the chancellorship. Yet the Western powers, riven with guilt about having imposed what was described as a 'Carthaginian peace' on Germany in 1919, allowed the Germans to enter Rhineland unopposed".*

It is an important admission that Hitler could have been stopped so easily. However, Mr. Roberts, being yet another biased Anglo-American historian, again assumed the best intentions of the democratic powers.

The published British cabinet notes and other documents tell a very different story. The documents show that the French did not feel any "guilt" and actually wanted to kick Hitler out of the Rhineland, but they did not dare to do it without British approval. The German reoccupation of the Rhineland violated the Versailles and Locarno treaties, but the enforcement of these agreements, in Baldwin's opinion, could lead to war. Baldwin argued that with Russian help, the French might defeat Germany, however "it would probably result in Germany going Bolshevik".

Of course, as Mr. Roberts showed, Baldwin was exaggerating. Hitler occupied the Rhineland with little force and was prepared to retreat if French called his bluff. The point that Baldwin was actually making was that weakening Hitler was unacceptable for geopolitical reasons, since it would empower communists.

By applying pressure on Germany early on, England and France could have avoided war, but as a result their beloved Hitler might lose power. In fact, German generals were already preparing the coup to remove their "insane" leader who challenged the existing world order. The democracies did not act not because they were afraid of war or because they were indecisive, but because they needed Hitler. As a result, the political climate changed in Hitler's favor. German generals at first thought that Hitler was reckless, but when they saw him succeed diplomatically and militarily, they started to believe that he was genius.

Covert Support for Hitler

Let us go back to 1922, when Hitler was just a little known Bavarian radical who desperately looked for money to fund his tiny Nazi party. New political parties always struggle to find wealthy donors, and Nazis needed even more money than traditional parties since they had to feed, dress and train "brownshirts", their signature paramilitary force.

The question of who financed Hitler has interested historians for a long time, and there has never been a conclusive answer, especially for the early period of Nazi rise to power. The intelligence services of major powers are the obvious suspects to fill the gap, but understandably, there was not much information about their activity.

History left us with the mostly circumstantial evidence, such as the fact that Hitler made a trip to Switzerland to solicit funds in early 1922. Switzerland, which managed to remain neutral during both World Wars despite its location in the middle of Europe, was always the place where the intelligence services of various countries made their international contacts. For example, Allen Dulles (1893-1969), the infamous head of the CIA, worked in Switzerland for American intelligence during both world wars.

It is well known that when the Nazi party became the mighty force, German industrialists put their bet on it. However, early in

The True Origins of World War II

the game they should have had little interest in funding a small group of radicals. Intelligence services, on the other hand, are always interested in the activity of radical groups. In 1922, Captain Truman Smith, an American intelligence officer and the U.S. military attaché in Germany, visited Adolf Hitler for an interview. At the meeting, Hitler tried to persuade Truman Smith that he could be useful to the United States.

According to Smith report Hitler described his movement as a "union of Hand and Brain workers to oppose Marxism". He stated that it was

> "much better for America and England that the decisive struggle between our civilization and Marxism be fought out on German soil rather than on American and English soil. If we (America) do not help German Nationalism, Bolshevism will conquer Germany. Then there will be no more reparations and Russia and German Bolshevism, out of motives of self-preservation must attack the western nations."

Much impressed, Truman Smith became convinced that Hitler was going to be an important factor in German politics. Then the American officer did Hitler a huge favor by introducing him to Ernst Hanfstaengl, who would guide Hitler into the world of politics. The half-German, half-American Hanfstaengl had connections in higher societies of Germany, England and the United States. Among his ancestors was a Civil War general who had carried Lincoln's coffin. Among his friends was American president Franklin D. Roosevelt, whom he had met at Harvard University. Hanfstaengl worked as a successful art publisher and was a gifted pianist. After meeting with Hitler, Hanfstaengl became one of his most intimate followers. Hitler enjoyed Hanfstaengl's piano playing, befriended Hanfstaengl's

American wife Helene and played with Hanfstaengl's son Egon, who adored "Uncle Dolf".

Hanfstaengl introduced Hitler to high society and helped polish his image. He also helped to finance the official newspaper of Nazi Party, providing Hitler with funds at a time when he needed them most. Later, he also financed the publication of Mein Kampf. Hanfstaengl also composed Brownshirt and Hitler Youth marches that resembled his early work, the songs composed for Harvard's football team. After the failed Beer Hall Putsch, the injured Hitler sought refuge in Hanfstaengl's home, where Helene dissuaded Hitler from committing suicide.

In 1931, Hitler gave Hanfstaengl the post of foreign press chief in the Nazi Party. "You have all the connections and could render us a great service", said Hitler. Hanfstaengl connections were indeed remarkable. Apart from dealing with the foreign press, he also served as a go-between for Hitler with very important people, including Mussolini and Churchill. Churchill wrote in his memoirs that he met "a lively and talkative fellow"—the name was not mentioned—by chance in the restaurant while on visit in Germany. In reality the meeting was arranged by Churchill's son Randolph who flew with Hitler during Nazi election tours. According to Hanfstaengl, they had very interesting conversation that Churchill did not included in his memoirs:

"Tell me", he [Churchill] asked, "how does your chief [Hitler] feel about an alliance between your country, France and England?" ... "What about Italy?" I asked in the attempt to assess the full range of Churchill's ideas. "No, no", he said... You cannot have everybody joining a club at once."

Over time, Hanfstaengl fell out of favor with Hitler, perhaps because he kept trying to mentor Hitler about foreign politics. In 1937, Hitler decided to humiliate Hanfstaengl by ordering him to jump from a plane on a fake mission to Spain during the country's civil war. It was too much for Hanfstaengl, who managed to escape to Switzerland and then to England. During World War II, he worked for President Roosevelt in the United States revealing the information about Nazi leaders. In the United States, Hanfstaengl was reunited with his son Egon, who despite having Hitler as his godfather had received American citizenship and joined American army.

It has never been definitively proven that Hanfstaengl was an American spy, whose task was guide Hitler, although he almost certainly acted as one. Ordinary people do not write reports for American intelligence, make a detailed list of books on Hitler's bookshelf or meet Hitler's relatives to ask questions about his childhood. It's known that Hanfstaengl received a letter from President Roosevelt that stated, "If things start getting awkward, please get in touch with our ambassador at once." And, as good spies always do, Hanfstaengl had the passports of several countries handy, which helped him to escape when the time came.

It is likely that Hanfstaengl was not just an American spy, but also a truly devoted follower of Hitler who thought that Nazi Germany should ally with the United States. Apparently, at the time there was no contradiction in having both Roosevelt and Hitler as one's friend. To deepen the Nazi-American friendship, Hanfstaengl even acted as matchmaker for Hitler:

> *"He phoned Martha Dodd, the attractive daughter of the American ambassador, and announced: 'Hitler should have an American woman – a lovely lady could change the whole destiny of Europe. Martha, you are the woman!' Martha Dodd was 'rather excited by the opportunity that presented itself' and agreed to meet the Fuhrer and attempt 'to change the History of Europe'".*

Martha failed to court Hitler, but it is telling that the daughter of an American ambassador would be so willing and proud to try.

Funding the German War Machine

After World War I, Germany to a large degree lost the control over its economy and finance. Prominent German industrialists, such as the nationalist and anti-communist Fritz Thyssen (1873-1951), were dependent on Wall Street. The German central bank fell under Allied control, while large enterprises crucial for the war machine became international corporations. Professor Antony Sutton wrote in the Wall Street & the Rise of Hitler:

> "In the early 1930s financial assistance to Hitler began to flow more readily... The critical point is that the German industrialists financing Hitler were predominantly directors of cartels with American associations, ownership, participation, or some form of subsidiary connection. The Hitler backers were not, by and large, firms of purely German origin ... in most cases they were the German multinational firms — i.e., I.G. Farben, A.E.G., DAPAG, etc. These multi-nationals had been built up by American loans in the 1920s, and in the early 1930s had American directors and heavy American financial participation."

Such German and American financial connections were extremely common. Fritz Thyssen, the typical German industrialist who brought Hitler to power, had Wall Street banking connections through Brown Brothers Harriman, where Roosevelt advisor Averell Harriman and scion of two future US presidents Prescott Bush were senior partners. German financier and politician Hjalmar Schacht was intimately involved almost on a monthly basis with Wall Street and was the personal friend of

The True Origins of World War II

Montagu Norman, the king of international finance. Schacht and Thyssen were the main organizers of a November 1932 petition to President Hindenburg that asked him to appoint Hitler as Chancellor "to combat Bolshevism". Then, while Thyssen was busy with German rearmament, Schacht financed it as the President of the Reichsbank.

The most notorious example of German-American corporate collaboration was chemical conglomerate I.G. Farben. Apart from financing Hitler's election and playing a crucial role in the German rearmament, it also produced the poison gas Zyklon B, which eventually killed millions of people in the gas chambers of the Nazi extermination camps. The board of directors of I.G. Farben contained representatives of such well-known American enterprises as the Ford Motor Company, the Federal Reserve Bank, the Standard Oil Company, and President Franklin D. Roosevelt's Georgia Warm Springs Foundation. While some German directors of I.G. Farben were convicted after the war, the American directors were not even questioned about the funds that I.G. Farben made available for the Hitler's election.

In 1941, when World War II was already in full swing, 250 American firms owned more than $450 million worth of German assets. Among those firms were such big names as Standard Oil, Ford Motor Company, Woolworth, IT&T, Singer, International Harvester, Eastman Kodak, Gillette, Coca-Cola, Kraft, Westinghouse, and the main owner of "banana republics" United Fruit. Standard Oil, Ford and Chase continued their business with Nazis even after America declared war on Germany. In 1942 Senator Harry Truman (1884-1972) led investigation into a Standard Oil practice that "approached treason", giving patents to I.G. Farben but withholding them from U.S. military and industry. John D. Rockefeller, Jr (1874-1960), owner of Standard Oil, claimed ignorance of the day-to-day operations and avoided prosecution. When in 1942 the U.S. government ordered the seizure of Nazi German banking operations in New York City, Harriman and his partner Prescott Bush (1895-1972), the father and the grandfather of two American presidents, were among those who lost their shares in Nazi business.

Curiously enough, the prominent "International Jewish bankers", the Warburg brothers, whom Ford attacked in his anti-Semitic publications, were also on the board of directors of I.G. Farben. Paul Warburg was director of I.G. Farben in the United States, while his brother Max Warburg was director of I.G. Farben in Germany. Paul died in 1932, before Hitler came to power, but Max had a chance to work for Nazi government. Starting in 1933, he served on the board of the Reichsbank, reporting directly to Schacht.

On March 27, 1933, two months after Hitler came to power, in the attempt to sooth anti-Nazi sentiment in the United States Max Warburg wrote a letter to American businessman Averell Harriman (1891-1986) and his associates at Brown Brothers:

> *"For the last few years business was considerably better than we anticipated, but a reaction is making itself felt for some months. We are actually suffering also under the very active propaganda against Germany, caused by some unpleasant circumstances. These occurrences were the natural consequence of the very excited election campaign, but were extraordinarily exaggerated in the foreign press. The Government is firmly resolved to maintain public peace and order in Germany, and I feel perfectly convinced in this respect that there is no cause for any alarm whatsoever."*

Two days later Max Warburg's son Eric (1900-1990) contacted his cousin Frederick M. Warburg, a director of the Harriman railroad system in the United States, asking him to "use all [his] influence" to stop anti-Nazi activity in America.

The True Origins of World War II

Did these very prominent and influential Jews not believe Hitler's anti-Semitic rhetoric? Did they simply think they could control him, or did their business profits blind them? It is certainly possible that they did not realize that Nazism was not a game, and Hitler was not their pawn. Unlike the less fortunate Jews who perished in Holocaust, Max and Eric Warburg immigrated to the United States when the need arose. During World War II, Eric served as an intelligence officer in the U.S. Army and even interrogated top Nazis at Nuremberg.

Among those war criminals tried at Nuremberg were Fritz Thyssen and Hjalmar Schacht. Unlike other prominent Nazis who were executed, Schacht was acquitted, despite objections of the Russians. Thyssen was convicted, but only paid a fine for mistreatment of his Jewish employees. It should be noted that Schacht and Thyssen went into opposition to Hitler when Nazi politics came into conflict with Anglo-Americans at the end of 1930s and were even sent into Nazi concentration camps. However, their biographies only prove the significant initial support of Hitler by Anglo-Americans. We can see that those Nazi supporters who did not betray their real masters had their sin of bringing Hitler to power forgiven.

How did Americans gain control over German industry and finance in the first place? By supplying the Allies during World War I, the United States was able to take possession of most of the Europe's gold, making the U.S. dollar the leading world currency. Meanwhile, Germany was obligated to pay large reparations to the Allies, in addition to its own large internal debt acquired during the war. England, France and others in turn had to repay their war loans to the United States. However, nobody had the money or will to pay the debt, so meet its financial needs the German government resorted to practice of printing money, causing unthinkable hyperinflation. By November 1923, the American dollar was worth more than 4 trillion German marks. The hyperinflation was blamed on foreigners who forced Germany to pay reparations; however, that was only part of the problem. In fact, hyperinflation allowed German government to wipe out internal debt and confiscate the savings of its own middle class citizens.

In line with the previously discussed geopolitical games, German inability to pay reparations was met with understanding in England and the United States, but not in France. The conflict came to a head in January 1923, when France and Belgium occupied Ruhr, the industrial German area, to extract reparations themselves. French occupation caused a surge of German nationalism and was condemned by Anglo-Americans, who as we know always oppose the strongest power in Europe by uniting all the lesser powers against it. New York's Wall Street and the City of London, the financial centers of Anglo-Americans, put pressure on the French franc, demanding the country's withdrawal from the Ruhr.

In April 1924, Charles Gates Dawes (1865 – 1951), an American banker and politician, made an offer to resolve the dispute that no one could refuse. The Dawes plan called for the lowering of German reparations and the evacuation of the Allied troops from the Ruhr. It also put the Reichsbank under Allied supervision and provided Germany with additional loans from the US. On the surface, it seemed like the Americans resolved the conflict between Germany and France with a reasonable compromise. In 1925, Dawes would even receive the Nobel Peace Prize for his plan. Looking deeper, we can see that Anglo-American financial oligarchy defined international politics. Playing "divide and conquer" again, it restrained French power and seized control of German finance. As a matter of fact "Norman insisted that neither British nor American bankers

The True Origins of World War II

touch the [French] loan "until the French are out of the Ruhr bag and baggage", which actually means that Anglo-American bankers controlled the movement of French troops!

In 1929, the Dawes plan was modified by American Owen D. Young (1894-1962), the chairman of General Electric. Young Committee suggested the opening of the Bank for International Settlements (BIS), which was established on May 17, 1930 by an intergovernmental agreement of Germany, Belgium, France, England, Italy, Japan, the United States and Switzerland. The BIS headquarters were conveniently located in forever neutral Switzerland, and it enjoyed immunity in all the contacting states even if they were at war with each other. The bank soon became a convenient outlet to fund Hitler and his war machine. During World War II, the bank remained open and, while soldiers were killing each other at the front, the BIS bankers from the United States, England, Germany, Italy and Japan were sitting in the meetings together and conducting business as usual. The BIS also helped Nazis launder loot from the occupied Europe, including the gold stolen from Jews killed in the concentration camps.

Historians commonly say that after World War I America became isolationist and was not involved into the European affairs because of their lack of participation in the League of Nations. In reality, American bankers and industrialists were not only involved in the international politics, they defined it to a large degree. In 1924, Dawes devised a financial version of "musical chairs". The American investors from Morgan trust would give Germany credits from which Germany would pay its reparations to England and France, who in turn would repay its war loans.

"No one was willing to predict what would happen once the music stopped." "The music" stopped after Great Depression kicked in 1929 and Americans recalled their loans. Germany fell into the recession that helped to bring Hitler to power. Then Hitler refused to pay reparations, and no one objected. The stage was set for the next war.

Conclusion

Hitler's rise to power and the subsequent rapid rearmament of Nazi Germany happened with the approval of elites in Great Britain and the United States. The ties of Nazis with London and New York were much stronger than one might think. Thyssen, Schacht, Hanfstaengl, Norman, Dulles brothers, Lloyd George and British King Edward VIII were only the tip of the iceberg.

The geopolitical reasons for supporting Hitler were simple. A strong Germany was viewed as the best defense against communism; it supposed to be the counterbalance to Russia and to less extend counterbalance to France.

The idea that Hitler might become the enemy of England and the United States was not seriously considered because Hitler always underlined his hostility to Communist Russia and his desire to respect British interests.

Chapter 6:
Countdown to War

Article in American newspaper Milwaukee Sentinel
"Europe, Ripe for Strife, Faces Menace of Russian Red Forces"
United States, 9 June 1935.

The solution to the "menace" suggested in the article, illustrated with large portrait of Soviet defense commissar Voroshilov, is that Americans and British should help Nazi Germany invade Russia. The cartoon on the left mocks French-Soviet treaty of mutual assistance that was aimed against the growing German threat. (The caption says "cultivated people must hang together")

Pop Quiz

What was the main cause of World War II?

    a) Hitler, Stalin and the Japanese decided to conquer the world and threatened democracy.

    b) The expansionist ambitions of the dictatorships (Germany, Italy, Japan and the Soviet Union) magnified by the unwillingness of the democratic powers (Great Britain, France and United States) to stop the aggressors in the attempt to avoid war.

    c) The world's top imperialists (Great Britain and United States) played "divide and conquer" with the up-and-coming fascists and encouraged them to be the "bulwark against communism".

"Will a leader appear who will have the eloquence appeal and driving power to bond together these discordant nationalities and set the armed forces marching under a single banner? Germany in sum an alliance must become the great organizer and industrial producer. In her factories the instruments of war on a colossal scale could be turned out. The resources of the world can be assured to such an alliance only through the command of the seas. This would be obtained should Great Britain throw in her sword on that side. With the seas open for trade, the American markets could not be expected to remain closed. In the guise of such a great crusade, maybe yet inarticulate in men's thoughts, cannot one see the outlines of a daring plan, not only forever laying the ghost of Bolshevism but for opening up the fertile lands of Russia to a crowed and industrially hungry Europe?"

U.S. Rear Admiral Yates Stirling, Jr.
The Milwaukee Sentinel, United States, 9 June 1935

American historian Alan Axelrod described the politics of years leading up to World War II in this way:

"By the mid 1930s, the planet was divided into dictatorships with rattling sabers and democracies seeking nothing but peace... the democracies so feared renewing the terrors of a world war that they were inclined to do almost anything to avoid pushing the aggressors into armed conflict. Instead of averting war, this policy of avoidance - it would be called 'appeasement' - virtually ensured war."

Seeking peace brought war. Strange, isn't it? This paradox can be resolved, however, if we analyze the events that led to the war without naive assumption that the democracies had only good intentions. Only then are we able to see that the alleged "peace seeking" was actually the "divide and conquer" politics, as the quote from Admiral Stirling, Jr., above indicates.

The Start of Japanese Expansion

After the Wall Street crash in 1929, the first country that resorted to force to solve her economic problems was Japan. On September 18, 1931, in a staged event, a Japanese-owned railroad was dynamited near Mukden, the city in Chinese province of Manchuria. The Mukden Incident was used by Japanese military as an excuse to invade and occupy Manchuria.

In 1932, a Japanese puppet state was created in the province, with deposed Qing Emperor Puyi (1906-1967) as the figurehead leader. When the League of Nations condemned Japanese aggression, Japan became the first country to leave the powerless organization. No meaningful sanctions against Japan followed.

There were a few consistent themes in Japanese reasoning that were used to justify the Empire's expansion. The first was that Japan helped maintain order in disorganized China to the benefit of all imperialists. The numerous episodes of pacification of the Chinese by the British and other imperialists were cited as precedents.

In an address defending Japanese actions in Manchuria to the League of Nations on December 6, 1932, Yosuke Matsuoka explicitly blamed China for Japanese aggression:

> *"Our Government was still persisting earnestly in efforts to induce the Chinese Government ... to see the light of reason when the incident of September 18th, 1931, took place. We wanted no such situation as has developed. We sought in Manchuria only the observance of our treaty*

> *rights and the safety of the lives of our people and their property. We wanted from China the right to trade, according to existing treaties, free from unwarranted interference and molestation. But our policy of patience and our efforts at persuasion were misinterpreted by the Chinese people. Our attitude was regarded as weakness, and provocations became persistently more unbearable."*

The second theme that often recurred is that Japan only did what other great powers routinely do to protect their "interests". In other words, western powers that disapproved of Japanese expansion were being hypocritical. In the same League of Nations speech, Matsuoka noted sharply that when the interest of British, French and American imperialists were threatened in China, those countries never hesitated to use force. Matsuoka described in details the events that happened in China in 1927 and drew a very convincing parallel between British and Japanese actions in China:

> "In dealing with China, Japan is dealing with a State in a menacing condition. We have acted also with a view to promoting and preserving peace. If it is contended that the League could have afforded Japan adequate protection, why was it — may I be permitted to ask — that the League Council gave its approval, with no dissenting voice, when the United Kingdom, with France, the United States and Japan, sent troops to Shanghai in 1927? ... The Government then welcomed the presence of the British and other troops at Shanghai as of possible service to them in staying the advance of the Nationalist forces then hostile to them..."

Later, in objecting to proposed international control of Manchuria, the Japanese representative asked,

> "Would the American people agree to such control of the Panama Canal Zone? Would the British permit it over Egypt?"

Unlike the polite Japanese, Hitler was more straightforward in pointing out western hypocrisy, stating the following on January 30, 1939:

> "But to assume that God has permitted some nations first to acquire a world by force and then to defend this robbery with moralizing theories is perhaps comforting and above all comfortable for the 'haves', but for the 'have nots' it is just as unimportant as it is uninteresting and lays no obligation upon them."

The third theme was that Japan provided a much needed containment of Russia and communism in China. Matsuoka of course played this trump card in his League of Nations speech as well:

> "The communist movement controls as many provinces as the recognized Government. I might even say that communism is to-day eating into the very heart of China. In this connection, we would say that Japan cannot afford to shut her eyes to the possibilities of the future. Our action in recognizing the State of Manchukuo was the only and the surest way for us to take in the present circumstances. In the absence of any other means of stabilizing conditions in that territory — where we have interests, both strategic and economic, which we cannot sacrifice — we had no other recourse."

Of these themes, this last one proved the most resonant. The great powers could not appreciate Japan's desire to become their equal. Japanese references to Panama and Egypt left them unmoved. However, Japan as a counterbalance to

Communist Russia made much more sense. It was perhaps one of the main reasons why Japan was allowed to continue her aggression against China for years to come.

For example, on September 1, 1934, Neville Chamberlain proposed a pact with Japan, arguing that it had "anxieties about Soviet Government" and that the Soviet Union is "the only Power which really menaces their present acquisitions or their future ambitions." Professor Clement Leibovitz, co-author of In Our Time: The Chamberlain-Hitler Collusion, observed that Chamberlain used the mild words "acquisitions" and "ambitions" to describe Japanese occupation and aggression, while the mere presence of the Soviet Union constituted "menace". Also note, that Soviet Union was the only "menace" in the path of Japanese aggression that the West would allow it to take on.

Admiral Stirling, Jr also appreciated Japan as the counterbalance to Communist Russia, noting in his infamous article:

> *"Japan in the Far East finding the Red tide in China most inconvenient, and Germany can count on her to keep occupied or immobilized a Red army in the Russian eastern provinces."*

Moreover, history shows that "seeking peace" was actually never on the agenda of the democracies. They used "divide and conquer" politics that required igniting a conflict between their opponents, and then preventing either side of the conflict from a decisive win. That way, the democracies could keep all sides of the conflict exhausted, dependent and thus under control.

In 1939, Stalin summarized this tactic:

> *"The policy of non-intervention reveals an eagerness, a desire, not to hinder the aggressors in their nefarious work : not to hinder Japan, say, from embroiling herself in a war with China, or, better still, with the Soviet Union : to*

allow all the belligerents to sink deeply into the mire of war, to encourage them surreptitiously in this, to allow them to weaken and exhaust one another; and then, when they have become weak enough, to appear on the scene with fresh strength, to appear, of course, 'in the interests of peace,' and to dictate conditions to the enfeebled belligerents."

A Period of Change

Japan made the first move in 1932, but 1933 started a period of intense change in the geopolitical landscape when both Adolf Hitler and Franklin D. Roosevelt came to power.

On March 22, 1933, the first concentration camp for "political prisoners", Dachau, opened in Germany. Communists and Jews were the first victims of Nazi persecution. Academics such as Albert Einstein decided to immigrate right away, but some businessmen such as Max Warburg decided to serve in the new Nazi government. On April 27, 1933, three months after Hitler came to power, the Germany economy was given a boost when a British-German trade agreement was signed.

After Japan's withdrawal from League of Nations, Germany followed suit on October 19, 1933. Italy, Spain, Romania, Hungary and France also withdrew over the following decade. In 1934, a year after establishing diplomatic relations with the United States for the first time, the Soviet Union was admitted into League of Nations. While fascists were leaving the peace-keeping organization, the communists had finally joined.

On January 26, 1934, the German–Polish Non-Aggression Pact was signed, signaling the improvement of German-Polish relations. It was the first Non-Aggression pact signed by Nazi Germany, and the first of many it would violate. Poland and Nazi Germany had grounds for friendship, their mutual hostility

The True Origins of World War II

towards Soviet Union being only one. In 1930s, Poland was also ruled by a dictatorial and anti-Semitic regime; there were even Jewish boycotts and pogroms. In 1938, Poland joined Germany in dismembering Czechoslovakia and it did not seem improbable that one day Germany and Poland may join hands in an invasion of the Soviet Union.

On February 6, 1934, fascist riots broke out in Paris. The government fell, but anti-fascist forces soon prevailed in France as socialists and communists united into Popular Front. The political situation in France was a good example of a global clash between the communist and fascist political forces all around the globe. This global clash of the left and right wing forces was much more real than the invented "democracy vs. dictatorship" propaganda from America and Britain.

On July 25, 1934, the Nazis assassinated Austrian Chancellor Engelbert Dollfuss (1892 – 1934) in response to his ban of the Austrian Nazi Party, which called for unification with Germany. Annexation seemed imminent, but this time the Austrian independence was saved not by Western democracies, but by Fascist Italy. Mussolini ordered mobilization of the Italian army on the Austrian border and announced to the world:

> "The independence of Austria, for which he [Dollfuss] has fallen, is a principle that has been defended and will be defended by Italy even more strenuously".

Thanks to Mussolini, the coup failed and Austria kept its independence for the moment. In four years, after Fascist Italy had allied with Nazi Germany, Hitler would have no problem annexing Austria. Great Britain and France did not act in either instance. They were "seeking nothing but peace", of course, and did not mind the stronger Nazi Germany as the precondition, despite the fact that they themselves forbade the unification of Germany and Austria after World War I.

On October 9, 1934 King of Yugoslavia Alexander I (1888-1934) was assassinated in Marseille by a professional terrorist Velicko Kerin (1897-1934), who shot King at point blank range as he drove in a car, just like Franz Ferdinand in Sarajevo. Foreign Minister Louis Barthou (1862-1934), who was in the car with King, was also shot and killed. Barthou had been an ardent supporter of an alliance between France and the Soviet Union, so the assassination weakened international stance of France in the face of growing German and Italian threats.

The threat became evident when, on November 1, 1936, the Rome-Berlin "Axis" were introduced in Mussolini's speech in Milan:

"This Berlin-Rome vertical line is not an obstacle but rather an axis around which can revolve all those European states with a will to collaboration and peace."

Soon Japan joined the fascist club. On November 25, 1936 Germany and Japan signed the Anti-Comintern Pact, directed against the Soviet Union and the international Communist movement.

On March 16, 1935, Hitler announced the reintroduction of conscription and the creation of an army of more than 100,000 men, in violation of the Treaty of Versailles. In response, on May 2, 1935, France and the Soviet Union concluded a pact of mutual assistance.

On June 18, 1935, the world was shocked by the sudden conclusion of Anglo-German Naval Pact signed in London by German Ambassador Joachim von Ribbentrop. The agreement fixed a ratio of the total tonnage of German Navy to be no more than 35% of British Navy. Being a disarmament measure by its face value, it actually marked the beginning of Anglo-German alliance against France and the Soviet Union.

The 35:100 tonnage ratio allowed German the right to build a Navy beyond the limits set by the Treaty of Versailles; Germany was even allowed to build submarines. Additionally, the British had made the agreement without consulting France or Italy, thus betraying its World War I allies. Britain unilaterally threw away the disarmament clauses of the Treaty of Versailles, and while they set the limits on the German Navy, no such limits were mandated for the German Army and the Air Force. Everyone could see that as long as Germany respected British interests, England was going to ignore the security concerns of other European nations. As an additional insult, the Naval Pact was concluded at 120th anniversary of Napoleon's defeat at Waterloo, when the French army was defeated by British and German (Prussian) forces. A century later, England and Germany once again humiliated France.

The significance of Anglo-German Naval Treaty was universally understood. After concluding the Munich Pact in 1938 Chamberlain and Hitler issued the joint statement that said:

> *"We regard the agreement signed last night and the Anglo-German Naval Agreement as symbolic of the desire of our two peoples never to go to war with one another again."*

Indeed after Hitler renounced the Naval Pact on April 28, 1939, war followed. In essence, the Anglo-German Naval Pact was yet another forgotten Non-Aggression agreement concluded with Nazi Germany. In return for the peace with England, Germany was receiving a "free hand" elsewhere.

Not surprisingly Soviet Union's reaction to the Naval Pact was almost as violent as the French. Russians also had another reason to worry. In addition to concluding the pact, the British yielded the control of Baltic Sea to Nazi Germany. Thus, a German invasion of the Soviet Union through Baltic States became more probable.

By promising not to challenge British Navy, Hitler fixed the mistake that German Kaiser made at the dawn of World War I. So far everything was going according to Hitler's prediction in Mein Kampf, where he explicitly stated that by respecting British naval supremacy Germany could count on British support. As historian Alan Axelrod noted:

> "Indeed, the Hitler government persuaded many in the British government that a strong Germany was the West's best defense against the spread of Soviet Communism, and in 1935 the Anglo-German Naval Pact allowed Germany increased tonnage in warships. The treaty led Hitler to believe that Britain and Germany might one day – and soon – become allies"

The Ethiopian Precedent,

On October 3, 1935 Fascist Italy invaded Ethiopia, the only independent nation on the African continent and a member of the League of Nations. The Italian army easily defeated the Ethiopians, who were armed with rifles, spears and bows, but had few modern weapons. Meanwhile Italians had tanks, planes and artillery pieces, and on the top of it used illegal chemical weapons.

Slowly advancing ahead the Italian army reached the Ethiopian capital, Addis Ababa, on May 5, 1936. Four days later, on May 9, Italy officially annexed Ethiopia.

The Emperor of Ethiopia, Haile Selassie I, escaped to Europe and arrived to Geneva to personally address the League

The True Origins of World War II

of Nations. In a stirring speech, the Emperor warned humanity that the world was no longer safe for peace:

> *"I, Haile Selassie I, Emperor of Ethiopia, am here today to claim that justice which is due to my people, and the assistance promised to it eight months ago, when fifty nations asserted that aggression had been committed in violation of international treaties...*
>
> *I pray to Almighty God that He may spare nations the terrible sufferings that have just been inflicted on my people, and of which the chiefs who accompany me here have been the horrified witnesses...*
>
> *Special sprayers were installed on board aircraft so that they could vaporize, over vast areas of territory, a fine, death-dealing rain. Groups of nine, fifteen, eighteen aircraft followed one another so that the fog issuing from them formed a continuous sheet. It was thus that, as from the end of January, 1936, soldiers, women, children, cattle, rivers, lakes and pastures were drenched continually with this deadly rain. In order to kill off systematically all living creatures, in order to more surely to poison waters and pastures, the Italian command made its aircraft pass over and over again. That was its chief method of warfare...*
>
> *I ask the fifty-two nations not to forget today the policy upon which they embarked eight months ago, and on faith of which I directed the resistance of my people against the aggressor whom they had denounced to the world. Despite the inferiority of my weapons, the complete lack of aircraft, artillery, munitions, hospital services, my confidence in the League was absolute. I thought it to be impossible that fifty-two nations, including the most powerful in the world, should be successfully opposed by a single aggressor. Counting on the faith due to treaties, I had made no preparation for war, and that is the case with certain small countries in Europe...*

> *It is collective security: it is the very existence of the League of Nations. It is the confidence that each State is to place in international treaties. It is the value of promises made to small States that their integrity and their independence shall be respected and ensured. It is the principle of the equality of States on the one hand, or otherwise the obligation laid upon small Powers to accept the bonds of vassalship. In a word, it is international morality that is at stake. Have the signatures appended to a Treaty value only in so far as the signatory Powers have a personal, direct and immediate interest involved? ...*
>
> *I ask the fifty-two nations, who have given the Ethiopian people a promise to help them in their resistance to the aggressor, what are they willing to do for Ethiopia? And the great Powers who have promised the guarantee of collective security to small States on whom weighs the threat that they may one day suffer the fate of Ethiopia, I ask what measures do you intend to take?"*

Despite stirring the anti-fascist sentiment around the world, the Emperor archived nothing. The democracies could not care less about the fate of smaller states, particularly African ones. The ineffective sanctions imposed on Italy were soon lifted, and most countries recognized the Italian conquest. Apparently, the friendship of Italy was more important for the democracies than the fate of Ethiopia. Another warning made to the world was ignored.

The Spanish Civil War

On May 3, 1936, the Popular Front of socialists, communists and other left-wing parties won elections in France. Leon Blum (1872-1950) became the first socialist and Jewish Prime Minister of the country. Blum and his government polarized the nation and being a Jew, he was an object of particular hatred to

The True Origins of World War II

the anti-Semitic right. During his campaign in February 1936, Blum had almost been beaten to death. After coming to power, Blum dissolved the far-right fascist leagues in retaliation.

Blum's new government introduced a forty-hour workweek, two week's paid holidays and other social reforms. Despite these reforms, the economic situation in France continued to worsen as businessmen took their funds out of the country. Blum and the Popular Front government quickly fell out of favor.

The Popular Front of Socialists, Communists and other left-wing parties won the 1936 elections not only in France, but also in Spain. If in France the political situation was unstable, in Spain it went out of control. On July 18, 1936, the fascist and conservative forces, a.k.a. Nationalists, rebelled against Popular Front government, a.k.a. Republicans. The rebellion led to a long and bloody civil war. On September 28, rebel generals chose a charismatic new leader, General Francisco Franco (1892-1975).

The Spanish Civil War "seized the fears and hopes of the world". Fascist Italy, Nazi Germany and the right all over the world supported the Nationalists as a way to stop the spread of communism. In turn, Soviet Union and the left all over the world supported the Republicans as a way to stop the spread of fascism. While the societies in the democratic countries were split on the issue of the Spanish Civil War, the elites preferred fascists.

(By the way, the term "fifth column" was originated during the Spanish Civil War, when a Nationalist general told the press that while four columns of troops approached Madrid, a "fifth column" of Nationalists supporters waited inside the city.)

Thousands and thousands foreign nationals participated in the Spanish Civil War, Ernest Hemingway (1899-1961) and George Orwell (1903-1950) among them. Volunteers from various countries who came to fight against fascists formed international brigades. Germany and Italy sent the Nationalists money, military advisers, planes, tanks and even large number of combat troops. The Soviet Union in turn provided all types of the military help to the Republicans. In anticipation of the coming global clash between fascism and communism, the Spanish Civil War became "the dress rehearsal" of World War II.

One might think that the democratic powers should have supported the democratically elected government and tried to prevent the establishment of a dictatorship in Spain. Right? Wrong. The United States and Great Britain proclaimed neutrality and non-intervention in the Spanish Civil War, prohibiting the sales of arms to Spain. France, once again pressured by her English-speaking big brother, reluctantly went along.

The legitimate government of Spain found itself in virtual blockage, as so-called democratic countries once again betrayed democracy. British government covertly supported the fascists, for example by forbidding refueling Republican ships. Meanwhile, fascists were able to receive oil and trucks from the United States, sometimes even on credit! Among Nationalist suppliers were such familiar names as Texaco, Standard Oil, Ford, Studebaker, and General Motors.

The bloody civil war in Spain went on for three years, resulting in fascist victory on April 1, 1939. England, France and the United States promptly recognized new Franco's fascist government. Spain became the classic "totalitarian state" with only one party, concentration camps, and executions of ideological enemies. Franco ruled Spain as a dictator for 36 years until his death in 1975.

Conclusion

"By the mid-1930s, the planet was divided into dictatorships with rattling sabers and democracies seeking nothing but peace," wrote Alan Axelrod. Not exactly. By mid 1930s the world was actually divided into three groups of powers.

The first group, the democracies, was represented by the leading imperialists—Great Britain, France, and the United States—who wanted to keep their privileged position. While relying on each other to support the existing world order, the democracies were also undermining each other fighting for the most privileged position in the club.

England and the United States were allies of France, but at the same time they were undermining the dominating position of France in Europe by supporting fascists in Germany and Spain. The United States in turn could help England to deal with the threats in Europe and the Far East, but in return England would have to give up her empire.

The second group, the fascists—Germany, Italy and Japan—wanted to redraw the map of the world. Initially they did not dare to directly challenge the main imperialists and thus sought conquest outside the established spheres of the influence of the great powers: in Russia, China and Ethiopia. Among themselves, they agreed that Asia should belong to Japan, Central and Eastern Europe to Germany, and the Mediterranean to Italy.

The third group, the communists, was represented by one country, Soviet Union. It was not the most powerful state, but its communist ideology was rapidly spreading all over the world, threatening the established empires from within.

Hindered by the global economic crises, and seeking to preserve their hegemony over the world, the leading imperialists, in accordance with "divide and conquer" strategy saw the best chance for "peace" in the big war between fascists and communists.

To encourage the aggressors, the democracies played a game of "neutrality" and "appeasement. Fascists initially played along, pretending that all they wanted was to fight communists, but over time the dominating position of the democracies began to be threatened.

Part III
Peace in Our Time
1937-1939

World War II emerged slowly but steadily from isolated incidents and local conflicts. On July 7, 1937, yet another minor Sino-Japanese incident quite suddenly grew into full-scale war between Japan and China. Even more surprisingly, it actually was the start of the Pacific part of the coming global conflict. Meanwhile in Europe, despite of the British Prime Minister Chamberlain's assurances of the "peace in our time" Nazi Germany annexed Czechoslovakia and then demanded port city of Danzig from Poland. Could the world war start because of Danzig?

Chapter 7: The Second Sino-Japanese War

"Bloody Saturday"
A crying baby at Shanghai South Railway Station bombed-out by Japanese military. August 28, 1937

Japan's invasion of China in 1937 was the beginning of World War II in Pacific.

Pop Quiz

What country was first to fight the aggressors back and never gave up even while fighting alone?

a) The United States fought the bad guys alone.

b) After the fall of France in 1940, Great Britain fought Hitler alone for a year.

c) China fought Japanese aggression alone for four years since 1937.

"Fascists are preparing a new world bloody carnage and organize an attack on the Soviet Union... Japanese imperialists are seizing the land of China, exterminating civilians, enslaving the Chinese people. Bloody dogs of fascism gone mad. They want to turn the millions of working people of the world into their slaves"

Alexander Kosarev, leader of Soviet Komsomol,
September 12, 1937

On July 7, 1937, a minor skirmish happened at Marco Polo Bridge near Beijing in China. The bridge was an important junction on the border between the annexed by Japan province of Manchuria and the mainland China. In the middle of the night, Chinese troops were alarmed by the unexpected Japanese military training maneuvers and fired few shots. Nobody got hurt and one Japanese soldier, who was reported missing, later returned to his unit. Amazingly, those few shots became the first shots of World War II.

A Century of Humiliation

While Japan was on the rise since the end of the nineteenth century, China was on the decline, subject to foreign invasions, partial colonization and unequal treaties. The British invasion of 1839 in the First Opium War marked the beginning of a "century of humiliation" with China paying indemnities and giving concessions to the number of foreign aggressors.

As we saw in Chapter 1, at the dawn of the twentieth century, the Boxer Rebellion in China against foreigners was put down by an eight-nation alliance. The members of the alliance were Japan, Russia, Great Britain, France, United States, Germany, Austria-Hungary and Italy. While most third world nations were fully colonized by a particular imperialist nation, China was "shared" by democracies and monarchies alike with an "open door" policy. When Japan later claimed exclusive rights in China, it alienated the other great powers and Chinese received support from a number of her former adversaries.

After failing to solve internal and external problems in the wake of the Boxer Rebellion, the Qing dynasty was overthrown in 1911, ending thousands of years of imperial rule in China. As it often happens after revolutions, the new republic failed to become a democracy, and the country quickly disintegrated into provinces ruled by the local warlords. In 1925, after death of the leader of revolution Sun Yat-sen (1866-1925), political and military leadership of nationalist Kuomintang party went to Chiang Kai-shek (1887-1975), who united the country with an iron fist.

Chiang Kai-shek's career was as complex as Chinese politics at the time. He studied in military school in Japan and even served in the Imperial Japanese army. He met with Trotsky and other Soviet leaders in Moscow. Chiang's first son Ching-kuo lived in Russia for twelve years, where he married and had two children. Meanwhile Chiang's second adopted son Wei-kuo went to serve in the army of Nazi Germany and was recalled back to China only in 1938.

It should be noted that since 1922 Kuomintang was allied with the communists and received significant help from Russia. But, on April 12, 1927, Chiang carried out a purge of communists in Shanghai, which was followed by massacres across the country. The long civil war between nationalists and communists had begun. Even after Japan invaded Manchuria in 1931, Chiang Kai-Shek was determined to deal with communists first, adopting the slogan "first internal pacification, then external resistance". He also said, "Japanese are disease of the skin, while communists are disease at the heart".

In 1934, Chiang's forces attacked the Chinese Soviet Republic, the area controlled by communists in Jiangxi province. The Communists's Red Army escaped in a circling retreat to the west and north, traversing some 12,500 kilometers over 370 days in the famous Long March. During this difficult march, Mao Zedong (1893-1976), the future leader of communist China, ascended to power in Chinese Communist Party. However, in 1936 as the threat from Japanese intensified, Chiang Kai-Shek was forced by the nationalist generals to agree on cease-fire with the communists that lasted until the end of World War II. The fight against Japanese invaders became a priority for China.

The Limit of Endurance

The fateful shots fired on Marco Polo Bridge on July 7, 1937 soon escalated into a fight for the bridge itself, followed by a small-scale Japanese invasion and the occupation of Beijing. Local Japanese commanders would not tolerate Chinese "stirring trouble", responding in force even without orders from Tokyo, while Chinese resistance only escalated the conflict even further. The history knew a number of "incidents" like the one at the bridge, but they always ended with Chinese retreats and confessions.

This time, however, the Chinese decided to resist. The Japanese were happy with their gains in the north, and major war could have been avoided if the Chinese accepted another local defeat. However, after century of Chinese humiliation and six years of Japanese invasion, Chinese society came to realize that the policy of continuous concessions leads nowhere. In fact, it amounted to a step-by-step colonization of the country. Although the enemy was still much stronger, and the tasks of the internal pacification and rearmament were not yet complete, Chiang Kai-shek could no longer retreat without losing his credibility. With its large territory and population, China held out hope that they could win a war of attrition against a militarily superior Japan.

Ten days after the Marco Polo bridge incident, Chiang Kai-shek outlined the new desperate strategy. As if he knew that conflict in China was the prelude to a new world war, Chiang started his speech by noting,

> *"The consequences of this [Marco Polo Bridge] incident threatened not only the very existence of China, but the peace and prosperity of mankind."*

Admitting that China was "a weak nation" and that "peace is an absolute essential for the reconstruction of the nation", he also explained that after the "limit of endurance" is reached they had to "fight to the bitter end". Realizing "extent of sacrifice implied" he cautioned against "stopping midway to seek peace" as it would imply "the complete surrender, which would mean the complete annihilation of our race".

> *"Since we are a weak country, there is only one thing to do when we reach the limit of endurance: we must throw every ounce of energy into the struggle for our national existence and independence... If we allow one inch more of our territory to be lost, or our sovereignty to be again infringed, we shall be guilty of committing an unpardonable offense against our race. There will then be no way left but to throw all the resources of our nation into a grim struggle for ultimate victory."*

The Japanese had no idea of the new Chinese determination and were prepared to press on thus widening the war. It would in turn threaten foreign interests in China, giving hope for the international involvement. However, as the history of fruitless Chinese appeals to the League of Nations has shown, helpless victims of aggression get nowhere. To win support from other countries, China had to demonstrate her ability to fight.

The Battle of Shanghai

As had happened with World War I, when everyone is ready for the big war, all it takes is one shot to start it. On August 9, 1937, a Japanese officer was shot dead in Shanghai, the heart of China where Chiang Kai-Shek had his best forces and the strongest support base. The incident predictably met with Japanese demands of removing Chinese forces and dismantling the defenses around the city. However, Chiang Kai-shek was no longer going to acquiesce to any Japanese demands.

On August 13, 1937, instead of accepting another humiliating peace deal, the Chinese attacked Japanese marines in Shanghai, escalating the conflict into full-blown war. The plan was to take Japanese troops by surprise with the overwhelming force and "push them into the river", but lacking heavy artillery the Chinese could not penetrate Japanese concrete fortifications. The fight ended in a standstill.

In ten days, Japanese reinforcements arrived, and amphibious landings started in metropolitan Shanghai, supported by the heavy naval and air bombardment of the costal defenses. On August 23, Japanese also started a bombing campaign, targeting various cities in Central China. The Chinese had no heavy firepower to respond, but they still engaged in house-to-house fighting for three months until they had to retreat to avoid encirclement. As neither side declared war, the full-scale fighting drag for years.

From the Japanese point of view, the Chinese were to blame for the start of the war, since it was China who violated the status-quo of Japan's domination. In some sense, it wasn't just the war of Japanese conquest, but also the war of Chinese national uprising against foreign domination that Japan was bound to suppress. Japanese officials stressed that, like in Boxer Rebellion, the Chinese were actually trying to "drive all foreigners into the sea". British, French and American interests were thus threatened by the Chinese action, and those interests would be more secure when Japan "restores order".

As in the Manchurian incident, the Japanese again played on Western fears of communist domination. The Chinese—and indeed the whole world—should be thankful to Japan for their efforts to contain communism and the threat they presented to the Soviet Union. And of course, all Japan wished for was "peace". On September 5, 1937, Japanese Prime Minister Prince Fumimaro Konoe (1891-1945) stated:

> *"For the people of East Asia, there can be no happiness without a just peace in this part of the world. The Chinese people themselves by no means form the objective of our actions, which directive is against the Chinese Government and its army who are carrying out such erroneous, anti-foreign policies."*

With regards of Shanghai situation, the Japanese position was quite understandable. First the Chinese killed a Japanese officer, then they violated the existing agreement and attacked Japanese marines. What was Japan supposed to do under those circumstances? Swallow the humiliation and retreat? Of course, Japanese decided to teach Chinese a lesson; after being severely beaten, the Chinese would have no choice but to surrender. The Japanese Emperor was promised by the army command that the whole operation in China would not take more than three months, so there was not much to worry about. The new Chinese resolve to fight on no matter what for the independence of their country, however, was not taken into account.

The Failure of Collective Security

On September 12, 1937, one month after the start of the Battle of Shanghai, China challenged Japanese aggression in the League of Nations. Like in the case of Italian aggression against Ethiopia, the League was of little help. All it produced was an October 4 statement of "spiritual support" to China.

The next day, on October 5, President Franklin Roosevelt gave his famous Quarantine Speech, creating an impression that US may take a stand against the aggressors:

> *"The political situation in the world, which of late has been growing progressively worse, is such as to cause grave concern and anxiety to all the peoples and nations who wish to live in peace and amity with their neighbors...*
>
> *Without a declaration of war and without warning or justification of any kind, civilians, including vast numbers of women and children, are being ruthlessly murdered with bombs from the air. In times of so-called peace, ships are being attacked and sunk by submarines without cause or notice. Nations are fomenting and taking sides in civil warfare in nations that have never done them any harm. Nations claiming freedom for themselves deny it to others. Innocent peoples, innocent nations, are being cruelly sacrificed to a greed for power and supremacy which is devoid of all sense of justice and humane considerations...*

> It seems to be unfortunately true that the epidemic of world lawlessness is spreading. When an epidemic of physical disease starts to spread, the community approves and joins in a quarantine of the patients in order to protect the health of the community against the spread of the disease...
>
> It is my determination to pursue a policy of peace. It is my determination to adopt every practicable measure to avoid involvement in war...
>
> If civilization is to survive the principles of the Prince of Peace must be restored. Trust between nations must be revived. Most important of all, the will for peace on the part of peace-loving nations must express itself to the end that nations that may be tempted to violate their agreements and the rights of others will desist from such a course. There must be positive endeavors to preserve peace. America hates war. America hopes for peace. Therefore, America actively engages in the search for peace."

The speech raised China's morale, but in reality Roosevelt meant no action. No countries were mentioned in the speech by name, and the actual meaning of the word "quarantine" was not clarified.

In a private letter, Prime Minister Neville Chamberlain confessed that he had "mixed feelings" about Roosevelt's speech. He was unclear about the intended meaning, since "it was contradictory in parts & very vague in essentials". It seemed that Roosevelt's speech "was intended to sound out the ground" only. Indeed, the speech only intensified isolationist mood in America.

Western powers saw the whole conflict as Japan violating the "open door" policy and trying to grab more than was her fair share in China. On the other hand, Japan was clearly an effective counterbalance to Russia and communism in Asia, so for the time being most were unwilling to take real measures against Japanese aggression. Despite all the articles in the press and passionate speeches, the United States, Great Britain and France remained indifferent to Chinese plight. The profitable trading of war materials with Japan would go on.

One may argue that Roosevelt was sincere in his desire to help China, but he was handicapped by the domestic isolationist public opinion. Indeed the idea of collective security, that helping victims of aggression made the world safer, never truly captivated the public opinion of the democracies. However, when the aggressors moved against the selfish national interests of the democracies, the isolationist public opinion never presented any obstacle for the decisive actions of the democratic governments. It is therefore clear where the real priorities of the "democratic" countries lie.

The Soviets were much more passionate and specific about the situation in China, knowing full well that German and Japanese expansion would be directed against them as well. A speech by the Young Communist League (Komsomol) leader Alexander Kosarev (1903-1939) was published in Pravda on September 13, 1937, that captured Soviet feelings at the time:

> *"The struggle for peace and happiness of millions of working people is the supreme law to the Soviet citizen, to the Komsomol members. Fascists are preparing a new world bloody carnage and organize an attack on the Soviet Union. They reached the monstrous impudence. They are creating provocations all over the world by sinking peaceful merchant ships. Fascists of Germany and Italy for the second year are waging a criminal war against the Spanish people. They destroy the peaceful towns and villages. These killers and gangsters are torturing and killing women, children and the elderly. Japanese imperialists are seizing the land of China, exterminating civilians, enslaving the Chinese people. Bloody dogs of fascism gone*

> mad. They want to turn the millions of working people of the world into their slaves.
>
> Young people should to upmost to help break these plans of fascist barbarians. Our hearts are with you, valiant soldiers of the Spanish Republic, fighting for the freedom and independence of your homeland! Our hearts are with you, the young heroes of China, giving resistance to the Japanese invaders!"

As we can see, it was communists who really raised their voice against the fascist aggressors, while the democracies just wanted to stay away from the trouble using words like "quarantine". In the Anglo-American perspective, the fascist aggressors were going after the democracies, but the democracies were indecisive at first, trying to save peace. In reality, the fascists were going after the communists and weak countries like China and Ethiopia, while the democracies were the mere bystanders.

The pretense of international involvement continued with the opening of the Nine Power Treaty Conference of Pacific Powers, which included United States. American entry brought new hope to the Chinese. Although by mid-October Japanese had made significant gains in Shanghai, Chiang Kai-shek insisted on holding the city to prove to the world that China was worth fighting for.

On November 3, the Conference finally started in Brussels. While the Conference dragged on with little productivity, the Chinese troops were dying in Shanghai, waiting in vain for the western intervention. Japan declined the invitation to the conference, thus mediation between China and Japan was out of question. Western powers weren't prepared to do more than that.

On November 24, the Nine-Power Treaty Conference ended without producing any measures against Japanese aggression.

The True Origins of World War II

Two days later, the Battle of Shanghai was over as last Chinese troops left the city. Idea of collective security suffered another severe blow diminishing hopes for the world's peace.

The Rape of Nanking

Despite being a military defeat, Battle of Shanghai symbolized high point for Chinese resistance. For the first time, Japanese had to fight hard and suffer high number of casualties from Chinese whom they considered inferior to them. No longer China was going to swallow humiliation by allowing Japan to conquer its territories piece by piece without a fight. No longer was China going to surrender even in the face of overwhelming firepower, determined to "outlive the menace of tyranny, if necessary for years, if necessary alone", like Churchill later said about England. However, in the short term, Chiang Kai-shek's insistence on holding Shanghai in the hope of international involvement worn out his strength, and now he had neither troops nor supplies for the defense of the capital, Nanking.

With little opposition Japanese army marched towards Chinese capital covering almost 400 kilometers in about the month. The expensive "Chinese Hindenburg Line", the last line of defense between Shanghai and Nanking, collapsed in only two weeks. The victorious Japanese entered Nanking on December 13, 1937. This victory was followed by the so-called Rape of Nanking—the mass murder of civilians and disarmed soldiers, widespread rape, and looting. The total number of victims was estimated by Chinese as high as 300,000 people. Among murder methods were bayonet practices and burning alive. Some Japanese historians deny or downplay the massacre, which to this day remains the sore point in relations between Japan and China.

Tigran Khalatyan

Stalemate

With the fall of Nanking, the Japanese expected Chinese surrender, but it never materialized. Instead, Chiang Kai-shek consolidated his forces in Wuhan, gathering more than one million troops. The Japanese were reluctant to widen the war even more, but they eventually attacked Wuhan in the summer of 1938. Engagements spread across vast areas of the several provinces and lasted for four and half months. The battle for Wuhan became the longest, largest and one of the most significant battles of the entire war.

To slow Japanese advance, Chiang Kai-shek ordered destruction of a dike on Yellow River that caused serious flooding and the hundreds of thousands of casualties among local civilians. When Chiang Kai-shek talked about sacrifice required to stop Japanese, he really meant it.

The Japanese captured Wuhan on October 27, 1938, but they still failed to achieve final victory. Chiang Kai-shek retreated further inland to Chongqing, and still refused to negotiate, saying he would only consider talks if Japan agreed to withdraw to pre-1937 borders.

The Japanese then attempted to break Chinese resistance by launching a massive bombing campaign on Chongqing and other major cities in unoccupied China, leaving millions dead, injured, and homeless. But although Japanese bombed Chongqing, they had no strength to make another long march for it. By this time they had really overstretched their supply lines. Japanese troops could occupy only big cities and major highways, while Chinese could still ravage the countryside unopposed.

At the end of 1938, the war in China reached stalemate. By 1940 Japanese pretended that they already won and established the puppet government in occupied China led by Wang

The True Origins of World War II

Jingwei (1883-1944), the top level Chinese defector who after the death of Sun Yat-sen was the main rival to Chiang Kai-Shek for control over the Kuomintang. The war in China would drag on for six more years.

Foreign Intervention

Foreign powers were heavily involved in China's fighting. In 1930s, China had close military cooperation with Nazi Germany. Germany was helping China modernize its industry and military in exchange for raw materials. It was German military advisers who trained Chiang Kai-shek troops that fought in Shanghai. However, German support faded away by 1938 as Hitler was forming an alliance with Japan against the Soviet Union.

With the start of the war in 1937, the Soviet Union became the primary supporter of China. Japanese troops massing in the North of China meant Japanese troops massing on the Southern Russian border, and it was no secret that the Japanese had plans to invade Russian Siberia. There is a theory that Chinese General Zhang Zhizhong (1895-1969) provoked the war with Japan in Shanghai because he was communist agent who received the orders from Moscow to move the war away from the Soviet borders. True or not, the Soviet Union had an interest to tie the Japanese down in China.

In September 1937, the Sino-Soviet Non-Aggression Pact was signed, and China had started to secretly receive large amount of munitions and other supplies from Russia. Thousands of Russian military advisers arrived to China including Soviet general Vasily Chuikov (1900-1982), the future famous defender of Stalingrad.

Until 1941, the Russians provided the largest amount of foreign aid to China. What on the surface was just a war between China and Japan, under the cover was also a proxy war between Japan and Russia. If you also add into equation that Japan was importing much of its war materials and 90% of oil from the United States during that period, then the geopolitical situation looked even more curious.

Soviet Union and Japan not only fought a proxy war in China, but they directly clashed as well. The Japanese were planning an invasion and occupation of Russian Siberia, but like in China it started with a series of "incidents". The first major incident occurred near Lake Hasan on the Soviet Manchurian border in the summer of 1938. The Soviets decided to reinforce the part of the border which had not been clearly marked and were attacked by Japanese troops who believed that Russia went little too far. Local battle raged from July 29, 1938 until August 11, 1938 and resulted in a Russian victory.

The Japanese military decided to test Soviet resilience once more in the much larger border war in Mongolia, the Russian ally in the Far East. The battle of Khalkhin Gol, a.k.a. Nomonhah Incident occurred in the summer 1939, just before the start of the war in Europe. This time Russian victory was delivered by Georgy Zhukov (1896-1974), a career officer in the Red Army who had served with distinction in cavalry during World War I and would become the top military commander of World War II. Even before the Germans unleashed the blitz on Europe, Zhukov pioneered the encirclement of the enemy with panzer strikes, which resulted in the complete annihilation of the invading Japanese army. This defeat left the Japanese army reluctant to fight the Soviets again and was a major factor in the Japanese decision not to join Germany when it invaded the Soviet Union in 1941. However, Soviet aid to China ended that

The True Origins of World War II

same year as a result of the Soviet-Japanese Neutrality Pact and the beginning of the Soviet-German war. Soon Japan moved against the Americans in Pacific, and the United States became the main provider of the foreign aid to China until the end of the war. American aid went not only to the Chiang Kai Shi but also to the communist Mao Zedong. By the way, Chinese Communists increased their party membership from 100,000 in 1937 to 1.2 million by 1945.

The Aftermath

World War II become global in December 1941, and in the Declaration by the United Nations, signed on 1 January 1942, China was presented as the fourth major allied power after the United States, Great Britain, and the Soviet Union. Chiang Kai-shek personally met with Roosevelt and Churchill. At the end of the day, Chinese contribution to the Allied victory was not as significant as was expected; however, the Chinese did tie down the largest chunk of Japanese army. Meanwhile Chinese casualties, especially among civilians, were among the largest in the war.

During the war, the nationalists of Chiang Kai-shek and communists of Mao Zedong competed for domestic and international support by presenting themselves as the main force that fought Japanese aggressors. However, after the war become global, both sides tried to preserve their strength for the future civil war and let Americans, Russians and other Allies to win the war over Japan for them.

The stubborn Chinese resistance eventually paid off with the long awaited change of the international situation, despite the fact that Chinese army lost most of the battles on the ground. In 1943, Great Britain and the United States abrogated extraterritoriality rights in China, the first step of undoing the unequal treaties and ending the "century of humiliation".

By 1945 China would become great independent power and one of the five members of the United Nations with the permanent seat in the Security Council and veto power. However, once Japanese were driven out of China, the anticipated civil war was reactivated, resulting in communist victory in 1949. Chiang Kai-shek and his nationalist forces escaped to Taiwan Island, which became a de-facto independent Chinese state protected by the United States. Chiang ruled Taiwan as a dictator until his death in 1975. His son Ching-kuo succeeded him.

Conclusion

The Second Sino-Japanese war (1937-1945) was the longest and one of the bloodiest struggles of World War II. It sapped Japanese strength and allowed China to complete the task of national liberation that ended its "century of humiliation".

China's involvement has not been heavily distorted by the Anglo-American perspective of World War II, because it has largely been neglected outright. In western culture, World War II begins in Europe on September 1, 1939, and in Pacific on December 7, 1941, with the Japanese attack on Pearl Harbor. When war in China is mentioned, as a rule, its complexity is ignored and it is presented as merely Japanese aggression and Chinese defense. Soviet participation in the war in China is usually omitted.

Chapter 8:
The Munich Pact

Leaders of Europe meet to satisfy Hitler's demands to Czechoslovakia. Munich, 29 September 1938.

Leaders from left to right: Chamberlain (England), Daladier (France), Hitler (Germany), Mussolini (Italy) and Ciano (Italy, foreign minister).

The Munich Pact became the highest point of the appeasement, collusion between the democracies and Hitler, that empowered Nazi Germany and at the expense of Czechoslovakia and the Soviet Union.

Pop Quiz

What was the policy of appeasement about?

a) Appeasement is when naïve, good-willing democracies trust tyrants forgetting in their sincere desire to save peace that tyrants cannot be appeased!

b) Appeasement was the policy of giving in to aggressor's demands in order to avoid war.

c) Appeasement was the policy of befriending aggressors at the expense of their victims.

> "My good friends, for the second time in our history, a British Prime Minister has returned from Germany bringing peace with honor. I believe it is peace for our time."
>
> Neville Chamberlain, September 30, 1938

On September 30, 1938, British Prime Minister Neville Chamberlain returned from Germany to a hero's welcome in London. It seemed that he had just prevented European war with skillful diplomacy and a reasonable compromise. At the aerodrome, Chamberlain spoke to the crowds:

> "The settlement of the Czechoslovakian problem, which has now been achieved is, in my view, only the prelude to a larger settlement in which all Europe may find peace. This morning I had another talk with the German Chancellor, Herr Hitler, and here is the paper, which bears his name upon it as well as mine. Some of you, perhaps, have already heard what it contains but I would just like to read it to you:

> "We, the German Fuhrer and Chancellor, and the British Prime Minister, have had a further meeting today and are agreed in recognizing that the question of Anglo-German relations is of the first importance for our two countries and for Europe. We regard the agreement signed last night and the Anglo-German Naval Agreement as symbolic of the desire of our two peoples never to go to war with one another again. We are resolved that the method of consultation shall be the method adopted to deal with any other questions that may concern our two countries, and we are determined to continue our efforts to remove possible sources of difference, and thus to contribute to assure the peace of Europe."

Much impressed King George issued a statement to his people,

> "After the magnificent efforts of the Prime Minister in the cause of peace it is my fervent hope that a new era of friendship and prosperity may be dawning among the peoples of the world."

Most newspapers supported Chamberlain, and grateful citizens sent him thousands of gifts, including many of his trademark umbrellas. Only Churchill remained unconvinced, calling the agreement "a total and unmitigated defeat".

Meanwhile in Communist Russia, a cartoon was published depicting the British and the French offering Czechoslovakia on a plate to the German wolf, waving the flag "Go to the East" (i.e., "Attack Russia").

Appeasement

The policy of appeasement was first formulated in a speech by the prominent British politician Anthony Eden (1897-1977) shortly after Hitler came to power. This is how Wikipedia describes it:

> "Like many of his generation who had served in World War I, Eden was strongly anti-war, and strove to work through the League of Nations to preserve European peace. His ruling National Government, led by Prime Minister Ramsay MacDonald, failed to recognize the threat that an ascendant Nazi Party and Adolf Hitler posed, and proposed measures, in contravention of existing international agreements, that would allow Germany to rearm. In response to sharp criticism of this policy by Winston Churchill in the House of Commons on 23 March 1933, he defended this appeasement policy toward Adolf Hitler's Germany by arguing that Britain needed to "secure for Europe that period of appeasement which is needed",

a speech that brought him a standing ovation in the House."

Here we again see the typical fairy tale about anti-war peace loving democracy that had to wait for Hitler to come to power to start the policy of appeasement towards Germany. Think about it: There had been no talk about appeasement while there was a democratic government in Germany, but the moment Hitler came to power, British politicians started to talk about allowing Germany to rearm. Perfect timing!

Anglo-American historians and commentators always find excuses for their politicians. Just as Grey "failed to realize" that World War I was coming, by the same token Eden "failed to recognize the threat that an ascendant Nazi Party and Adolf Hitler posed". There is no hint as to why they were so unwise. Didn't British read Mein Kampf? Perhaps they did, but only came away impressed by Hitler's proposed Anglo-German alliance and his respect of British interests.

Likewise, what did British think about Hitler's plans to conquer Russia? Was it "the threat" to "peace"? Well, on November 28, 1934, senior British politician Lloyd George explained it very well in the House of Commons:

"In a very short time, perhaps in a year or two, the Conservative elements in this country will be looking to Germany as the bulwark against Communism in Europe. She is planted right in the center of Europe ... only two or three years ago a very distinguished German statesman said to me: "I am not afraid of Nazism, but of Communism' - and if Germany is seized by the Communists, Europe will follow. ... Do not let us be in a hurry to condemn Germany. We shall be welcoming Germany as our friend."

Moreover, the first appeasement proposals were aimed at disarming France, to which Churchill objected by arguing that a strong democratic France actually helped to maintain peace and security in Europe. Churchill went so far as to remark "Thank God for the French Army", and later recalled "the look of pain and aversion which I saw on the faces of members in all parts of the House" as he uttered those words.

Never mind that France was a democracy and a British ally, while Germany was ruled by a Nazi dictatorship. British geopolitical rule "to oppose the strongest power in Europe by uniting all the lesser powers against it" worked not only against Russia but against France as well. Nobody was going to listen to Churchill until Germany in fact became the strongest nation in Europe.

Therefore, the appeasement went ahead. Nazi Germany was allowed to rearm, build an air force and submarines, and even reoccupy the Rhineland. Then the time came to satisfy German territorial demands to its neighboring states, Austria, Czechoslovakia and Poland. German expansion into these three states would increase Germany's geopolitical stance and, as Chamberlain hoped, make it ready for a big war with Russia.

On May 10, 1937 Neville Henderson (1882-1942), the new British ambassador in Germany, wrote a remarkable memo to Anthony Eden's Foreign Office:

> "... On the other hand, through Germany must be regarded as the most formidable menace of all at the present moment, there is no reason, provided she does not ruthlessly disregard the vital principles of the League of Nations or revert to a policy of naval and overseas rivalry or of a renewed push to the West, or deliberately threatens us by air, why – restless and troublesome she is bound to be – she should perpetually constitute a danger of war for us"

As author Clement Leibovitz observed, it was typical for the diplomats like Henderson to talk a lot about "peace" and then use coded language to suggest that if Germany did not threaten British interests in the West she should be allowed to wage the war in the East. Then, as if unafraid to reveal the true meaning of appeasement, Henderson suddenly forgets the coded language and concludes:

> *"To put it quite bluntly, Eastern Europe emphatically is neither definitely settled for all time, nor is it a vital British interest and the German is certainly more civilized than the Slav, and in the end, if properly handled, also less potentially dangerous to British interests – One might even go so far as to asset that it is not even just to endeavour to prevent Germany from completing her unity or from being prepared for war against the Slav provided her preparations are such as to reassure the British Empire that they are not simultaneously designed against it".*

Henderson did not even bother to find an excuse in "communist danger" and instead simply laid bare his racist views about Slav inferiority. To Henderson, those "less civilized" Slavs included not only Russians, but Poles and Czechs as well. Here was the true face of the British democracy—the face of the plotting arrogant racist aristocrats, privileged Eton college graduates, who presumably were "seeking nothing but peace".

Halifax - Hitler Deal

The key points of territorial changes in Europe had to be discussed between British and Nazis on the highest level. The occasion was found when another arrogant aristocrat, the senior representative of British government and former vice king of India Lord Halifax (1881-1959). While attending a hunting exhibition in Germany in November 1937, Halifax had an opportunity to meet Hitler behind the close doors and discuss all the pressing matters.

The Halifax - Hitler meeting on November 19, 1937, was recorded for history by Hitler's interpreter, as well as Halifax's own notes. Curiously, it almost started in disaster, as Halifax mistaked Hitler for a footman and handed him his coat. At the last moment, someone whispered "Fuhrer, Fuhrer", preventing the embarrassment.

Lord Halifax began the discussion with Hitler by stressing the importance of good British – German relations for "European civilization", and his and the British government's conviction that all misunderstandings between the two countries could be resolved by a frank discussion between the two men. Then Halifax stated that British government acknowledged that Fuhrer had made great achievements in Germany and beyond. Halifax specifically noted that, by destroying communism in his country, Hitler prevented it from spreading into Western Europe. That was why Germany fully deserved to be called the bulwark against Bolshevism.

Halifax was no doubt referring to the fact that Nazis threw the communists into concentration camps, where they stayed indefinitely without trial. In Halifax's view, the politics of Nazi Germany did not cause any serious concerns in the democratic England. The British worried less about treatment of Jews than about the Nazis' anti-church and anti-union policies. When you read next time that "dictators threatened democracy", remember how thankful the democracy was to Hitler for his "achievements", and how little British government was bothered by Hitler's methods.

Then Halifax proposed that France and Italy should be invited to join the British-German agreement, since they should not feel excluded and think that British-German cooperation was aimed against them. Halifax believed that only if all four countries coordinated their foreign politics could a lasting peace be assured in Europe. Halifax clearly did not care if Soviet Union felt excluded; "peace" in Europe could be achieved without Russian participation.

Hitler responded that an agreement between the four powers would be very easy to achieve if Germany were treated as a great nation. Halifax agreed with Hitler that "mistakes" committed in the Versailles treaty should be fixed, and took credit for the British pro-German position in resolving the questions of the Rhineland and reparations. Of course, during the meeting Hitler missed no opportunity to underscore his hostility towards Russia to make it crystal clear the common enemy that Germany and England would share.

There were other questions Halifax and Hitler discussed, including the colonial problem, but the most important was Halifax's concession that British did not mind territorial changes in Poland, Austria and Czechoslovakia as long as those changes were done without "causing trouble". The British preferred political bullying and covert action to blatant war, since it could allow them to save face if they refused to help the victims of aggression. Thus, Hitler received carte blanche for all of his planned territorial changes in Europe. The smaller states could resist German pressure only with the support of the great powers, but with England on Germany's side they had no chance.

At the end of the friendly discussion, Hitler assured his guest that he should not be afraid of a new European war. In Hitler's view, the only threat was Bolshevism; everything else could be regulated. Halifax did not object, and in diplomacy, silence may speak louder than thousands of words. German expansion into Austria, Czechoslovakia and Poland was tacitly approved; the informal British-German alliance aimed against Communist Russia was confirmed. Appeasement thus moved into its active phase.

It should be noted that at the time intelligent observers could understand the true nature of appeasement, even though the details of the secret negotiations were not published in the press. For example, on February 21, 1938, the member of the opposition Mr. J. Griffiths asked in the House of Commons:

> "The Prime Minister, speaking of the future, said, "I want to bring Italy, Germany, France and ourselves together," but can we get peace in Europe if we leave Soviet Russia outside? Can we get peace in Europe by leaving Czechoslovakia outside? Why this proposal to bring two Fascist Powers and France and ourselves together? Is this a Western Pact? Is this telling Germany, "You leave us alone in the West and good luck to you in the East"? Is that behind it? The Prime Minister said not a word about Soviet Russia. We here feel that you cannot settle the peace of Europe without bringing in Russia."

Well, decades later British and American kids still learn in school that the democracies "were seeking nothing, but peace", and are never told that the British essentially gave Hitler a free hand in the East.

Anschluss

On February 4, 1938, Hitler assumed personal control over the army and purged the High Command of the C-in-C and thirteen other senior officers. He also replaced the foreign minister von Neurath (1873-1956) with the fervent Nazi Joachim von Ribbentrop, who would be the first major war criminal to be hanged at Nuremberg in October 1946. Sex scandals, which are still so popular in politics, were used as the pretext for the purge; Minister of War Blomberg (1878-1946) had to resign for marrying a former prostitute, while unmarried Commander of the Army Fritsch (1880-1939) was accused of engaging in homosexual activity.

Hitler was getting ready to use force and got rid of those who were hesitant or not completely obedient. Wilhelm Keitel (1882-1946) who was appointed the chief of Supreme Command of the Armed Forces after the purge, obtained the nickname "Lackeitel" for being an "obedient lackey" of Hitler. In 1945, Keitel would sign the final act of German surrender and be hanged at Nuremberg shortly after Ribbentrop.

Back in 1938, though, Hitler's task of the day was Anschluss (which means Unity in German), the popular term for the annexation of Austria, the independent German state. After collapse of the Austro-Hungarian Empire in 1918, Austria, where Hitler was born, wanted to unite with Germany. However, in violation of Wilson's principle of self-determination, unity was explicitly forbidden by the Allies, who at the time simply did not want a stronger Germany.

After Hitler came to power, he brought back the question of German-Austrian unity. With the benefit of appeasement, Anschluss became a feasible goal for Germany, since unlike her democratic predecessor Nazi Germany was allowed to rearm and expand. On the wave of Nazi success in Germany, Austrian Nazis were expected to do very well in the upcoming elections and even had a chance to win them, thus bringing closer the dream of Anschluss.

However, in March 1933 Austrian Chancellor Engelbert Dollfuss, an anti-Nazi Catholic, shut down parliament, banned the Austrian Nazi party and assumed dictatorial powers. The new regime was allied with Fascist Italy and was not only anti-Nazi, but anti-Communist and anti-Socialist as well. Although later Nazi Germany and Fascist Italy became close allies, early in the game tensions between Nazis and Catholics seemed like a big deal.

On July 25, 1934, Austrian Nazis staged a coup and wounded Chancellor Dollfuss, who then slowly bled to death. The coup failed because of the decisive action of Mussolini who vowed to defend Austrian independence and moved Italian army to Austrian border to scare off a possible German invasion. In 1938, however, Anschluss had a better chance for success since Mussolini had become Hitler's ally. On February 12, 1938 Dollfuss successor, Chancellor Kurt Schuschinigg (1897-1977), arrived at Hitler's residence at Berchtesgaden where he was presented with a set of demands that included appointing Austrian Nazis to key positions in the Austrian government. While bullying his guest into submission, Hitler did not miss an opportunity to tell Schuschinigg that three months earlier Halifax had signed off on the Anschluss:

> "Don't think for one moment that anybody on earth is going to thwart my decisions. Italy? I see eye to eye with Mussolini, the closest ties of friendship bind me to Italy. And England? England will not lift one finger for Austria. Not long ago an English diplomat sat in the very chair you are now sitting in. No, you can't expect any help from England."

Confirming this, Chamberlain publicly stated in the House of Commons on February 22, 1938:

> "I am confident I am, in saying that the League as constituted to-day is unable to provide collective security for anybody, then I say we must not try to delude ourselves, and, still more, we must not try to delude small weak na-

tions, into thinking that they will be protected by the League against aggression and acting accordingly, when we know that nothing of the kind can be expected."

The idea of collective security adopted after First World War was now officially dead, but in an act of a desperate defiance Schuschnigg scheduled a plebiscite to confirm the Austrian independence. An outraged Hitler declared that any referendum would be subject to major fraud and that Germany would not accept it. And Hitler had a point. The question on the ballot was formulated in the way that presumed a "yes" answer, and the minimum voting age was set to 24 years, since younger generation was believed to be mostly pro-Nazi.

On March 11, Hitler sent an ultimatum to Schuschnigg, demanding that he cancel the plebiscite and hand power over to the Austrian Nazis or face an invasion. Schuschnigg desperately sought support for Austrian independence from London, but Chamberlain sent him a chilling reply that suggested surrender:

"His Majesty's government cannot take responsibility of advising the Chancellor to take any action which might expose his country to dangers against which His Majesty's Government are unable to guarantee protection."

Realizing that this time neither Italy, nor France nor England were willing to offer any assistance, Schuschnigg resigned. Austrian Nazi Seyss-Inquart (1992-1946) was appointed chancellor, and quickly sent a pre-drafted telegram requesting that German troops enter Austria to help "restore order". Seyss-Inquart would be also hanged at Nuremberg in October 1946.

Hitler was not afraid of how England and France would react thanks to his meeting with Halifax, but he could not disregard Mussolini's opinion and asked him to bless the invasion. Upon receiving the positive response from Italy, a grateful Hitler told his envoy on the telephone:

> *"Tell Mussolini I will never forget him for this! Never, never, never, no matter what happens... I shall stick to him whatever may happen, even if the whole world gangs up on him!"*

On the morning of March 12, the German army crossed the border into Austria. The troops were greeted by cheering Austrians with Nazi salutes, Nazi flags, and flowers. Hitler himself soon arrived and was given an enthusiastic welcome. Next day, the unity of Austria and Germany was officially announced. Of course, Jews and political opponents of the new regime were promptly thrown into concentration camps.

It should be pointed out that Hitler, the Nazis and the idea of unity with Germany were definitely not unpopular in Austria and might have been won by voting if given a chance. On the other hand, Austrian sovereignty was clearly compromised. However, the democracies cared neither for the will of Austrian people nor for the rights of small states. They certainly cared little for the fate of Jews. They only cared about their own strategic interests, and at the time Nazi expansion seemed fine to them. Another great chance to stop Hitler and World War II was lost.

The Sudeten Crisis

Now that Austria was in the fold, Hitler turned his sights to the next border. The democratic Republic of Czechoslovakia had been created by the Allies after World War I out of the remnants of the Austro-Hungarian Empire. The split up of multiethnic Austria-Hungary was justified by the principle of self-determination, but the newly created Czechoslovakia was mul-

The True Origins of World War II

tiethnic as well. Apart from dominating ethnic groups of Czechs and Slovaks, the new country had sizeable German, Hungarian, Ukrainian and Polish minorities. The ethnic Germans lived mostly in the western part of Czechoslovakia, known as the Sudetenland, and like Austrian Germans they had strong desire to unite with Nazi Germany.

Apart from usual benefits of taking over Czech armament production and gold reserves, the country was of great strategic value to Hitler since it was the part of French-Czech-Soviet defensive alliance that had to be broken if Hitler wanted to dominate Europe. If Hitler attacked Czechoslovakia, France and the Soviet Union should have come to her aid, just as Russia had done for Serbia in World War I. The British, however, insisted that Czechoslovakia renounce its alliances with the Soviet Union and France and become neutral state like Switzerland. Hitler was also able to get Poland and Hungary on his side by promising them the parts of Czechoslovakia where Polish and Hungarian minorities lived. Although Poland was destined to become Hitler's next target, in 1938 it allied with Nazi Germany in the task of dismembering of Czechoslovakia and keeping the Soviets away from interfering into "European affairs".

Shortly after completing the absorption of Austria, Hitler ordered Sudetenland Nazis to start actions of civil disobedience. German propaganda spread the news of Sudetenland Germans fighting against oppression, while German generals were ordered to prepare a military attack on Czechoslovakia. It should be noted that the same three-step method of aggression that includes provoking internal unrest, spreading propaganda about oppression and military "liberation" is still in active use today, mostly by Americans in the Middle East.

Hitler's aggression against Czechoslovakia was a risky venture, since at the time the German army was comparable in size to Czech army, and with French and Soviet forces greatly outnumbering them. In addition, there was also a heavily fortified defensive line along the Czech-German border.

Some top German generals including Ludwig Beck (1880-144), Franz Halder (1884-1972) and the Chief of German Intelligence Admiral Wilhelm Canaris (1887-1945) were sure that the war would lead to the certain German defeat and formed a conspiracy to remove Hitler from power after he gave the actual invasion order. The conspirators send their agents to London to inform "the bosses" about the plot and ask them to adopt an openly aggressive stance toward Hitler to justify the action against him.

Beck and Canaris would lose their heads for conspiring against Hitler several years later, but in 1938 their plot was doomed because of British efforts to save the German Fuhrer. Britain was not interested in removing Hitler but proposed mediation between Czech government and Sudetenland Germans, which of course achieved nothing expect further escalation of the conflict.

When the situation around the Sudetenland reached the boiling point with the Czech government imposing martial law and Hitler threatening invasion, British Prime Minister Chamberlain made his "sudden and dramatic" entrance to the scene and proposed the cession of the Sudetenland to Nazi Germany. Chamberlain was going to sell public on the idea that "compromise" could avert war in Europe, although it was hardly doubtful to an intelligent observer that the Sudetenland alone could satisfy Hitler's appetite for conquest.

Here is something that American and British kids do not learn in school. On September 13, 1938, before presenting Hitler with his "peace plan" Chamberlain wrote King George VI the detailed report of what he was planning to do. Chamberlain wrote his King the following:

> " ... reports are daily received... Mainly of these (and of such authority as to make it impossible to dismiss them as unworthy of attention) declare positively that Herr Hitler had made up his mind to attack Czecho-Slovakia and **then to proceed further East**. He is convinced that the operation can be effected so rapidly that it will be all over before France and Great Britain could move and that they will not then to try to venture to try to upset a fait accompli...
>
> In these circumstances I have been considering the possibility of a sudden and dramatic step which might change the whole situation. The plan is that I should inform Herr Hitler that I propose at once to go over to Germany to see him...
>
> I should hope to persuade him that he had an unequled opportunity of raising his own prestige and fulfilling what he has so often declared to be his aim, namely the establishment of an Anglo-German understanding preceded by a settlement of the Czecho-Slovakian question... the prospect of **Germany and England as the two pillars of European peace and the buttresses against communism.**"

So Chamberlain knew that Hitler was planning to "attack Czecho-Slovakia" and even "proceed further East", but still saw Germany and England as "the two pillars of European peace" bound by their hatred of communism. How sweet!

No sooner said than done, on September 15, 1938, the elderly Chamberlain made his first trip on a plane to see Hitler in his luxurious mountain residence at Berchtesgaden. Chamberlain and Hitler sat in the same room with the big picture window and magnificent views of the Alps where Lord Halifax had sat before.

During the meeting, Chamberlain quickly agreed to Hitler's demand to respect the principle of self-determination in the Sudetenland and hand Germany all border areas where 50 percent of the population or more was German. Chamberlain only asked Hitler to refrain from military action while he went back to London to consult with his Cabinet and bring French and Czech in line.

This part of the Hitler-Chamberlain meeting is well known in Anglo-American perspective, but the following Chamberlain's notes are rarely analyzed:

> "He [Hitler] then launched into a long speech ... all he wanted was Sudetenland Germans. As regards the "spearhead in his side" he would not feel he had got rid of the danger until the abolition of the treaty between Russia and Czechoslovakia. I [Chamberlain] said: "Supposing it were modified, so that Czechoslovakia were no longer bound to go to the assistance of Russia if Russia was attacked, and on the other hand Czechoslovakia was debarred from giving asylum to Russian forces in her aerodromes or elsewhere; would that remove your difficulty?"

Despite the sugarcoated diplomatic language, we can clearly see that Hitler complained to Chamberlain that Czechoslovakia may come to Russia's aid during his planned attack on the Soviets, and Chamberlain promised to help to abrogate the Czech - Russian defensive treaty. According to Hitler's translator, Hitler also said during the meeting:

> "we will not stand in the way of your pursuit of your non-European interests and you may without harm let us have a free hand on the European continent in central and South-East Europe."

The True Origins of World War II

Chamberlain did not directly respond to the comment about Hitler's "free hand," but his silence was worth a thousand words. The essence of Hitler-Chamberlain agreement was that Hitler was allowed to attack East towards Russia if he did not threaten British interests in the West.

Chamberlain had every reason to believe that Hitler would be satisfied with the proposal. It had nothing to do with his alleged "naivety"; it was a calculation of mutual interests. After all, this was the plan that had been steadily unfolding for years since the early days of Mein Kampf. This is how serious politicians do their non-sentimental business.

Hitler Raises the Stakes

Chamberlain returned to London and got his Majesty's government approval for the Sudetenland concession. Then Chamberlain pressed French Prime Minister Edouard Daladier (1884-1970) to force him abandon his obligations towards Czechoslovakia. Daladier was reluctant to give in to the bullying, but Chamberlain explained that in the case of the war France would not receive British help. The desperate French contacted President Roosevelt, asking him to guarantee Czech sovereignty, but Americans refused to help. Losing Anglo-American support, France once again gave in to appeasement and agreed to Chamberlain's "peace plan".

Britain and France, having agreed to give Hitler the Sudetenland, now together confronted the Czech government. President Edvard Benes (1884-1948) was awoken at 2 a.m. to receive the Anglo-French ultimatum that Czechoslovakia had to give up Sudetenland or face German invasion without the prospect of French or British support. In return, Britain and France pledged to defend what would remain of Czechoslovakia from aggression—a promise that they were quick to forget.

The Czech government, realizing it had been abandoned by its Western Allies, gave in and agreed to the terms. The Czechs could not rely solely on the Soviet Union, since "world opinion" was going to make them not the victims of Nazi aggression who defend their country but the friends of communist outcasts who bring Bolshevik danger into the middle of Europe. This was confirmed by M. Vavrecka, the Czech minister of propaganda, who in a broadcast on September 30, 1938, explained that:

> "... our war by the side of Soviet Russia would have been not only a fight against Germany but it would have been interpreted as a fight on the side of Bolshevism. And then perhaps all of Europe would have been drawn into the war against us and Russia."

This is how cunning British diplomacy was transforming Hitler's aggression into a European crusade against Bolsheviks.

On September 22, the happy Chamberlain returned to Germany to report to Hitler that he could have his Sudetenland after all formalities for territory transfer were completed. However, Hitler suddenly raised the stakes and demanded immediate German occupation of the Sudetenland, claiming that the Czech government had started a massive ethnic cleansing of Germans and thus he could not wait. (The expulsion of Germans from the Sudetenland would actually start in 1945 out of retribution after Germany lost the war). Hitler also mentioned a possible Bolshevik uprising in Czechoslovakia.

The immediate German occupation of the Sudetenland meant that people who did not want to live under Nazi rule would have to abandon their property and run for their lives. Meanwhile, the Czech army would have to abandon heavy equipment, leaving the rest of Czechoslovakia defenseless. Furthermore, by adding new demands Hitler was actually bullying the head of the government of the powerful British Empire. This was simply unacceptable for British prestige and the existing world order. However, being so successful before, Hitler was keep raising his stakes.

Chamberlain returned to London empty handed as stunned British, French and Czech governments rejected new Hitler's ultimatum. The Czechs and their allies started to mobilize while Hitler set the deadline for Czech acceptance of his new terms on September 28 and invasion on October 1.

Hitler's uncompromising position was outlined in his speech on September 26 that as usual was full of drama:

> *"And now we are faced with the final problem that must be solved and will be solved! It is the final territorial demand which I shall make of Europe, but it is the demand which I shall not give up and which with God's help I shall ensure is fulfilled!"*

Presenting himself as a champion of all oppressed, Hitler said that during the creation of Czechoslovakia in 1918

> *"they simply took three and a half million Germans in violation of their right to self-determination and their will to decide their own fate."*

Hitler even expressed sympathy for non-German "suppressed people" in Czechoslovakia.

> *"I feel sympathy with the Slovaks, the Poles, Hungarians and Ukrainians"*, he stated. *"And now finally England and France have made the only possible demand of Czechoslovakia: release the German territory and cede it to the Reich."*

Of course, Hitler could not avoid the theme of communist danger that helped him so many times before, and explained why he could no longer wait:

> "And now Bolshevism is using this state as its front gate. We did not seek contact with Bolshevism; Bolshevism is using this state to gain access to Central Europe... Mr Benes ... resumed his campaign of military suppression, only with even greater severity... Entire stretches of land are being depopulated"

The British public, however, was not buying Hitler's claim of atrocities in the Sudetenland. Leader of Labor opposition Clement Attlee (1883-1967) wrote a letter to Chamberlain urging firmness:

> "The British Government must leave no doubt in the mind of the German Government that it will unite with the French and Soviet Governments to resist any attack upon Czechoslovakia... Whatever the risks involved, Great Britain must make its stand against aggression."

War seemed imminent, but Chamberlain did not give up on the idea to grant Hitler what he wanted without a fight. Uniting with the Soviet Government against Germany was precisely what he was trying to avoid. President Roosevelt added his two cents by writing Hitler a couple of letters in which he did not deny the validity of Hitler's demands, but reiterated the need to find a peaceful resolution to the issue. Roosevelt concluded with the following:

> "Should you agree to a solution in this peaceful manner I am convinced that hundreds of millions throughout the world would recognize your action as an outstanding historic service to all humanity. Allow me to state my

The True Origins of World War II

unqualified conviction that history, and the souls of every man, woman, and child whose lives will be lost in the threatened war will hold us and all of us accountable should we omit any appeal for its prevention. The Government of the United States has no political involvements in Europe, and will assume no obligations in the conduct of the present negotiations. Yet in our own right we recognize our responsibilities as a part of a world of neighbors. The conscience and the impelling desire of the people of my country demand that the voice of their government be raised again and yet again to avert and to avoid war."

As we can see, Roosevelt's letter does not sound like a principled stand against aggression. In fact, it explicitly mentioned that United States was going to stay neutral in the case of war, exactly what Hitler needed. Meanwhile, Chamberlain decided to turn around public opinion by telling his people that the coming war would be horrible and meaningless:

"... How horrible, fantastic, incredible it is that we should be digging trenches and trying on gas-masks here because of a quarrel in a far-away country between people of whom we know nothing. It seems still more impossible that a quarrel which has already been settled in principle should be the subject of war. ... I shall not give up the hope of a peaceful solution, or abandon my efforts for peace, as long as any chance for peace remains. I would not hesitate to pay even a third visit to Germany if I thought it would do any good. ... However much we may sympathise with a small nation confronted by a big and powerful neighbour, we cannot in all circumstances undertake to involve the whole British Empire in war simply on her account. If we have to fight it must be on larger issues than that. I am myself a man of peace to the depths of my soul. Armed conflict between nations is a nightmare to me; but if I were convinced that any nation had made up its mind to dominate the world by fear of its force, I

should feel that it must be resisted. Under such a domination life for people who believe in liberty would not be worth living; but war is a fearful thing, and we must be very clear, before we embark on it, that it is really the great issues that are at stake, and that the call to risk everything in their defence, when all the consequences are weighed, is irresistible."

Somehow it was not yet obvious to Chamberlain that Hitler "made up its mind to dominate the world by fear of its force", and whole issue was just a "quarrel in a far-away country between people of whom we know nothing". Who says that public opinion is not easy to manipulate?

Also, note that the Czech people who had to face direct German attack and suffer the most casualties were more ready for the "nightmare" of the war than the relatively safe British. Was it because British loved peace more or because Czech were more motivated to see Hitler defeated? If Chamberlain's peace was so wonderful, why were the Czech people not eager to obtain it?

The Munich Conference

After turning public opinion in the needed direction, Chamberlain contacted Mussolini and asked him to intercede with Hitler on his behalf. The flattered Mussolini agreed to help and proposed an urgent conference of Germany, England, France and Italy. Hitler could not refuse his friend Mussolini, so he postponed the ultimatum deadline to Czechoslovakia for 24 hours and invited leaders of England, France and Italy to Munich.

Before leaving England for his third trip to Germany, Chamberlain declared:

The True Origins of World War II

> *"When I was a little boy, I used to repeat, 'If at first you don't succeed, try, try, try again.' That's what I am doing. When I come back I hope I may be able to say, as Hotspur says in Henry IV, 'Out of this nettle, danger, we plucked this flower, safely.'"*

Indeed, the whole affair was starting to resemble a well-rehearsed play.

The Munich conference took place on September 29, attended by Hitler, Chamberlain, Mussolini, and Daladier. Czech representatives also arrived, but they were forbidden to enter the meeting room where great powers were deciding the fate of their country.

The "compromise" proposed by Mussolini was in fact written by the Germans and differed very little from Hitler's ultimatum, which had been rejected a week earlier. However, the staged mediation of Mussolini allowed the British and French to accept Hitler's demands.

Just after 1 a.m. on September 30, the four leaders signed the Munich Pact, allowing the German Army to immediately start occupation of the Sudetenland as Hitler wanted. Half an hour later, the humiliated and betrayed Czech representatives were informed of the terms and forced to comply.

Chamberlain returned to London receiving the hero welcome, while one of the sober British observed,

> *"You might think that we had won a major victory instead of betraying a minor country"*

After the announced agreement, the German generals who were conspiring to oust Hitler gave up their plan in dismay. On October 1, on Hitler's original schedule, the German Army invaded the Sudetenland without firing a single shot. President Benes resigned and went into exile.

The new, smaller Czechoslovakia, prostrated defenseless before Hitler, had no choice but to become German puppet state. One of the voices of dissent in Britain was of course Winston Churchill, who stated in the House of Commons:

> *"We have suffered a total and unmitigated defeat. You will find that in a period of time, which may be measured by years, but may be measured by months, Czechoslovakia will be engulfed in the Nazi régime. We are in the presence of a disaster of the first magnitude. We have sustained a defeat without a war, the consequences of which will travel far with us along our road. We have passed an awful milestone in our history, when the whole equilibrium of Europe has been deranged, and that the terrible words have for the time being been pronounced against the Western democracies: "Thou art weighed in the balance and found wanting". [citation from Bible that means that one was found deficient, lacking important qualities] And do not suppose that this is the end. This is only the beginning of the reckoning. This is only the first sip, the first foretaste of a bitter cup which will be proffered to us year by year unless by a supreme recovery of moral health and martial vigor, we arise again and take our stand for freedom as in the olden time."*

Churchill stressed the important point that England had submitted to Hitler's bullying, which was a sure way to lose the status of great power. However, Churchill did not correctly explain Chamberlain's motivation and backed up the false Chamberlain's claim that all he wanted was to save peace.

In Anglo-American mythology, you can find numerous excuses for the British capitulation at Munich. Chamberlain "wanted to avoid war at any cost"; he "overestimated German strength"; he "underestimated Czechoslovakia's strategic value"; or he "was trying to buy time for rearmament". Those excuses beg the question of why British did not act earlier when Nazi Germany was not yet strong military and there was no need to play coward.

The Anglo-American perspective ignores the most likely version that Chamberlain simply wanted to channel German aggression towards Russia. It overlooks the fact that there was no Soviet representative in Munich and that an anti-Russian western pact became a reality. The new political situation was illustrated in a famous cartoon by David Low showing Hitler, Mussolini, Chamberlain and Daladier sitting around globe, and Stalin entering the room and asking "What, no chair for me?" Although Americans were also not present at the Munich Conference, President Roosevelt actually blessed the idea and its outcome, calling Chamberlain "good man".

The mainstream Anglo-American propaganda hardly even mentions the undeniably significant factor of Russia, but at the same time, it may seriously consider the naive version that Chamberlain trusted Hitler's word that all he wanted was the Sudetenland. For example, the popular book *The Complete Idiots Guide to World War II* by Professor Mitchell Bard claims:

> "In hindsight, Munich has become a symbol of naiveté in dealing with despots, but to give some perspective, it is important to realize the only alternative to negotiation was war. Chamberlain and the rest of democratic leaders hoped to find an agreement that would satisfy Hitler's ambitions and avoid a broader conflict. Simultaneously, they hoped to deter his aggression without provoking it. The lesson, which few leaders have assimilated in the succeeding 60 years, is that tyrants cannot be pacified."

This very typical claim above is perhaps really made for idiots. Like all biased ideological generalizations, it fails to take into account specific circumstances and personalities. It is no better than, for example, communist claims that leaders of capitalist countries cannot be trusted because they serve the interests of big money, while communist leaders can be trusted because they serve common people. Dogma about "democracy versus tyrants" is no better than any other dogma.

Moreover, false lessons "learned" from appeasement are often used in modern propaganda to manipulate public opinion. After deciding to start another war, American hawks usually warn about the danger of appeasement and argue that US cannot negotiate with this or that "dictator" they are going to attack.

The argument that Chamberlain wanted to save time for rearmament does not hold water either. Professor Bard himself gives the clue to the probable Chamberlain's motivation later in his book, forgetting for a minute about "naivety" and "despots", and turning to the reality of geopolitics:

> "The French and British were reluctant to cooperate with Stalin, and many in both countries hoped the Nazis and Communists might destroy each other. They also feared the opposite result: that a strictly European war would decimate the powers and leave the Soviet Union to dominate the Continent"

Chamberlain simply wanted to redirect Hitler's aggression to the East towards Russia and that explains everything. If there were only two great powers in Europe, England and Germany, British would probably prefer to engage Nazi Germany sooner than later. But if they dreamt how "the Nazis and Communists might destroy each other" than they would be motivated to avoid engagement with Hitler at any cost. Moreover, we should remember that in 1933 when Hitler came to power, Germany was disarmed, so if the democracies wanted the Nazis and

Communists "destroy each other", they first had to help the Nazis rearm.

Marshal Keitel was asked at Nuremberg trial

"Would the Reich have attacked Czechoslovakia in 1938 if the Western Powers had stood by Prague?"

Keitel answered

"Certainly not. We were not strong enough military. The object of Munich was to get Russia out of Europe, to gain time, and to complete the German armaments".

The main object of Munich was to get Russia out of Europe. But our democratic historians hardly even mention Russia when they teach kids about Munich. This is the way to create a big lie; you just omit the most important evidence.

Indeed the Russian factor as a missing piece of the puzzle glues all the conflicting explanations of Chamberlain's appeasement together. Everyone is amazed why Chamberlain was so naïve in his trust of Hitler. It was indeed naïve to think that Hitler was going to stop his territorial acquisitions after getting the Sudetenland, but it was reasonable to believe that after getting Czechoslovakia Hitler should head East and leave British alone. They say that Chamberlain underestimated Czechoslovakia's strategic and military value. It was indeed shortsighted to give up Czechoslovakia if war with Hitler could be expected soon. But if Hitler was expected to attack East, then Czechoslovakia could be safely sacrificed.

Tigran Khalatyan

Conclusion

In 1930s, the democracies appeased Hitler allegedly to save peace, however that "peace" implied a war between Nazi Germany and the Soviet Union. The culmination of appeasement was the Munich pact that delivered the democratic Czechoslovakia to the Nazi wolf on a silver platter.

On the geopolitical level, Munich broke the defensive alliance between France, Czechoslovakia and the Soviet Union and replaced it with the pact of England, France, Germany and Italy aimed against Soviet Union. Then, according to the classic "divide and conquer" principle, Germany and Russia had to destroy each other.

Anglo-American mainstream historians distort the story about appeasement using the simple trick; they just ignore the factor of Communist Russia. Without Russia in the picture, the actions of the democracies look like an honest, if mistaken, attempt to save peace.

Chapter 9: The Sudden End of Appeasement

New German Stroke in Central Europe
New York Times, 14 March 1939

Hitler's invasion of Czechoslovakia was supposedly sudden and shocking for the leaders of the democracies, although it was openly discussed in newspapers. This article in New York Times predicts split up of the country into Bohemia, Slovakia and Carpatho-Ukraine, and it also shows anticipated movement of German troops. What they could not anticipate that there would be no Carpatho-Ukraine, and that turned out to be very, very important...

Pop Quiz

Why did the policy of appeasement suddenly end in March 1939?

a) The democracies finally realized that Hitler wanted to rule the world.

b) After Hitler occupied Czechoslovakia on March 15, 1939 in violation of the Munich agreement, France and Great Britain realized that he must be stopped.

c) Realizing that Hitler changed his plans to attack Russia in near future, Neville Chamberlain, who had calmly accepted Hitler's occupation of Czechoslovakia, abruptly ended the policy of appeasement.

> *"Is this the last attack upon a small State, or is it to be followed by others? Is this, in fact, a step in the direction of an attempt to dominate the world by force?"*
>
> Neville Chamberlain, Birmingham, England
> March 17, 1939

On November 10, 1938, the rosy "peace in our time" attitude was shaken by a mass Jewish pogrom in Germany called Kristallnacht, "the night of broken glass". Then it became obvious that Hitler was going to absorb the rest of Czechoslovakia. Nevertheless, British Prime Minister Neville Chamberlain continued to have "more optimistic view of the situation", and appeasement continued on course. Nobody expected that in March 1939, appeasement would be abruptly terminated thanks to a single telegram.

Kristallnacht

Apart from cooperating in the question of dismemberment of Czechoslovakia, Germany and Poland also had similar anti-Semitic policies. In August 1938, the government of Nazi Germany announced the mandatory renewal of all residential permits for foreigners, and it was obvious that Jews were going to be denied new permits. Trying to avoid mass re-immigration of Jews from Germany, Poland authorities in turn announced that Polish citizens who "lost connection" with the country will be denied reentry unless they confirm their citizenship by October 31.

On October 26, trying to beat the deadline, the Gestapo arrested and deported 12,000 Polish Jews residing in Germany. However, when deportees reached the border, Polish authorities refused to let most of them in. Thousands of men, women and children were stuck in the border zone living in miserable conditions, unable to pass into either Poland or Germany.

Among Jewish families stuck at the border was the Grynszpan family. The seventeen-year-old member of the family Herschel Grynszpan (1921 - 1944) lived in Paris where he received the news of his family misfortune. On November 7, 1938, the outraged young man bought a revolver, went to the German Embassy and shot the junior embassy official Ernst vom Rath. Grynszpan was arrested and caused a world sensation when he said that his motive was to avenge the persecuted German Jews.

Vom Rath died of his wounds on November 9. The news reached Hitler and other top Nazis when they were commemorating the 15th anniversary of the Beer Hall Putsch. Goebbels announced the decision to organize a "spontaneous" Jewish pogrom to avenge Vom Rath's murder. During the night on November 10, Nazis shattered the storefronts of Jewish stores and businesses, burnt synagogues and arrested Jewish men. Some were killed. The emigration of Jews from Germany accelerated, but many Jewish refugees soon found that other countries were not so eager to let them in.

Nazi brutality during Kristallnacht did not alter the course of appeasement. On December 6, 1938 German foreign minister Ribbentrop arrived to Paris where with his French counterpart George Bonet they signed an agreement in which they confirmed French-German border and pledged to resolve all disputes by negotiations. The document stated:

"The French Government and the German Government fully share the conviction that pacific and neighborly relations between France and Germany constitute one of the essential elements of the consolidation of the situation in Europe and of the preservation of general peace. Conse-

quently both Governments will endeavor with all their might to assure the development of the relations between their countries in this direction."

Complementing Hitler-Chamberlain pact signed on September 30, Bonet-Ribbentrop pact confirmed new understanding of "security" and "peace" in Europe: Hitler had no claims in the West, but got free hand in the East.

The Nazi occupation of Czechoslovakia had to come next and British and French thought hard how to break their promise to defend their former ally. The formula was found that England, France, Germany and Italy should together guarantee borders of Czechoslovakia, and take action only if three or four countries agree that its independence was threatened.

On February 12, 1939, just a month before a start of a new crisis that would end appeasement and lead directly to World War II, Chamberlain wrote to his sister, "So you see I continue to take a more optimistic view of the situation".

The Birmingham Speech

One of the most important Anglo-American legends about World War II origins goes like this: On March 15, 1939 German troops suddenly occupied Czechoslovakia. Everyone was shocked that Hitler broke his promise to leave Czech alone after they gave up Sudetenland. Chamberlain realized that Hitler could not be trusted, and on March 17 he ended the policy appeasement with strong words against aggression, as spoken in his famous Birmingham speech:

"... Who can fail to feel his heart go out in sympathy to the proud and brave people who have so suddenly been subjected to this invasion, whose liberties are curtailed,

whose national independence has gone? What has become of this declaration of "No further territorial ambition"? What has become of the assurance "We don't want Czechs in the Reich"? What regard had been paid here to that principle of self-determination on which Herr Hitler argued so vehemently with me at Berchtesgaden when he was asking for the severance of Sudetenland from Czecho-Slovakia and its inclusion in the German Reich?

Now we are told that this seizure of territory has been necessitated by disturbances in Czecho-Slovakia. We are told that the proclamation of this new German Protectorate against the will of its inhabitants has been rendered inevitable by disorders which threatened the peace and security of her mighty neighbour. If there were disorders, were they not fomented from without? And can anybody outside Germany take seriously the idea that they could be a danger to that great country, that they could provide any justification for what has happened? Does not the question inevitably arise in our minds, if it is so easy to discover good reasons for ignoring assurances so solemnly and so repeatedly given, what reliance can be placed upon any other assurances that come from the same source?

There is another set of questions which almost inevitably must occur in our minds and to the minds of others, perhaps even in Germany herself. Germany, under her present regime, has sprung a series of unpleasant surprises upon the world. The Rhineland, the Austrian Anschluss, the severance of Sudetenland-all these things shocked and affronted public opinion throughout the world. Yet, however much we might take exception to the methods which were adopted in each of those cases, there was something to be said, whether on account of racial affinity or of just claims too long resisted-there was something to be said for the necessity of a change in the existing situation. But the events which have taken place this week in complete disregard of the principles laid down by the German Government itself seem to fall into a

> *different category, and they must cause us all to be asking ourselves: "Is this the end of an old adventure, or is it the beginning of a new?" "Is this the last attack upon a small State, or is it to be followed by others? Is this, in fact, a step in the direction of an attempt to dominate the world by force?"*

The speech was followed by a British guarantee to smaller states that could become victims of Hitler's next attack. So when Hitler invaded Poland several months later, England and France declared war on Germany to retaliate against his aggression.

The legend that the democracies were outraged when Hitler occupied Czechoslovakia is very important for Anglo-Americans, because it allows them to present appeasement as an honest, if mistaken, attempt to save peace. If Chamberlain indeed accepted Hitler's aggression in the East, why would he suddenly change his policy after the fall of Prague?

Let's go back from the legend to the real life and re-check the facts. First, German occupation of Czechoslovakia was neither sudden nor surprising. British and French governments decided in advance that they are not going to defend the country and kept low profile while Hitler was preparing his not so secret invasion.

Not without Hitler's help political situation in Czechoslovakia continued to boil after Munich. After getting the Sudetenland, Hitler started supporting Slovak and Ukrainian separatists in the country. Slovak leader Joseph Tiso (1887-1947) was invited to Berlin on March 13, where Hitler told him that Slovakia had to become an independent country under German protection. Without further delay, Slovakia declared its independence on March 14. British and French governments did not raise their voice to defend territorial integrity of Czechoslovakia, but actually accepted the breakup of the country.

Then came the turn of Czech remnants of the country, Bohemia and Moravia. President of Czechoslovakia Emeil Hacha (1872-1945) was also summoned to Berlin where he was informed of the imminent German invasion. Threatening to bomb Prague, Hitler, Goering and Ribbentrop bullied Hacha into ordering the capitulation of the Czechoslovak army and accepting annexation of his country by Germany. During the ongoing negotiation, the elderly Hacha suffered a heart attack and had to receive medical help, but he eventually gave in and signed the surrender terms. German troops entered Czechoslovakia on March 15, meeting practically no resistance.

The next day, Hitler went to Prague and proclaimed the creation of German protectorate of Bohemia and Moravia. Czechoslovakia was annexed by Germany but retained some limited autonomy. Hacha kept his post as head of state. A joint Czech-German press release stated the following:

> *"Both [Czech and German] sides gave expression to their mutual conviction that the aim of all efforts in this part of Central Europe should be the safeguarding of calm, order and peace. The Czecho-Slovak President declared that in order to serve this purpose and in order to secure final pacification, he placed the destiny of the Czech people and country with confidence in the hands of the German Reich.*
>
> *Herr Hitler accepted this declaration and expressed his determination to take the Czech people under the protection of the German Reich, and to guarantee to it an autonomous development of its national life in accordance with its peculiar characteristics."*

During the Nuremberg trial after the war, there was an interesting dispute about whether the events on March 15 were an act of German aggression or if German troops were invited by the head of state. Ribbentrop was asked by British prosecutor:

> "What further pressure could you put on the head of a country beyond threatening him that your Army would march in, in overwhelming strength, and your air force would bomb his capital?"

Ribbentrop's answer was: "War, for instance." To this, Goering remarked that Ribbentrop deserved to be hanged, if only for his stupidity. Hacha did not live to hear Ribbentrop's testimony; in 1945, he was arrested for collaborating with Nazis and died in prison.

Back in 1939, Chamberlain knew about movement of German troops and did not lift a finger to prevent the invasion. If all the secret reports Chamberlain was receiving as a head of state were not enough, he could just read the newspapers. Newspapers all around the world reported that Hitler was sending troops toward the border of Czechoslovakia. The maps clearly showed how the once-strongest state in Central Europe was about to be dismembered by the black arrows representing the anticipated German invasion force.

On March 14, the editorial board of the New York Times bluntly stated:

> "It now appears that the present situation is to be used by Hitler as the pretext for another thrust: having destroyed the defenses of Czecho-Slovakia last September, he would now destroy the independence of that state and bring it wholly within the power of German Reich."

The newspaper also admitted that the democracies were going to allow Hitler to do whatever he wanted:

> *"There is complete confidence here that in the end the Czech Government will do whatever the Germans may command; it has no choice in the matter. Prime Minister Neville Chamberlain had made up his mind that there is going to be no crises in Europe at the present time and really believes that general conditions in Europe justify optimism"*

Indeed, on the same day when Chamberlain was asked in the House of Commons if he is going to do something about the new threat, the answer showed Chamberlain's determination to do nothing.

> *Atlee: "Does the Prime Minister say that the Government are merely awaiting for a fait accompli, and have they taken any steps to have any consultation with the representatives of the Czecho-Slovak Government or with the French Government or any other guarantor, seeing that there are rumours and implications, which can hardly be disregarded altogether, of a possible break up of Czecho-Slovakia, which this country has guaranteed?"*
>
> *Chamberlain: "I am not sure what the right hon. Gentleman thinks that we should do. I might remind him that the proposed guarantee is one against unprovoked aggression on Czecho-Slovakia. No such aggression has yet taken place."*

Next day, on March 15, after German troops entered Prague, Chamberlain gave very feeble response to Hitler's aggression. Chamberlain actually backed up Hitler's claim that Czechoslovakia's problems were created at Versailles "20 years earlier" and the state broke up due to internal reasons. While disapproving Hitler's methods he accepted what had happened as fait accompli and in effect urged to continue the politics of appeasement:

The True Origins of World War II

"In considering these events and their relation to the events which preceded them, we must remember that at Munich, and at the discussions which went on before it, we were not dealing with a situation which had just been created. We were dealing with events and with a set of circumstances which had resulted from forces set in motion 20 years earlier...

The State which under that settlement we hoped might begin a new and more stable career, has become disintegrated. The attempt to preserve a State containing Czechs, Slovaks, as well as minorities of other nationalities, was liable to the same possibilities of change as was the Constitution which was drafted when the State was originally framed under the Treaty of Versailles. And it has not survived...

They [Germans] have now, without, so far as I know, any communication with the other three signatories to the Munich Agreement, sent their troops beyond the frontier there laid down. But even though it may now be claimed that what has taken place has occurred with the acquiescence of the Czech Government, I cannot regard the manner and the method by which these changes have been brought about as in accord with the spirit of the Munich Agreement. A further point which I would make is this: Hitherto the German Government in extending the area of their military control have defended their action by the contention that they were only incorporating in the Reich neighbouring masses of people of German race. Now for the first time they are effecting a military occupation of territory inhabited by people with whom they have no racial connection. These events cannot fail to be a cause of disturbance to the international situation. They are bound to administer a shock to confidence, all the more regrettable because confidence was beginning to revive and to offer a prospect of concrete measures which would be of general benefit. It is natural, therefore, that I should bitterly regret what has now occurred. But do not let us on that account be deflected from our course. Let us remember that the desire of all the peoples of the

> *world still remains concentrated on the hopes of peace and a return to the atmosphere of understanding and good will which has so often been disturbed. The aim of this Government is now, as it has always been, to promote that desire and to substitute the method of discussion for the method of force in the settlement of differences. Though we may have to suffer checks and disappointments, from time to time, the object that we have in mind is of too great significance to the happiness of mankind for us lightly to give it up or set it on one side."*

In respect to British guarantee to Czechoslovakia against unprovoked aggression, Chamberlain proclaimed that it was no longer valid because the state that British promised to protect no longer exists:

> *"In our opinion the situation has radically altered since the Slovak Diet [parliament] declared the independence of Slovakia. The effect of this declaration put an end by internal disruption to the State whose frontiers we had proposed to guarantee and, accordingly, the condition of affairs described by my right hon. Friend the Secretary of State for the Dominions, which was always regarded by us as being only of a transitory nature has now ceased to exist, and His Majesty's Government cannot accordingly hold themselves any longer bound by this obligation."*

This sneaky diplomatic language doesn't sound like outrage against aggression, does it? For whatever reason, Chamberlain waited two days to speak much stronger words at Birmingham. Churchill noticed sharp change in Chamberlain's attitude, although he did not explain it:

> *"It is not easy to imagine a greater contradiction to the mood of the Prime Minister's statement two days earlier in the House of Commons. He must have been through a period of intense stress. On the fifteenth he had said: 'Do*

not let us be deflected from our course.' But this was 'Right-about-turn.'"

Meanwhile, Americans only recalled their ambassador from Germany to protest the annexation of Czechoslovakia on March 20, five days after the aggression. This strange delay of "outrage" is usually just ignored or explained away, which indicates that some critical information is missing.

For example, some argue that Chamberlain had to change his position under the pressure of public opinion. In the past, however, Chamberlain had no problem bucking public opinion. This time, it seemed that he in fact felt fooled and betrayed by Hitler's actions, yet he still hesitated to act.

A few days later, Chamberlain himself acknowledged that his first statement on March 15 was inadequate, explaining in a private letter that:

> *"It was like the stupidity of the Opposition to insist on a debate before we knew all that had happened and when we had had no time to consider our attitudes."*

Chamberlain never specified, however, just what "before we knew all that had happened" actually meant. What significant information he did not know on March 15, but knew on March 17? Wasn't everyone anticipating the subjugation of Czechoslovakia in one way or another?

There was nothing surprising in Hitler's occupation of Czechoslovakia, however the initial calmness of British and French governments, followed by sudden outrage, was indeed surprising. On March 27, when the "Stop Hitler" campaign began to gain momentum, Time magazine published an article with the telling title "Surprise? Surprise?" The article openly questioned why British and French were initially so inert in their reactions:

> "The swift, smooth pace of the occupation showed that the Germans had made organized preparations for it well in advance. If the British and French secret services did not know all this they were not worth their pay. That they did know it and did report it was made fairly evident at week's end ... Next question the world wanted answered was: If Neville Chamberlain knew what was going to happen, why did he act as though he didn't? ... when the German troops marched into Prague, the Prime Minister was still cucumber-cool."

The question of why the Prime Minister was "cucumber cool" was never answered, though it's reasonable to suggest that Chamberlain had decided in advance to tolerate German aggression. Even on March 16, the British government did not officially protest the invasion, and nothing indicated that it was going to. When asked by a member of the House whether the British government would warn the German government not to harm the Czech leaders, Chamberlain responded: "I think it wrong to assume that the German Government have any such intention". There was every indication that the German occupation of Czechoslovakia would be accepted by British government with only token protest.

Why was Chamberlain so calm on March 14, when the subjugation of Czechoslovakia was about to proceed? Why was he so calm on March 15, when the occupation of Czechoslovakia became a fact? Why was he so calm on March 16, when the formal annexation of Bohemia and Moravia was proclaimed? And why did he suddenly became outraged on March 17, when nothing significant happened?

There can be only one explanation: on March 17, Chamberlain finally received proof that Hitler no longer planned to head East towards Russia. His policy of appeasement, therefore, stood no chance.

Carpatho-Ukraine

At the beginning of 1939, it was obvious to an intelligent observer that Europe was headed to war. On January 30, in his infamous Reichstag speech, Hitler predicted the coming World War and the Holocaust. The following passage was especially notorious:

> *"The world has sufficient space for settlements, but we must once and for all get rid of the opinion that the Jewish race was only created by God for the purpose of being in a certain percentage a parasite living on the body and the productive work of other nations. The Jewish race will have to adapt itself to sound constructive activity as other nations do, or sooner or later it will succumb to a crisis of an inconceivable magnitude. One thing I should like to say on this day which may be memorable for others as well as for us Germans: In the course of my life I have very often been a prophet, and have usually been ridiculed for it. During the time of my struggle for power it was in the first instance only the Jewish race that received my prophecies with laughter when I said that I would one day take over the leadership of the State, and with it that of the whole nation, and that I would then among other things settle the Jewish problem. Their laughter was uproarious, but I think that for some time now they have been laughing on the other side of their face. Today I will once more be a prophet: if the international Jewish financiers in and outside Europe should succeed in plunging the nations once more into a world war, then the result will not be the Bolshevizing of the*

> earth, and thus the victory of Jewry, but the annihilation of the Jewish race in Europe!"

As usual, the speech was full of the vehement anti-Communism that was closely linked to Hitler's anti-Semitism:

> "Had the German Reich sunk into Bolshevik chaos it would at that very moment have plunged the whole of Western civilization into a crisis of inconceivable magnitude. Only islanders with the most limited vision can imagine that the Red Plague would have stopped of its own accord before the sacredness of the democratic idea or at the boundaries of disinterested states... Thus our relationship with Japan is determined by the recognition of the need to stem, as we are determined to do, the tide of the threatened bolshevization of a world gone blind with all the resolution at our command. The Anti-Comintern Pact will perhaps one day become the crystallization point of a group of powers whose ultimate aim is none other than to eliminate the menace to the peace and culture of the world instigated by a satanic apparition."

According to Chamberlain, at the time this speech was given his "confidence was beginning to revive" and he had "a more optimistic view of the situation". Chamberlain in fact had a very favorable opinion of Hitler's speech, because the Fuhrer had added a few words about "long peace" between Germany and England:

> "We believe that if the Jewish international campaign of hatred by press and propaganda could be checked, good understanding could very quickly be established between the peoples. It is only such elements that hope steadfastly for a war. I however believe in a long peace. For in what way do the interests of England and Germany for example conflict!

> *I have stated over and over again that there is no German and above all, no National Socialist, who even in his most secret thoughts has the intention of causing the British Empire any kind of difficulties. From England, too, the voices of men who think reasonably and calmly express a similar attitude with regard to Germany. It would be a blessing for the whole world if mutual confidence and cooperation could be established between the two peoples."*

Once again, Hitler employed his secret formula for success: attack communists while offering friendship to England. The formula still worked, but the time was coming to show his cards. It was obvious that Europe was headed to war, but it was still not obvious where Hitler was going to attack first, in the East or in the West. The appeasement had to ensure Hitler's attack in the East, but the realities of geopolitics tempted Hitler to attack in the West first. There were serious strategic reasons why at the dawn of World War I Germany had tried to quickly eliminate the French threat in the West and then turn East without fear of a stab in the back.

Despite all Chamberlain's efforts, Hitler had very little trust in the democracies and their promises. For example, on October 9, 1938 Hitler noted,

> *"It only needs that in England instead of Chamberlain, Mr. Duff Cooper or Mr. Eden or Mr. Churchill should come to power, and then we know quite well that it would be the aim of these men immediately to begin a new World War."*

Reading Mein Kampf, the blueprint for the world conquest that Hitler followed almost to a letter, we can see that he wanted to defeat France to eliminate the threat from the west. Only England and Italy were on the list of his friends, and slow German naval rearmament actually indicated that Hitler had no desire to conquer England.

There was, however, one condition that could guarantee British-German "long peace": England had to allow Germany to defeat France and dominate Europe, something that England was never prepared to do. Thus Hitler had to constantly demonstrate his hostility towards Communist Russia, or there would be no appeasement.

Moreover, after Munich there was common "understanding" of how German aggression towards Russia should proceed. Hitler was expected to support Ukrainian separatists in Soviet Ukraine and Poland in order to create "independent" pro-German Ukraine. The whole affair could have been presented as another case of self-determination—tie Nazis and the Communists in a proxy or even full-scale war and keep moralizing western democracies away from the trouble. The plan was openly discussed in the world press and in the diplomatic circles. In one of many examples of the anticipation of the Hitler's next move towards Ukraine, The Sydney Morning Herald reported on November 24, 1938:

> *"The German diplomatic and military strategists had already commenced at drawing the Russian and the Polish Ukraine directly within the political and military sphere of influence of Greater Germany."*

On November 30, 1938, the Soviet ambassador in England Ivan Maiskiy (1884-1975) reported his discussion with Chamberlain's adviser Wilson:

> *"England in the near future is not threatened by war, because, according to Wilson, the Hitler's next big blow is against Ukraine. The technique will be approximately the same as in the case of Czechoslovakia. First, the rise of nationalism, the outbreaks, the uprising of the Ukrainian*

> *population, and then the "liberation" of Ukraine by Hitler under the slogan of "self-determination".*

German aggression against the Soviet Union through Ukraine was thus anticipated and welcomed by the democracies. This was the "peace" that they were waiting for. Britain only had to make sure that France would not get involved on the Russian side, because of the existing Soviet-French defensive treaty. The "mistake" made at the dawn of World War I had to be avoided.

On November 24, 1938 Chamberlain met with French foreign minister Georges Bonet (1889-1973) and told him that "it would be unfortunate" if France became "entangled" in German-Soviet dispute over the Ukraine. Chamberlain then directly asked:

> *"What the position would be if Russia were to ask France for assistance on the grounds that a separatist movement in the Ukraine was provoked by Germany. M. Bonnet explained that French obligations towards Russia only came into force if there was a direct attack by Germany on Russian territory. Mr. Chamberlain said that he considered M. Bonnet's reply entirely satisfactory."*

Thus, the plan for Ukraine was approved by all major parties. There was even designated spearhead for the future "independent" Ukraine, the province of Ruthenia. Previously part of Austria-Hungary, Ruthenia became the easternmost district of Czechoslovakia after World War I. After Munich, Hungary wanted to annex Ruthenia, but Hitler vetoed the idea since he needed the province for the "Greater Ukraine" project.

Hungary got only piece of Ruthenia, while the rest was renamed to Carpatho-Ukraine and, as Time magazine reported,

> *"became an "autonomous" region with only loose connections with Prague but with very definite though unofficial links with Berlin":*
>
> *"The Nazis' Ukrainian blueprints nominated it as the generating center for a movement to "liberate" all Ukrainians from their present Polish, Rumanian and Russian masters and bring them under the benevolent protection of Führer Hitler. Well-heeled Nazi organizers began to appear in Chust, capital of the Carpatho-Ukraine. A military mission arrived to teach the hastily arming Ruthenians the art of warfare."*

Indeed, the western press was not shy to describe plans for "Greater Ukraine" in detail. The article cited above, titled "Liberation", was published on January 23, 1939, perhaps explaining why Mr. Chamberlain was so optimistic at that time. The article explained that after Munich, Czechoslovakia became a German puppet state and that Carpatho-Ukraine was going to be used by the Nazis as the spearhead against Soviet Union, which was only 90 miles away. Time also reported Nazi activity in the region and indicated that Hitler would not allow Poland and Hungary to invade Ruthenia as they wished. It was also noted that the Nazi-backed press had started a "Freedom for the Ukraine" campaign.

So when on March 14 Hitler sent troops toward Czechoslovakia border, everyone expected not only the creation of an "independent" Slovakia, but an "independent" Carpatho-Ukraine as well. The New York Times specifically stated:

> *"Chancellor Hitler in Virtual Ultimatum to Czecho-Slovakia is understood to have demanded the independence of Slovakia as forerunner to the break up of the nation into three countries Bohemia, Slovakia (which would share with Germany what is now Moravia) and Carpatho-Ukraine."*

On March 15, following the example of Slovakia, Carpatho-Ukraine declared its independence. The president of the new country, Avgustin Voloshyn (1874-1945), immediately sent Hitler a telegram requesting German protection.

Then something unexpected happened. Hitler abandoned Carpatho-Ukraine and let Hungary occupy it. Invading Hungarian troops quickly crashed local resistance and annexed the one-day-old Ukrainian state. Voloshyn escaped to Romania and then moved to German occupied Prague. When Soviets entered Prague in 1945, they arrested Voloshyn, who soon died in Moscow prison. The project of "Greater Ukraine" that Hitler abandoned would be completed by Stalin, who by the end of the war had joined Polish Western Ukraine, Soviet Eastern Ukraine, as well as Carpatho-Ukraine into one big Soviet Ukraine.

The world was surprised that Hitler abandoned Carpatho-Ukraine, but soon everyone forgot about the tiny region. However, the hidden effect of Hitler's abandonment of his Ukrainian project was tremendous. The governments of the democratic countries suddenly realized that they could not predict Hitler's next move and lost all confidence in him. Had Hitler decided to attack in the west first? Had he decided to bring all the small states in Eastern Europe into the German orbit? The world press that had been so confident in predicting Hitler's march on Ukraine was now full of guesses about his next move. Chamberlain, who thought that he understood Hitler, was utterly disappointed.

The timing of this realization coincides perfectly with the change in tone at Birmingham. As author Clement Leibovitz pointed out:

> *"On March 17 at 7:30pm Halifax received a telegram from the British ambassador to Budapest, who informed him that the German ambassador had confirmed that Germany was uninterested in Ruthenia and prepared to let Hungary occupy the area. Eighty minutes after receiving the news, Halifax sent Henderson a telegram with a message to be conveyed to the German government. The message was that the British government not only regarded the invasion of Czechoslovakia as a violation of the spirit of Munich but also considered the changes effected in Czechoslovakia 'devoid of any basis of legality'"*

The night of March 17 was when Chamberlain suddenly decided to publicly end his appeasement policy. Of course, he did not even mention Carpatho-Ukraine in his Birmingham speech, but its importance becomes even more evident if one remembers Stalin's famous "Chestnut" speech spoken just a week earlier on March 10, 1939. In his speech Stalin suggested that Germany should abandon its game with Carpatho-Ukraine. Hitler, it seems, was listening. Chamberlain could no longer trust that he had the ear of the Fuhrer.

Conclusion

On March 17, the democracies suddenly made a sharp turn from appeasement to containment. Anglo-American histories say that it happened because Hitler broke his word and everyone realized he was planning conquest of the world.

In reality, Hitler's plans of conquest were well-known to everyone for a long time, and it was not the first time he broke his word. As a matter of fact, Chamberlain was at first "cucumber cool" when Hitler occupied Czechoslovakia, and his sudden outrage at Birmingham was rather surprising. It's doubtful that

The True Origins of World War II

Chamberlain changed his attitude due to public opinion alone. Everything indicated that he was genuinely shocked by Hitler's betrayal. The only probable explanation of this sudden change of mind was the fact that Hitler let Hungary occupy Carpatho-Ukraine, thus abandoning the Greater Ukraine project that was meant to be a springboard to war between Russia and Germany. If Hitler was not planning to attack Russia in the near future, then what he was up to?

Chapter 10:
The Non-Aggression Treaty

A cartoon on the Soviet-German Non-aggression treaty published in Japan 1939

The cartoon correctly depicts the world's astonishment at the sudden agreement of the sworn enemies Communist Russia and Nazi Germany. Among the consequences of the treaty was the fall of the Japanese government that felt betrayed by Hitler.

Pop Quiz

What was the significance of the Soviet-German Non-Aggression treaty?

a) Nazi Germany and Soviet Union became allies and together started World War II.

b) The pact directly led to World War II as it gave Hitler freedom to attack Poland. Moreover, in the secret protocol of the pact Soviet Union and Nazi Germany divided the spheres of influence in Eastern Europe.

c) The Non-Aggression treaty was in essence proclamation of the Soviet neutrality in the coming war between Nazi Germany and the West. The democracies wanted to provoke war between Nazi Germany and Communist Russia, but Hitler decided attack in the West first, which suited Soviets well.

> *"People were unpleasantly affected by the thought of having to **pull England's chestnuts out of the fire;** as though there ever could be an alliance on any other basis than a mutual business deal."*
>
> Adolf Hitler, Mein Kampf, 1925

> *"The tasks of the Party in the sphere of foreign policy are : ... To be cautious and not allow our country to be drawn into conflicts by warmongers who are accustomed to have **others pull the chestnuts out of the fire** for them"*
>
> Joseph Stalin, March 10, 1939

In the spring and summer of 1939, the complex geopolitical game reached its climax. After many years of confrontation between Nazi Germany and Communist Russia, Hitler suddenly reached an agreement with the Soviet Union and collided with the West instead.

The 18th Congress of the Communist Party

On March 10, 1939, only a week before Chamberlain's speech in Birmingham that marked the end of appeasement, Stalin made report to the Eighteen Congress of the Communist Party that started with description of the international situation. Below are some lengthy excerpts from the report, which serves as a good overview of the origins of World War II and the meaning of Carpatho-Ukrainian game:

> *"The new economic crisis must lead, and is actually leading, to a further sharpening of the imperialist struggle. It is no longer a question of competition in the markets, of a commercial war, of dumping. These methods of struggle*

have long been recognized as inadequate. It is now a question of a new re-division of the world, of spheres of influence and colonies, by military action.

[. . .]

Here is a list of the most important events during the period under review, which mark the beginning of the new imperialist war. In 1935 Italy attacked and seized Abyssinia. In the summer of 1936 Germany and Italy organized military intervention in Spain, Germany entrenching herself in the north of Spain and in Spanish Morocco, and Italy in the south of Spain and in the Balearic Islands. Having seized Manchuria, Japan in 1937 invaded North and Central China, occupied Peking, Tientsin and Shanghai and began to oust her foreign competitors from the occupied zone. In the beginning of 1938 Germany seized Austria, and in the autumn of 1938 the Sudeten region of Czechoslovakia. At the end of 1938 Japan seized Canton, and at the beginning of 1939 the Island of Hainan.

Thus the war, which has stolen so imperceptibly upon the nations, has drawn over five hundred million people into its orbit and has extended its sphere of action over a vast territory, stretching from Tientsin, Shanghai and Canton, through Abyssinia, to Gibraltar.

After the first imperialist war the victor states, primarily Britain, France and the United States, had set up a new regime in the relations between countries, the post-war regime of peace. The main props of this regime were the Nine-Power Pact in the Far East, and the Versailles Treaty and a number of other treaties in Europe. The League of Nations was set up to regulate relations between countries within the framework of this regime, on the basis of a united front of states, of collective defense of the security of states. However, three aggressive states, and the new imperialist war launched by them, have upset the entire system of this post-war peace regime.

Japan tore up the Nine-Power Pact, and Germany and Italy the Versailles Treaty. In order to have their hands free, these three states withdrew from the League of Nations.

[...]

It is not so easy in our day to suddenly break loose and plunge straight into war without regard for treaties of any kind or for public opinion. Bourgeois politicians know this very well. So do the fascist rulers. That is why the fascist rulers decided, before plunging into war, to frame public opinion to suit their ends, that is, to mislead it, to deceive it.

A military bloc of Germany and Italy against the interests of England and France in Europe? Bless us, do you call that a bloc? "We" have no military bloc.

All "we" have is an innocuous "Berlin-Rome axis"; that is, just a geometrical equation for an axis. (Laughter.)

A military bloc of Germany, Italy and Japan against the interests of the United States, Great Britain and France in the Far East? Nothing of the kind.

"We" have no military bloc. All "we" have is an innocuous "Berlin-Rome-Tokyo triangle"; that is, a slight penchant for geometry. (General laughter.)

A war against the interests of England, France, the United States? Nonsense! "We" are waging war on the Comintern, not on these states. If you don't believe it, read the "anti-Comintern pact" concluded between Italy, Germany and Japan.

That is how Messieurs the aggressors thought of framing public opinion, although it was not hard to see how preposterous this whole clumsy game of camouflage was; for it is ridiculous to look for Comintern "hotbeds" in the deserts of Mongolia, in the mountains of Abyssinia, or in the wilds of Spanish Morocco. (Laughter.)

But war is inexorable. It cannot be hidden under any guise. For no "axes," "triangles" or "anti-Comintern pacts" *can hide the fact that in this period Japan has seized a vast stretch of territory in China, that Italy has seized Abyssinia, that Germany has seized Austria and the Sudeten region, that Germany and Italy together have seized Spain - and all this in defiance of the interests of the non-aggressive states.*

The war remains a war; the military bloc of aggressors remains a military bloc; and the aggressors remain aggressors.

It is a distinguishing feature of the new imperialist war that it has not yet become universal, a world war. The war is being waged by aggressor states, who in every way infringe upon the interests of the non-aggressive states, primarily England, France and the U.S.A., while the latter draw back and retreat, making concession after concession to the aggressors.

Thus we are witnessing an open re-division of the world and spheres of influence at the expense of the non-aggressive states, without the least attempt at resistance, and even with a certain amount of connivance, on the part of the latter.

Incredible, but true.

To what are we to attribute this one-sided and strange character of the new imperialist war?

How is it that the non-aggressive countries, which possess such vast opportunities, have so easily, and without any resistance, abandoned their positions and their obligations to please the aggressors?

Is it to be attributed to the weakness of the nonaggressive states? Of course not. Combined, the nonaggressive, democratic states are unquestionably stronger than the fascist states, both economically and in the military sense.

To what then are we to attribute the systematic concessions made by these states to the aggressors?

The True Origins of World War II

It might be attributed, for example, to the fear that a revolution might break out if the non-aggressive states were to go to war and the war were to assume world - wide proportions. The bourgeois politicians know, of course, that the first imperialist world war led to the victory of the revolution in one of the largest countries. They are afraid that the second imperialist world war may also lead to the victory of the revolution in one or several countries.

But at present this is not the sole or even the chief reason. The chief reason is that the majority of the non-aggressive countries, particularly England and France, have rejected the policy of collective security, the policy of collective resistance to the aggressors, and have taken up a position of nonintervention, a position of "neutrality."

Formally speaking, the policy of non-intervention might be defined as follows: "Let each country defend itself from the aggressors as it likes and as best it can. That is not our affair. We shall trade both with the aggressors and with their victims." But actually speaking, the policy of non-intervention means conniving at aggression, giving free rein to war, and, consequently, transforming the war into a world war. The policy of non-intervention reveals an eagerness, a desire, not to hinder the aggressors in their nefarious work : not to hinder Japan, say, from embroiling herself in a war with China, or, better still, with the Soviet Union : to allow all the belligerents to sink deeply into the mire of war, to encourage them surreptitiously in this, to allow them to weaken and exhaust one another; and then, when they have become weak enough, to appear on the scene with fresh strength, to appear, of course, "in the interests of peace," and to dictate conditions to the enfeebled belligerents.

Cheap and easy!

Take Japan, for instance. It is characteristic that before Japan invaded North China all the influential French and British newspapers shouted about China's weakness and her inability to offer resistance, and declared that Japan with her army could subjugate China in two or three

253

months. Then the European and American politicians began to watch and wait. And then, when Japan started military operations, they let her have Shanghai, the vital center of foreign capital in China; they let her have Canton, a center of Britain's monopoly influence in South China; they let her have Hainan, and they allowed her to surround Hong Kong. Does not this look very much like encouraging the aggressor? It is as though they were saying:

"Embroil yourself deeper in war; then we shall see."

Or take Germany, for instance. They let her have Austria, despite the undertaking to defend her independence; they let her have the Sudeten region; they abandoned Czechoslovakia to her fate, thereby violating all their obligations; and then began to lie vociferously in the press about "the weakness of the Russian army," "the demoralization of the Russian air force," and "riots" in the Soviet Union, egging the Germans on to march farther east, promising them easy pickings, and prompting them : "Just start war on the Bolsheviks, and everything will be all right." It must be admitted that this too looks very much like egging on and encouraging the aggressor.

The hullabaloo raised by the British, French and American press over the Soviet Ukraine is characteristic.

The gentlemen of the press there shouted until they were hoarse that the Germans were marching on Soviet Ukraine, that they now had what is called the Carpathian Ukraine, with a population of some seven hundred thousand, and that not later than this spring the Germans would annex the Soviet Ukraine, which has a population of over thirty million, to this so-called Carpathian Ukraine. It looks as if the object of this suspicious hullabaloo was to incense the Soviet Union against Germany, to poison the atmosphere and to provoke a conflict with Germany without any visible grounds.

It is quite possible, of course, that there are madmen in Germany who dream of annexing the elephant, that is,

The True Origins of World War II

the Soviet Ukraine, to the gnat, namely, the so-called Carpathian Ukraine. If there really are such lunatics in Germany, rest assured that we shall find enough straitjackets for them in our country. (Thunderous applause.) But if we ignore the madmen and turn to normal people, is it not clearly absurd and foolish to seriously talk of annexing the Soviet Ukraine to this so-called Carpathian Ukraine? Imagine: The gnat comes to the elephant and says perkily : "Ah, brother, how sorry I am for you . . . Here you are without any landlords, without any capitalists, with no national oppression, without any fascist bosses. Is that a way to live? . . . As I look at you I can't help thinking that there is no hope for you unless you annex yourself to me . . . (General laughter.) Well, so be it :

I allow you to annex your tiny domain to my vast territories . . ." (General laughter and applause.)

Even more characteristic is the fact that certain European and American politicians and pressmen, having lost patience waiting for "the march on the Soviet Ukraine," are themselves beginning to disclose what is really behind the policy of non-intervention. They are saying quite openly, putting it down in black on white, that the Germans have cruelly "disappointed" them, for instead of marching farther east, against the Soviet Union, they have turned, you see, to the west and are demanding colonies. One might think that the districts of Czechoslovakia were yielded to Germany as the price of an undertaking to launch war on the Soviet Union, but that now the Germans are refusing to meet their bills and are sending them to Hades.

[...]

There is no doubt that any war, however small, started by the aggressors in any remote corner of the world constitutes a danger to the peaceable countries. All the more serious then is the danger arising from the new imperialist war, which has already drawn into its orbit over five hundred million people in Asia, Africa and Europe. In view of this, while our country is unswervingly pursuing a policy of preserving peace, it is at the same time doing a great deal to increase the preparedness of our Red Army and Red Navy ...

The tasks of the Party in the sphere of foreign policy are :

1. To continue the policy of peace and of strengthening business relations with all countries;

2. To be cautious and not allow our country to be drawn into conflicts by warmongers who are accustomed to have others pull the chestnuts out of the fire for them;

3. To strengthen the might of our Red Army and Red Navy to the utmost;

4. To strengthen the international bonds of friendship with the working people of all countries, who are interested in peace and friendship among nations."

Note item 2 above regarding "warmongers who are accustomed to have others pull the chestnuts out of the fire for them", the reference to the politics of the democratic countries who incite conflict between Germany and Russia. By coincidence or not, Hitler repeated this "pull the chestnuts out of the fire" idiom in his speech on April 1, 1939, this time warning Poland not to conflict with Germany in British and French interests.

Did Hitler forget that he himself promised "pull England's chestnuts out of the fire" in Mein Kampf? As we mentioned before, Hitler explicitly expressed regret in Mein Kampf that at the beginning of the century Germany did not became the British proxy instead of Japan to fight with Russia:

"... at the turn of the century London itself attempted to approach Germany. For the first time a thing became evident which in the last years we have had occasion to observe in a truly terrifying fashion. People were unpleasantly affected by the thought of having to pull England's chestnuts out of the fire; as though there ever could be an

The True Origins of World War II

alliance on any other basis than a mutual business deal. And with England such a deal could very well have been made. British diplomacy was still clever enough to realize that no service can be expected without a return. Just suppose that an astute German foreign policy had taken over the role of Japan in 1904, and we can scarcely measure the consequences this would have had for Germany. There would never have been any 'World War.' The bloodshed in the year 1904 would have saved ten times as much in the years 1914 to 1918. And what a position Germany would occupy in the world today!"

Just imagine Chamberlain's shock, then, when Hitler let Hungary occupy Carpatho-Ukraine. It looked like Hitler was no longer his friend, but Stalin's. England was not going to get those long promised "chestnuts"!

The true meaning of Carpatho-Ukraine game was very well understood behind the scenes. For example, a German diplomat noted on July 27, 1939,

"the solution of the Carpatho-Ukrainian question had shown that here we did not aim at anything there that would endanger Soviet interests."

Meanwhile, the prominent old Bolshevik Leon Trotsky, the leader of anti-Stalinist communists opposition in exile, wrote in his article "Problem of Ukraine" on April 22, 1939:

"We shall not pause here to analyze the motives that impelled Hitler to discard, for the time being at least, the slogan of a Greater Ukraine. These motives must be sought in the fraudulent combinations of German imperialism on the one hand and on the other in the fear of conjuring up an evil spirit whom it might be difficult to exorcize. Hitler gave Carpatho-Ukraine as a gift to the Hungarian butchers. This was done, if not with Moscow's open approval then in any case with confidence that ap-

> *proval would be forthcoming. It is as if Hitler had said to Stalin: "If I were preparing to attack Soviet Ukraine tomorrow I should have kept Carpatho-Ukraine in my own hands." In reply, Stalin at the 18th Party Congress openly came to Hitler's defense against the slanders of the "Western Democracies." Hitler intends to attack the Ukraine? Nothing of the sort! Fight with Hitler? Not the slightest reason for it. Stalin is obviously interpreting the handing over of Carpatho-Ukraine to Hungary as an act of peace."*

In the rest of the article, Trotsky argued that Soviet Ukraine should secede from the Soviet Union, all according with the principle of the self-determination.

Stalin must have been reading Trotsky's articles with great interest, because his response was swift and brutal. In 1940, the undercover NKVD agent Ramon Mercader (1913-1978) found Trotsky in Mexico and ended the life of the proponent for world revolution with a mountaineers' ice pick.

The Polish Question

On March 17, 1939, as Chamberlain felt insecure about Hitler's true intentions, British politics towards Germany had made sharp turn from appeasement to containment. As the pressure upon Germany increased, so did Hitler's defiance. Europe was headed to war.

Similar to the dawn of World War I, the intensive diplomatic game between the major parties had started. The Soviet Union was negotiating with England and France to create an alliance against Germany. Behind the scenes, England and Germany were trying to find another Munich-style compromise. Last but not least, Germany and Soviet Union started to look for ways to avoid confrontation.

The True Origins of World War II

After dismemberment of Czechoslovakia, it was Poland's turn to become the focal point of the great power's contest. Poland had difficult relations with its Eastern and Western neighbors for ages. In the seventeenth century, the Polish–Lithuanian Commonwealth was a large and powerful European state that included territories of modern Baltic States, Belorussia, and Ukraine. From 1610 to 1612, Polish troops even occupied Moscow. But then history changed its course. Russia was expanding, while Poland was shrinking. By the end of the eighteenth century, Poland was divided between Russia, Prussia and Austria. Central Poland with Warsaw became Russian province, Germans took Western and North parts of the country, and South Poland including Galicia (Western Ukraine) went to Austria.

Poland regained its independence only in 1918 after Russia, Germany and Austria-Hungary lost World War I. As a matter of fact, the day of Polish independence is the same as the day of the armistice: November 11, 1918. Western Polish borders were defined by the Treaty of Versailles. Poland was allowed to split Germany in order to get access to the sea with so-called Polish Corridor and to take control over German port city, Danzig. However, in the east, Polish borders remained undefined for another two years.

Poland did not intervene into Russian Civil War, having no desire to support either Whites or Reds. Polish nationalists equally hated the proponents of united Russia and the internationalist Jewish Bolsheviks. What they cared about was to expand Poland to the east into Belorussia and Ukraine. Given the circumstances, a large Polish offensive in the east started not in 1919 when it would help Denikin and could kill Bolshevik regime, but only in spring 1920 when Bolsheviks had started winning the Civil War.

On May 7, 1920, Polish troops took Kiev, the capital of Ukraine. Then military fortune shifted to the Soviet side, and on August 12, 1920, Soviet troops stormed Warsaw, the Polish capital. On the verge of collapse, the pendulum suddenly swung the other way and Polish troops managed to beat back the Soviets.

Military fortunes continued to swing back and forth until the 1921 Treaty of Riga was signed, which allowed Poland to annex western Ukraine and western Byelorussia, the territories located beyond so called Curzon Line where Polish ethnicity was in the minority. In 1920, while the Polish-Russian war was still going on, British Foreign Secretary Lord Curzon (1859-1925) proposed an armistice on a seemingly fair border line. Although his proposal was ignored at the time, this line played a big role in politics later on.

The German-Polish border disputes were resolved only when Hitler came to power and established friendly relations with the dictatorial and anti-Semitic Polish regime. In 1934, the German-Polish Non-Aggression Pact was signed, effectively excluding Poland from any anti-German defensive alliances in return for Hitler's recognition of the German-Polish border. During the Czechoslovakian crises, Poland acted as the German ally, preventing Russia from intervening into "European affairs" and grabbing a piece of Czechoslovakia.

Nevertheless, after Czechoslovakia, it was Poland's turn to receive Hitler's demands. However, unlike Czechoslovakia, Hitler's terms to the friendly Poland were more or less reasonable. Initially Hitler did not ask to return all former German territories; he wanted only the already semi-independent Danzig and the exterritorial highway over Polish Corridor to connect East Prussia to the rest of Germany. In return, Poland was promised the share of the future spoils in the Baltic States and Russia.

The True Origins of World War II

Much to Hitler's surprise, Poland rejected Fuhrer's "generous offer". Hitler's immediately ordered his generals to plan an invasion of Poland, while the German press had began an anti-Polish campaign. Poland's defiance was encouraged by British who used the burgeoning crisis to pressure Hitler into submission. On March 31, Chamberlain even announced a "blank check" guarantee to Poland's independence, which was unprecedented for British diplomacy. In response, on April 6 Hitler denounced the Anglo-German Naval Treaty and the German-Polish Non-Aggression Pact, protesting against the "encircling" of Germany.

A Soviet proposal to create a defensive alliance against Germany was rejected by Poland, and the British did not press them to comply. Marshal Rydz-Smigly (1886-1941) summed up the Polish attitude: "With the Germans we risk losing our freedom; with the Soviets we shall lose our souls."

Refusing to compromise with Germany or ally with Soviet Union, Poland decided to rely solely on British and French support. When the British ambassador asked the Polish foreign minister Jozef Beck (1894-1944) for his opinion about the British guarantee, Beck agreed without hesitation "between two flicks of the ash of his cigarette".

As a result, Hitler chose Poland as his next victim, and while Russian help was refused, not much could be expected from British and French, who were not ready to fight for Poland. Moreover if there were no British guarantee to Poland, Hitler might choose to attack France first, as he himself once told his generals. However in light of British-French-Polish alliance, Hitler had to eliminate the Polish threat first before he could attack France. Thus by promising help to Poland, England was actually diverting Hitler's attention from the west to the east.

Without realizing it, Poland was trapped in a big game in which she was only a pawn. Seemingly unaware of those geopolitical complications, on May 5, 1939, Beck publicly rejected Hitler demands, praised British guarantee and proudly concluded:

> *"Peace is a valuable and desirable thing. Our generation, which has shed its blood in several wars, surely deserves a period of peace. But peace, like almost everything in this world, has its price, high but definable. We in Poland do not recognize the conception of "peace at any price." There is only one thing in the life of men, nations and States which is without price, and that is honor."*

The Leningrad Conference

On March 18, the very next day after Chamberlain's Birmingham speech, Soviet foreign minister Litvinov put the British and French to the test, proposing a European conference on preventing aggression. Previous Soviet proposals made after annexation of Austria were ignored, but now appeasement was supposedly over. Three days later, Chamberlain reluctantly agreed to call the conference of Great Britain, France, the Soviet Union and Poland. But as Poland refused to negotiate with the Soviets, the idea was promptly dropped.

And so it went on. To satisfy the public opinion and to pressure Hitler, Chamberlain would pretend that he is negotiating with the Soviet Union, while in fact he did little to nothing to create an alliance with Russia against Germany. Poland's refusal to allow passage of Soviet troops presented one stumbling block of negotiations, while the questionable status of the Baltic States was another. The British and French guaranteed Polish independence, but they refused to do the same for the Baltic

The True Origins of World War II

States as the Soviets had insisted. Thus, Hitler hinted that he could attack Russia through Baltic States, while Poland strategically located between Germany and Russia had to insure that Hitler would respect British and French interests in the process.

Chamberlain's attitude towards Russia was clear from his private correspondence. On March 26, he wrote: "I must confess to the most profound distrust of Russia." On April 9: "I regard Russia as a very unreliable friend with very little capacity for active assistance but with enormous irritative power on others". On April 29: "Our problem therefore is to keep Russia in the background without antagonizing her". On July 15: "If we do get agreement [with Russia] I am afraid I shall not regard it as a triumph". Obviously, such an attitude did not help efforts to form a defensive pact against Germany.

Only in August 1939 did Britain and France send their delegations to Moscow to negotiate the creation of a military alliance against Germany, and even then it did not seem serious. The British and French delegations chose to travel by the slowest way possible, in a merchant ship to Leningrad, which took six days. Then, they went to Moscow by train. While on the Soviet side the chief negotiator was the defense commissar (minister) Voroshilov, the British and French delegations included no top-level officials. Chamberlain and Halifax, who were so eager to fly to Germany, now had more important business than negotiations with Stalin. Moreover, British promised to provide only few divisions in the case of war. It comes as no surprise that nothing came of the negotiations.

It's well known and understandable that Chamberlain was reluctant to ally with the Soviet Union. It also well known that the British and French ruling circles preferred that Nazis and Communists destroy each other. Still, it does not fully explain the western position, on the assumption that Russia was the only

263

hope in deterring Hitler's aggression. One quote may help us to clarify the situation, though. On April 3, 1939 Joseph E. Davies (1876-1958), former US Ambassador in Moscow, recorded in his diary the conversation with US Ambassador in London Joseph Kennedy (1888-1969), the father of the future President:

> *"... he [Kennedy] could tell Chamberlain from me that if they are not careful they would drive Stalin into Hitler's arms ... He [Kennedy] recognized the value of Russia in the military situation; but, as a matter of fact, Russia would have to fight for Poland or Rumania anyway, and regardless of whether there was a formal agreement with France and Britain or not, because it's vital to Russia's self-interest."*

The democracies were taking Russian involvement against Hitler for granted. One day they decided to appease Hitler at the expense of the Soviet Union, another day they decided to contain Hitler, and again Russians were supposed to pick up the bill. Smart, isn't it?

Stalin was even smarter. He didn't mind joining the British and French in crushing Germany, which would eliminate a major threat against his country and increase Russian influence in Eastern Europe. But without British and French commitment, fighting Hitler was risky.

The Whaling Conference

While the "democratic" Chamberlain did not want any agreement with the "totalitarian dictator" Stalin, he did not abandon hope of reaching an understanding with the no-less-totalitarian Hitler. In the same letter in which Chamberlain wrote "If we do get agreement [with Russia] as I rather think we shall I am afraid I shall not regard it as a triumph", he also wrote:

The True Origins of World War II

> *"The only question to which he [Hitler] is not sure of the answer is whether we meant to attack him as soon as we are strong enough. If he though we did he would naturally argue that he had better have the war when it suits him than wait till it suits us. But in various ways I am trying to get the truth conveyed to the only quarter where it matters."*

In fact, Chamberlain was keep trying to appease Hitler even after Birmingham. British-German negotiations continued in secret, carried by emissaries from neutral counties and low-key officials who travelled between Berlin and London.

In July, a German official named Dr. Wohltat arrived to London to participate in a whaling conference, resembling how Halifax once attended a hunting exhibition as a pretext for meeting with Hitler. He arranged a meeting with Chamberlain's adviser Sir Horace Wilson to discuss an agreement that included a German-British Non-Aggression Pact for twenty five years, the return of German colonies "in due course", a large loan to Germany, an acknowledgment of Eastern Europe as the German sphere of interests, and a trade deal for the export of German and British industrial products to the principal markets of the British Empire, China and even the Soviet Union.

Similar proposals were communicated to press secretary at the German embassy, Dr. Fritz Hesse. Ribbentrop was very impressed when Hesse told him about it:

> *"Did Hesse really think the British would go to war on Hitler's side in case the Soviets attacked Germany? Would they break off their conversations in Moscow before negotiating with Germany? Hesse believed they would"*

The proposal included many terms that Hitler had always wanted, but he still refused to go for it. Why? The proposed

265

agreement contained an important caveat. Hitler had to give up the use of force unless it was approved by the British, thus becoming a British puppet.

Doesn't it remind you the Anglo-American proposal made to German Kaiser before World War I? Geopolitics did not change much over the decades. And while both Hitler and Wilhelm II did not want war with England, no German ruler wants to become a British puppet.

Hitler wanted to crush Poland, but he still hoped to avoid war with England. An encouraging sign for Hitler was the fact that England seemed to be in no hurry to help Poland and only gave her a very small amount as financial aid. Hitler correctly calculated that England was not going to fight for Poland, but it brought him to the wrong conclusion that England would allow him to dominate in Europe. On September 10, after the war with Germany had started, Chamberlain summarized his attempts to reach a deal with Hitler:

> *"The communications with Hitler and Goering looked rather promising at one time but came to nothing in the end as Hitler apparently got carried away by the prospect of a short war in Poland & then a settlement"*

The Molotov-Ribbentrop Pact

Neither Hitler, nor the democracies were prepared to give in the case of Poland. Of course, it was not only about Poland. The stakes were much higher. Hitler had to be shown his proper place.

Behind the scenes, Americans urged defiance in London, Paris and Warsaw. Despite official U.S. neutrality, President Roosevelt secretly promised Chamberlain support in the case

The True Origins of World War II

of war. How naïve are those who think that the United States did not participate in the European affairs because of isolationism!

A disappointed Hitler told Swiss Commissioner to the League of Nations:

> *"Everything that I have in mind is directed against Russia; if the West is too stupid and blind to understand this then I will be forced to come to terms with the Russians, to crush the West and then after its defeat, turn all my forces against the Soviet Union. I need the Ukraine so they can't starve us out as in the last war".*

Indeed, to defy western pressure Hitler had no choice but "to come to terms with the Russians". The agreement with Moscow had to localize the German-Polish war and prevent England and France from intervening into the conflict. The Russians in turn could benefit from the quarrel between the West and Nazi Germany. In fact, the Soviet Union suddenly received the rare chance to play a more active role in the global game.

In return for the Soviet neutrality in the coming war, Stalin could demand concessions from Hitler. The agreement with Germany meant postponing of the war for the Soviet Union and the avoidance of yet another British-German compromise aimed against Russia. Of course after defeating the West, Stalin knew that Hitler might turn against Soviet Union. However that scenario seemed remote and under the circumstances could not outweigh the immediate benefits.

While in theory it was in everyone's interests to join hands against Hitler, the reality of the dirty geopolitics left the only open question as where Hitler was going to attack first, in the West or in the East. There were signs that the relations between Germany and Russia were warming up. For example, during an official event in Berlin, Hitler suddenly stopped next to the Soviet ambassador and had a pleasant little chat, to the amazement of all diplomats. Secret contacts between German and Soviet officials followed. Then on May 3, 1939 Stalin dismissed Litvinov from the position of the commissar (minister) of the foreign affairs. Another old Bolshevik Vyacheslav Molotov (1890-1986) took his post. The dismissal of Litvinov, the outspoken supporter of collective security, signaled the serious change in the foreign politics of the Soviet Union.

In the Anglo-American perspective, it often pointed out that being a Jew Litvinov was not fit to negotiate with Nazis. Actually, Molotov's wife was also Jewish. Litvinov's connections from his revolutionary past were much more important than his Jewish ancestry. Litvinov, who used to live in London, spoke fluent English, and even had British wife, was considered an unofficial representative of Anglo-Americans in the Bolshevik government. The importance of Litvinov in that regard was such that even after the dismissal, while his deputies were arrested and executed, he remained formally free. After Germany invaded Soviet Union in 1941, and the Russians allied with the English-speaking world, Litvinov was pardoned and became the Soviet ambassador to the United States.

Back in 1939, as the deadline to attack Poland came closer, Hitler became restless in his efforts to reach a deal with the Soviets. Stalin, who could now dictate his terms, insisted that the trade agreement between Russia and Germany must be signed first. It was rushed through and signed in Berlin in no time. According to the agreement, Nazi Germany granted the Soviet Union a credit of 200 million Reichmarks for seven years to finance Soviet Orders of valuable machine tools and industrial installations. Needless to say that Soviets never paid that money back.

The True Origins of World War II

Then the time came for the main event. On August 23, 1939, German foreign minister Ribbentrop arrived to Moscow and signed a non-aggression agreement with his counterpart Molotov. Soviet neutrality in the coming German-Polish war was assured. British and French military missions who were still negotiating in Moscow were sent home. Secretly Hitler also agreed to respect "Russian interests" in Eastern Europe. Stalin could now claim former Russian territories in Poland, Finland, Romania and the Baltic States.

Remarkably, when Ribbentrop's plane was preparing to take off to Moscow, next to him in the Berlin airport was Goering's plane, ready to take off to London. Both Moscow and London were ready to negotiate with top-level Nazis, but at the last moment Hitler chose Moscow, cancelling Goering's flight.

The world was stunned. The unbelievable happened, the sworn enemies, Nazis and Communists, reached a deal and were not going to fight each other in the near future.

"Everything that I have worked for, everything that I have hoped for, everything that I believed in during my public life has crashed into ruins",

complained Chamberlain ten days later, despite the fact that his desire of not having an agreement with Russia was fulfilled. As they say, be careful what you wish for.

The shock from the Soviet-German agreement was widespread among the foes and the allies alike. Among the consequences was the fall of the Japanese government, which resigned disoriented by the Hitler's betrayal of their anti-Russian alliance.

Since it broke the duplicitous game of the democracies the non-aggression pact was vilified ever since as "notorious" and "evil", the adjectives that were never used for the disgraceful agreements between the democracies and Nazi Germany, such as Anglo-German Naval Treaty (1935) or Munich Pact (1938). The Non-Aggression agreement was even presented as the reason for the start of World War II, to which Stalin once replayed:

> *"The American falsifiers and their British and French associates are trying to create the impression that the preparations for German aggression which developed into the Second World War were begun in the autumn of 1939. Who can swallow this bait nowadays but absolutely naive people prepared to believe any sensational fabrication?"*

Indeed when Nazis came to power in 1933 Germany was disarmed and bound by treaties, and Hitler, whose plans of conquest were known to everyone, could never prepare Germany for the war without support of the great democracies who considered him the "pillar of the peace" and the "bulwark against communism".

Conclusion

Anglo-American historians tells us that the democracies were trying to stop Hitler, but their efforts failed because of Soviet treachery. Stalin allied with Hitler, they say, and together they carved the Eastern Europe between them.

In reality, the democracies were trying to provoke war between Nazi Germany and Communist Russia, but Hitler decided to attack in the West first, which suited Soviets well. (Although Poland was located in the East, it was the part of the Western Alliance).

In its essence the Soviet – German Non-Aggression treaty was a declaration of Soviet neutrality in the coming war between Nazi Germany and the democracies. Although any deal with Hitler was a dirty one, it is important to remember that the much-vilified Soviet-German Non-Aggression treaty was the last treaty of its kind. England and France already had similar dirty deals with Hitler.

Soviets had not much choice actually. The attempts to create defensive alliance of the democracies and the Soviet Union were insincere as Russian involvement into the war against Nazi Germany was taken for granted. In the end, the democracies simply fell into the trap that they themselves were preparing for the Soviets. World War II was about to start.

Conclusion to
The True Origins of World War II

It's often difficult to comprehend how much interpretation of facts is based on implicit ideological perspectives. People need ideals and higher perspective, yet one of the main goals of an ideology is to explain why we are the good guys and our opponents are the bad guys. The human mind in general has an amazing capacity to excuse our own faults and blame others for our own wrongdoings.

Our opponents bombed someone? It only proves how bad they are and exposes the evil plans they have. We bombed someone? It was justified because we are the good guys and good guys don't bomb without a worthy cause. Our actions were not actually justified? Then it was only a mistake or the fault of a particular politician. If, God forbid, you see a pattern in how we bomb country after country for many years and assume that there is some evil plan behind it, then such observations can only be described as a conspiracy theory.

The Anglo-American perspective views World War II as the fight of good democratic countries against evil totalitarian dictatorships. The democratic countries were of course the United States, England and France. The dictatorships included Germany, Italy, Japan and the Soviet Union. The actual alliance between the democracies and Russia is either ignored or explained as an abnormality due to unusual circumstances.

In contrast, the Soviet perspective views World War II as the fight of common people against fascism, the extreme version of imperialism. The good fight of common people was of course headed by Communist Russia while fascist enslavers ruled in Germany, Italy and Japan. Meanwhile the United States, England and France are viewed not as democracies but as imperialists that oppressed people around the world and clashed with the fascists only due to a conflict of interests.

The Nazi perspective views World War II as the fight of pure-blood Germans against worldwide Jewish conspiracy. Jewish-Bolshevik Russia, populated by subhumans, was the main enemy, while mostly pure-blood yet under Jewish influence England and the United States could be either enemies or allies.

From an unbiased geopolitical perspective, World War II was simply another game of global domination where everybody undermines everybody. In return for help and alliance, England undermined France, while the United States in turn undermined England. The main conflict of the war was predetermined when, in accordance with the "divide and conquer" strategy, Nazi Germany received Anglo-American support to counterbalance the growing influence of Communist Russia.

The Anglo-American "democracy is good, dictatorship is bad" paradigm fails to explain the root causes of World War II, the place of the Soviet Union in it, and why the "democracies" were racists and needed colonies all around the world. The Soviet perspective is perhaps more realistic, but it fails to explain why German "workers and peasants" in army uniforms were so eager to kill their comrades in other countries. The perspective also failed to justify the Soviet-German non-aggression treaty and the serious damage it did to Russian diplomatic prestige ever since. We can simply discount Nazi perspective as evil nonsense, yet we have to understand it if we want to understand why millions of people were deliberately killed in gas chambers.

The True Origins of World War II

While geopolitical perspective is the most logical and objective, it cannot resolve moral dilemmas. When we decide what is good and what is evil, we have to step outside of cold geopolitical calculations. We feel sympathy towards the people who fight for freedom, progress and dignity, and we hate aggressors whose goal was to kill and enslave. We despise the gas chambers, although from the point of view of nationalism and self-interests they might be quite logical. After all, massacres and ethnic cleansings were not invented by Nazis; they just made them more "efficient".

In this book, we explored root causes of World War II and dispelled some common myths of the Anglo-American democratic perspective. The core myth to dispel is that the democracies strive to save piece while dictatorships start wars of aggression. The myth stuck although everybody understands that World War I was an imperialist war for world domination. After all, the Russian Czar would be very surprised to learn that he fought to make the world "safe for the democracy".

In the questions of war and peace the form of the government never actually mattered. So-called democracies were in fact racist empires that conquered and exploited numerous colonies all around the world. The main geopolitical strategy of Anglo-Saxon powers was to divide their opponents, provoke war between them and join late into the conflict to win it with the minimal casualties.

This is exactly what happened in the lead-up to World War II. Hitler's rise to power and the rapid rearmament of Nazi Germany could never have happened without the approval of elites of Great Britain and the United States. A strong Nazi Germany was viewed as the best defense against communism; it was supposed to be the counterbalance to Russia and to less extend counterbalance to France. The idea that Hitler might become the enemy of England and the United States was not seriously considered since Hitler always underlined his hostility to Communist Russia, his desire to respect British interests and become British ally.

Hindered by the global economic crises, and seeking to preserve their hegemony over the world, the leading imperialists, in accordance with "divide and conquer" strategy, saw the best chance for "peace" in a war between Nazi Germany and Communist Russia. To achieve their goals the democracies played the game of appeasement, which was "peace seeking" by its face value, but in reality was encouraging the aggression.

Although England and France were eventually forced to end the politics of appeasement, they did not want join hands with Russia to crush Germany. Appeasement or containment, Russia had to fight Germany alone without help from England and France. The democracies wanted to provoke war between Nazi Germany and Communist Russia, but Hitler decided attack in the West first, which suited Soviets well.

By September 1939, the stage was set for the Second World War. The course of the war, which we cover in the next book, was full of drama, unexpected turns and more geopolitical games. We will see how England and France betrayed Poland and why they declared war on Germany for invading Poland from the west, but actually approved of the Soviet invasion of Poland from the east. We will follow the Phoney War, the astonishing fall of France, and British defiance against the Blitz. We will see how Germany invaded Russia, and how the Russians managed to stop Germans at the gates of Moscow. We will explore how the United States provoked war with Japan and turned the war into a global conflict. We will uncover everything you never learned in school about World War II.

References

Author's Preface

[1] Churchill: "the abyss of a new Dark Age"
Their finest hour. Winston Churchill speech at House of Commons. London. 18 June 1940
https://winstonchurchill.org/resources/speeches/1940-the-finest-hour/their-finest-hour/

[2] Stalin: "How could it be that non aggressive countries"
Report on the Work of the Central Committee to the Eighteenth Congress of the C.P.S.U.(B.). Moscow, 10 March 1939. Marxists Internet Archive
https://www.marxists.org/reference/archive/stalin/works/1939/03/10.htm

[3] Churchill: "There never was a war in history"
The Sinews of Peace ("Iron Curtain Speech"). Westminster College, Fulton, Missouri, United States, 5 March 1946. The Churchill Centre
https://winstonchurchill.org/resources/speeches/1946-1963-elder-statesman/the-sinews-of-peace/

Prologue. History of World War II

[4] Churchill: "The Red Army celebrates its twenty-seventh"
Personal message for Marshall Stalin from Mr. Churchill. Received 23 February 1945. Marxists Internet Archive
https://www.marxists.org/reference/archive/stalin/works/correspondence/01/45.htm

The Anglo-American Perspective

[5] "Victory in Europe" – First Version
History of Our World. By Prentice Hall. Student Edition, 2004

Tigran Khalatyan

[6] "Victory in Europe" – Second Version
History of Our World. By Prentice Hall. Student Edition. 2006

[7] "World War II began in 1939"
Learn About the United States
Quick Civics Lessons for Naturalization Test.
By U.S. Citezenship and Immigration Services. 2011

[8] "After World War I, Americans were threatened"
America History of Our Nation Beginnings through 1877.
New Jersey Edition. By Prentice Hall, 2009

[9] "The second World War began"
The real history of World War II. By Alan Axelrod. 2011

Understanding World War II

[10] Doenitz: "German men and women"
Admiral Doenitz radio announcement of Hitler's death. 1 May 1945
http://www.ibiblio.org/pha/policy/1945/450501a.html

[11] "one tyranny for another"
Inferno: The World at War 1939-1945. By Max Hastings. 2012

[12] "lifetime of occupation"
The History Buff's Guide to World War II.
By Thomas R. Flagel. 2012, page 128

Double Standards

[13] Obama: "Respect for the right of peaceful protest"
Statement by the Press Secretary of President Barack Obama on Ukraine. Washington D.C. 21 February 2014
http://www.presidency.ucsb.edu/ws/index.php?pid=104743

Part I The War to End All Wars 1900-1919

Chapter 1. The Age of Empires

[14] Durnovo: "Strange as it may seem, England"
Peter Durnovo report to the Czar. Saint Petersburg, February 1914
http://www.pravoslavie.ru/36667.html

Democracies or Empires?

[15] Beveridge: "Mr. President, the times call for candor"
Speech in Congress "In Support of an American Empire".
Washington D.C. 9 January 1900
http://teachingamericanhistory.org/library/document/
in-support-of-an-american-empire/

[16] Rice: "it is time to abandon the excuses"
Condoleezza Rice speech at the American University in Cairo, Egypt, 21 June 2005
http://www.cnn.com/2005/WORLD/meast/06/20/mideast.rice/

The Great Game in Europe

[17] House: "The situation is extraordinary"
Colonel House's Report to President Wilson. Spring 1914
http://wwi.lib.byu.edu/index.php/
Colonel_House's_Report_to_President_Wilson

Chapter 2. World War I

[18] Wilson: "We are glad, now that we see"
Woodrow Wilson war massage to Congress.
Washigton D.C., 2 April 1917
https://wwi.lib.byu.edu/index.php/
Wilson%27s_War_Message_to_Congress

The July Crisis

[19] "For God's sake, what has happened to you?"
Memoir of Count Franz von Harrach
http://www.firstworldwar.com/source/harrachmemoir.htm

[20] Nicolas II: "In this serious moment"
Prewar correspondense between Russian and German monarchs ("The Willy-Nicky Telegrams") 29 July – 1 August 1914
https://wwi.lib.byu.edu/index.php/The_Willy-Nicky_Telegrams

[21] Wilhelm II: "It is with the gravest concern"
Ibid.

[22] Nicolas II: "these measures do not mean war"
Ibid.

[23] "The most effective work for peace"
Daily News, London, 29 July 1914
https://www.dailykos.com/stories/2014/7/29/1317561/-Countdown-to-World-War-I-July-29-1914

[24] "trouble now would be better than trouble later"
Who started World War I. By Alan Pacon

[25] "believed that a peaceful solution would be reached"
Europe's Last Summer: Who Started the Great War in 1914? By David Fromkin

[26] "made his hair stand on edge"
July Crisis: The World's Descent into War, Summer 1914. By T. G. Otte

[27] "a Serbian war meant a general European war"
The month that changed the world July 1914. By Gordon Martel.

[28] "Britain was not working in concord with France and Russia"
https://en.wikipedia.org/wiki/July_Crisis
Germany's Aims in the First World War. New York: W.W. Norton. By Fischer Fritz 1967

[29] "Grey failed to realize the urgency of situation"
https://en.wikipedia.org/wiki/Edward_Grey,_1st_Viscount_Grey_of_Fallodon
Christopher Clark, "Sir Edward Grey and the July Crisis." *International History Review* 38.2 (2016): 326-338.

[30] "I do not know whether this evening"
Statement of Paul Cambon, Ambassador of France.
London, *2 August 1914*
https://www.dailykos.com/stories/2014/8/2/1318572/
-Countdown-to-World-War-I-August-2-1914

[31] Wilhelm II: "Now we can go to war against Russia only."
Kaiser Wilhelm II conversation with Chief of Staff Moltke. Berlin, 1 August 1914
https://www.dailykos.com/stories/2014/8/1/1318306/
-Countdown-to-World-War-I-August-1-1914

[32] "Scrap of paper"
Chancellor von Bethmann-Hollweg meeting with British ambassador. Berlin, 4 August 1914
http://net.lib.byu.edu/~rdh7/wwi/1914/paperscrap.html.bak

The Great War

[33] Hitler: "Who, after all, speaks today"
Hitler's Obersalzberg Speech. 22 August 1939
http://www.armenian-genocide.org/hitler.html
https://en.wikipedia.org/wiki/Hitler%27s_Obersalzberg_Speech

The February Revolution

[34] Wilson: "Does not every American feel"
Ibid 18

[35] "One of England's goals has been achieved!"
My Mission to Russia and other diplomatic memories.
By George Buchanan.1923
https://archive.org/details/mymissiontorussi02buch

[36] "The saddest thing was that I learned"
Воспоминания великого князя Александра Михайловича Романова. Николай Стариков рекомендует прочитать. 2015.

Tigran Khalatyan

(Russian Language: The memoirs of Grand Duke Alexander Mikhailovich. Nikolay Starikov recommends to read. 2015)

For Democracy or For Money?

[37] "The Nye (Senate) Committee investigations"
The Untold History of the United States.
By Oliver Stone and Peter Kuznick 2013

[38] Wilson: "The world must be made safe for democracy"
Ibid 34

[39] "The United States intervened in the war"
U.S. Foreign Policy from the Founders' Perspective.
By George Friedman, Founder of Stratfor
https://worldview.stratfor.com/article/us-foreign-policy-founders-perspective

[40] Lloyd George: "I am glad; I am proud"
David Lloyd George on America's Entry into the War
American Club, London, 12 April 1917
http://www.firstworldwar.com/source/usawar_lloydgeorge.htm

The Bolshevik Revolution

[41] Trotsky 1917 trip to Russia
The Creature from Jekyll Island: A Second Look at the Federal Reserve, by Edward Griffin, 2002
Anion V.C. Sutton. Wall Street and the Bolshevik Revolution

[42] Wilson's 14 points
Declared on 8 January 1918
http://avalon.law.yale.edu/20th_century/wilson14.asp

"War is Peace"

[43] Blanque Check: "The Kaiser said he understood"
Report of the Austro-Hungarian ambassador in Berlin, Ladislaus Count von Szögyény-Marich, to Austro-Hungarian Foreign Minister

Leopold Count von Berchtold. Berlin, 5 July 1914
http://germanhistorydocs.ghi-dc.org/
sub_document.cfm?document_id=800

[44] Hitler: "Our love of peace"
Adolf Hitler "Rearmament" speech at Reichstag. Berlin, 21 May 1935
http://der-fuehrer.org/reden/english/35-05-21.htm

[45] Prince Konoe: "For the people of East Asia"
Speech of Konoe, prime minister of Japan,
at 72nd Session of the Imperial Diet. Tokyo, 5 September 1937
http://bhoffert.faculty.noctrl.edu/hst265/16.wwii.html
The Search for Modern China: A Documentary Collection
by Janet Chen (Editor), Pei-kai Cheng (Editor), Michael Lestz (Editor),

[46] Roosevelt: "America hates war. America hopes for peace."
President Roosevelt Quaranteen Speech. Chicago, 5 October 1937.
https://web.archive.org/web/20120509132052/
http://millercenter.org/president/speeches/detail/3310

[47] Chamberlain: "I believe it is peace for our time"
Statements of British Prime Minister, Neville Chamberlain.
London, 30 September 1938
http://www.emersonkent.com/speeches/peace_in_our_time.htm
https://eudocs.lib.byu.edu/index.php/
Neville_Chamberlain%27s_%22Peace_For_Our_Time%22_speech

[48] Hitler: "As always"
Adolf Hitler "War on Poland" speech at Reichstag.
Berlin, 1 September 1939
http://der-fuehrer.org/reden/english/39-09-01.htm

[49] Ribbentrop: "I wish peace to the world."
Last words of Foreign Minister of Nazi Germany Joachim
von Ribbentrop. Nuremberg, 16 October 1946
https://en.wikiquote.org/wiki/Joachim_von_Ribbentrop

Tigran Khalatyan

[50] Pilsudski: "the problem of the independence of Poland"
Meeting of Polish nationalists. Paris, January 1914
https://www.britannica.com/biography/Jozef-Pilsudski

Chapter 3. The Victory of the Democracy

[51] Wilson: "We have no quarrel with the German people"
Ibid 18

The Treaty of Versailles

[52] Wilson: "There shall be no annexations"
President Wilson address to Congress.
Washington D.C. 11 February 1918.
http://www.gwpda.org/1918/wilpeace.html

[53] Wilson: "seeks to punish"
Address at Memorial Hall in Columbus, Ohio, 4 September 1919.
http://www.presidency.ucsb.edu/ws/index.php?pid=117361

[54] Hitler: "Only through its internal dissensions"
Adolf Hitler: Declaration of War on the Soviet Union 22 June 1941
http://der-fuehrer.org/reden/deutsch/41-6-22.htm
http://der-fuehrer.org/reden/english/41-06-22.htm
https://www.jewishvirtuallibrary.org/adolf-hitler-declaration-of-war-on-the-soviet-union-june-1941

[55] Foch: "This is not a peace"
https://www.quora.com/After-the-Treaty-of-Versailles-Ferdinand-Foch-said-This-is-not-a-peace-It-is-an-armistice-for-twenty-years-What-did-he-know-at-the-time-that-allowed-him-to-make-this-prediction

The Victory of the Bolsheviks

[56] Churchill: "strangle Bolshevism in its cradle"
https://www.nationalchurchillmuseum.org/12-07-12-leadership-legacy.html

[57] Lloyd-George "Let us really face the difficulties."
The speech of British Prime-Minister in the House of Commons.
London, 17 November 1919
https://api.parliament.uk/historic-hansard/commons/1919/nov/17/govebnment-policy#S5CV0121P0_19191117_HOC_396

[58] House: "the rest of the world"
https://en.topwar.ru/65766-amerika-poteryala-rossiyu.html

[59] "All of Russia"
Ibid

Separatism versus Self Determination

[60] Wilson: "National aspirations must be respected"
Ibid 52

[61] Hitler: "Among the 14 points"
Adolf Hitler "Holocaust Prophecy" speech at Reichstag.
Berlin, 30 January 1939
http://www.emersonkent.com/speeches/the_jewish_question.htm

The Nazi Response to Bolshevism

[62] Hitler: "If land was desired in Europe"
Mein Kampf (My Fight) by Adolf Hitler. 1925
http://www.mondopolitico.com/library/meinkampf/v1c4.htm

[63] Hitler: "For such a policy there was but one ally in Europe"
Ibid

[64] Hitler: "at the turn of the century"
Ibid

The Secret of Isolationism

[65] Roosevelt: "Never before"
President Roosevelt "Arsenal of Democracy" speech.
29 December 1940

Tigran Khalatyan

http://www.americanrhetoric.com/speeches/
fdrarsenalofdemocracy.html

[66] Truman: "let them kill as many as possible"
Senator Truman, future U.S. President, statement on Nazi Germany invasion of Russia. New York Times, 24 June 1945
https://en.wikiquote.org/wiki/Harry_S._Truman

[67] "As most Americans saw it"
Ibid 9

[68] Churchill: "For 400 years the British policy"
Churchill, dismissing claims of Franco-philia, 1936
Churchill: The Wilderness Years.

[69] Churchill: "you must not underrate England"
Churchill memoirs about meeting with Nazi Germany ambassador Ribbentrop in 1937
https://winstonchurchill.org/publications/finest-hour/finest-hour-132/despatch-box-23/

Part II A Twenty-Year Armistice 1920-1937

Chapter 4. The Invisible Hand

[70] Stalin: "It is the jungle law of capitalism"
Joseph Stalin. "The Tasks of Business Executives"
Speech Delivered at the First All-Union Conference of Leading Personnel of Socialist Industry. Moscow, 4 *February 1931*
https://www.marxists.org/reference/arcive/stalin/works/1931/02/04.htm

[71] Churchill: "Thus, both in Europe and in Asia"
The Second World War, Volume 1 by Winston Churchill

The Great Depression

[72] "the Army would accept"
Lords of Finance: The Bankers Who Broke the World,
by Liaquat Ahamed, Penguin Books, 2009

[73] Arnold Toynbee: "In 1931"
Ibid

[74] Montagu Norman: "Unless drastic measures"
Ibid

[75] Franklin D. Roosevelt: "Only a foolish optimist"
Franklin D. Roosevelt first inaugural speech, 4 March 1933
https://millercenter.org/the-presidency/presidential-speeches/march-4-1933-first-inaugural-address

Communism vs. Capitalism

[76] Churchill: "the merciless, but perhaps not needless"
"The Gathering Storm" by Winston Churchill, 1948

The Rise of Fascism

[77] Churchill: "If I had been an Italian"
Churchill's press statement, praising Mussolini and fascism.
Rome, 20 January 1927
https://www.wsws.org/en/articles/2009/11/nbww-n18.html

[78] Tsuyoshi: "If I could speak you would understand"
Last words of Tsuyoshi. 15 May 1932.
https://en.wikipedia.org/wiki/May_15_Incident

[79] Henry Ford: "The only statement I care to make"
Henry Ford interview. February 1921
https://en.wikipedia.org/wiki/The_Dearborn_Independent

[80] Churchill: "A Struggle for the Soul of the Jewish People"
Illustrated Sunday Herald (London), 8 February 1920
https://en.wikisource.org/wiki/Zionism_versus_Bolshevism

[81] Hitler: "If the international Finance-Jewry"
Ibid 61

Chapter 5. Glory of Adolf Hitler

[82] David Lloyd George: "He is as immune from criticism"
"I talked to Hitler". By the Right Honourable David Lloyd George Daily Express. 17 September 1936
http://www.nationalists.org/library/hitler/
daily-express/lloyd-george-hitler.html

The Rise of Hitler

[83] Jessy Owens: "Hitler didn't snub me"
http://www.realclearsports.com/lists/united_states_olympians
/jesse_owens.html
http://www.rarenewspapers.com/view/594817?imagelist=1

[84] "Norman had to be one of the keys"
Ibid 72

[85] Lloyd George: "The fact that Hitler has rescued his country"
Ibid 82.

[86] Hitler: "How Germany has to work"
Adolf Hitler. Speech at Nuremberg rally. 12 September 1936
http://www.hitler.org/speeches/09-12-36.html

[87] Hitler: "I can come to no terms with a bolshevism"
Adolf Hitler. Speech at Nuremberg rally. 14 September 1936
http://www.hitler.org/speeches/09-14-36.html

[88] Lloyd George: "What then did the Führer mean"
Ibid 82.

Why the West Supported Hitler

[89] Halifax: "the achievement of keeping Communism"
Halifax-Hitler meeting, Hitler's Berghof residence, 19 Nov 1937.

https://www.historyextra.com/period/20th-century/prime-ministers-we-never-quite-had-neil-kinnock-labour-conservative-thatcher/

[90] "Illusion or not"
Paris 1919: Six Months That Changed the World.
By Margaret Macmillan. 2003

[91] Chamberlain: "In the end we succeeded"
The Neville Chamberlain Diary Letters.
By Neville Chamberlain. 2000

[92] Friedman: "The primordial interest of the United States"
The Chicago Council on Foreign Affairs. 4 February 2015
https://www.counterpunch.org/2015/03/18/washingtons-war-on-russia/

[93] "free hand in the East"
Adolf Hitler: The Definitive Biography
By John Toland. 2004

[94] "Hitler confident, solemn retort"
Ibid

[95] Hitler: "It is said Germany is threatened by nobody"
Adolf Hitler "Rearmamant" speech at Reichstag.
Berlin, 21 May 1935
http://comicism.tripod.com/350521.html

[96] Chamberlain "intensely relieved"
Ibid 91

[97] "Only two years"
Ibid 93

[98] "Europe, Ripe for Strife"
"Europe, Ripe for Strife, Faces Menace of Russian Red Forces".
By Rear Admiral Yates Stirling, Jr.
The Milwaukee Sentinel, 8 June 1935

[99] Churchill: "The Government simply cannot"
Winston Churchill speech at House of Commons.
London. 12 November 1936
http://www.churchill-society-london.org.uk/Locusts.html

[100] "Had the German Army been opposed"
By Andrew Roberts.
The Storm of War: A New History of the Second World War. 2011

[101] Baldwin: "it would probably result"
Source 1 - 5 FO 371/19892 - Minutes from the Foreign Office meeting on the Treaty of Locarno in 1936
https://nationalarchives.gov.uk/documents/education/rhineland.pdf

Covert Support for Hitler

[102] "Hitler had just returned"
Ibid 93

[103] "union of Hand and Brain workers to oppose Marxism"
Ibid 93

[104] Hitler: "You have all the connections"
Hitler: The Memoir of the Nazi Insider Who Turned against the Fuhrer. By Ernst Hanfstaengl

[105] Churchill: "Tell me"
Ibid

[106] Roosevelt: "If things start getting awkward"
Ibid

[107] "He phoned Martha Dodd"
Ibid 93

[108] "In the early 1930s"
Wall Street & the Rise of Hitler. By Antony Sutton.

[109] "For the last few years"
George Bush: The Unauthorized Biography
By Webster Griffin Tarpley and Anton Chaitkin 2004

[110] "Norman insisted"
Ibid 72

[111] "No one was willing to predict"
Ibid 72

Chapter 6. Countdown to war

[112] "Will a leader appear"
Ibid 98

[113] "By the mid 1930s"
Ibid 9

The Start of Japanese Expansion

[114] Matsuoka: "Our Government was still persisting"
Japan's case in the Sino-Japanese dispute as presented before the Special session of the Assembly of the League of Nations.
By League of Nations. Delegation from Japan. Geneva 1933
https://archive.org/details/japanscaseinsino00leag

[115] Hitler: "But to assume that God has permitted"
Ibid 61

[116] Chamberlain "anxieties about Soviet Government"
The Chamberlain-Hitler Collusion.
By Alvin Finkel and Clement Leibovitz, 1997

[117] "Japan in the Far East"
Ibid 112

[118] Stalin: "The policy of non-intervention"
Ibid 1

Tigran Khalatyan

A Period of Change

[119] Mussolini: "The independence of Austria"
https://www.imdb.com/name/nm0615907/bio

[120] Mussolini: "This vertical line between Rome and Berlin"
Mussolini "Axis" speech. Milan. 1 November 1936
https://rcg.org/realtruth/articles/160919-002.html
http://www.todayifoundout.com/index.php/2014/01/axis-allies-wwii-get-names/

[121] Chamberlain "We regard"
Ibid 47

[122] "Indeed, the Hitler government"
Ibid 9

The Ethiopian Precedent

[123] Selassie: "I, Haile Selassie I, Emperor of Ethiopia"
Appeal to the League of Nations. 30 June 1936
https://www.mtholyoke.edu/acad/intrel/selassie.htm

Part III Peace in Our Time 1937-1939

Chapter 7. China Incident

[124] Kosarev: "Fascists are preparing"
Alexander Kosarev, Moscow, 12 Sep 1937
Pravda. 13 September 1937
https://pravda37.files.wordpress.com/2018/08/pravda-1937-253.pdf

A Century of Humiliation

[125] Chiang Kai-Shek: "first internal pacification"
http://english.ningbo.gov.cn/art/2017/2/27/art_944_383177.html

The Limit of Endurance

[126] Chiang Kai-Shek: "Since we are a weak country"
Speech of Chiang Kai-Shek, China, 17 July 1937
Chinese Ministry of Information. 1946. The Collected Wartime Messages of Generalissimo Chiang Kai-shek: 1937-1945. Volume I. New York: The John Day Company. (pp. 21-25)
https://archive.org/stream/collectedwartime000856mbp/collectedwartime000856mbp_djvu.txt
https://teachwar.wordpress.com/resources/war-justifications-archive/sino-japanese-war-1937/

The Battle of Shanghai

[127] Konoe: "For the people of East Asia"
Prince Konoe, Prime Minister of Japan, Tokyo, 5 Sep 1937
Foreign Relations of the United States: Diplomatic Papers. Japan 1931-1941. Volume 1. Page 368. By United States. Department of State
https://books.google.com/books?id=a6spp-t_eMIC&pg=PA368&lpg=PA368#v=onepage&q&f=false

The Failure of Collective Security

[128] Roosevelt: "There must be positive endeavors"
Ibid 46

[129] Chamberlain: "mixed feelings"
Ibid 91

[130] Kosarev: "The struggle for peace"
Ibid 124

Chapter 8. Munich Pact

[131] Chamberlain: "My good friends"
Ibid 47

[132] Chamberlain: "The settlement"
Ibid 47

[133] King George: "After the magnificent efforts"
King George VI statement to his people. London. 30 Sept 1938
Munich, 1938: Appeasement and World War II. By David Faber
https://books.google.com/books?id=OaRF5yLeuZoC&pg=PA420&lpg=PA420%20-%20v=onepage&q&f=false#v=onepage&q&f=false

[134] Churchill: "Total and unmitigated defeat"
Speech in the House of Commons. Addressing the Munich Agreement and British Policy toward Germany. 5 Oct 1938
https://www.nationalchurchillmuseum.org/disaster-of-the-first-magnitude.html

[135] Soviet Cartoon: "Go to the East"
Kukryniksy, 1938
https://regnum.ru/pictures/2328677/1.html

Appeasement

[136] "Like many of his generation"
https://en.wikipedia.org/wiki/Anthony_Eden

[137] Lloyd George: "In a very short time"
Speech in House of Commons. London. 28 Nov 1934
https://api.parliament.uk/historic-hansard/commons/1934/nov/28/debate-on-the-address

[138] Churchill: "Thank God for the French Army"
Speech in House of Commons. London. 23 March 1933
https://link.springer.com/chapter/10.1057/9781137367822_8

[139] Henderson: "On the other hand"
Ibid 116

Halifax - Hitler Deal

[140] Halifax – Hitler meeting
Halifax-Hitler meeting, Hitler's Berghof residence, 19 Nov 1937.
https://www.historyextra.com/period/20th-century/prime-ministers-we-never-quite-had-neil-kinnock-labour-conservative-thatcher/

[141] Griffiths: "The Prime Minister"
Speech in House of Commons. London. 21 February 1938
https://api.parliament.uk/historic-hansard/commons/1938/feb/21/foreign-policy

Anschluss

[142] Hitler: "Don't think for one moment"
Hitler-Schuschinigg meeting, Hitler's Berghof residence, 12 February 1938
Ibid 133

[143] Chamberlain: "I am confident I am"
Speech in House of Commons. London. 22 February 1938
https://api.parliament.uk/historic-hansard/sittings/1938/feb/22

[144] Chamberlain: "His Majesty's government"
Ibid 93

[145] Hitler: "Tell Mussolini I will never"
Ibid 133

The Sudeten Crisis

[146] Chamberlain: "reports are daily received"
Ibid 116

[147] "He (Hitler) then launched into a long speech"
Ibid 116

[148] "we will not stand"
Ibid 116

Hitler Raises the Stakes

[149] "our war by the side of Soviet Russia"
Ibid 116

[150] "And now we face"
Hitler's speech. 26 September 1938
http://comicism.tripod.com/380926.html

[151] Atlee: "The British Government must leave no doubt"
https://scholarworks.umass.edu/cgi/viewcontent.cgi?article=2755&context=theses

[152] Roosevelt: "Should you agree to a solution"
Telegram of President Roosevelt to Hitler, 27 September 1938
https://www.mtholyoke.edu/acad/intrel/interwar/fdr14.htm

[153] Chamberlain: "How horrible, fantastic, incredible"
Chamberlain's Radio Broadcast. 27 September 1938
https://encyc.org/wiki/Chamberlain's_Radio_Broadcast,_September_27,_1938

The Munich Pact

[154] Chamberlain: "When I was a little boy"
Chamberlain's Statement at Aerodrom. 29 September 1938
https://www.youtube.com/watch?v=GCwm87gc5fQ

[155] "You might think"
Churchill and the King: The Wartime Alliance of Winston Churchill and George VI. By Kenneth Weisbrode
https://books.google.com/books?id=U0kCDAAAQBAJ&pg=PA55

[156] Churchill: "We have suffered"
Churchill speech in the House of Commons. Addressing the Munich Agreement and British Policy toward Germany. 5 October 1938
https://www.nationalchurchillmuseum.org/disaster-of-the-first-magnitude.html

[157] "In hindsight, Munich has become"
The Complete Idiot's Guide to World War II by Mitchell G. Bard

[158] "The French and British"
Ibid

[159] "Would the Reich have attacked Czechoslovakia"
Eleanor Roosevelt, Volume 2 by Blanche Wiesen Cook

Chapter 9. Birmingham Speech

[160] Chamberlain: ""Is this the last attack"
Chamberlain's speech at Birmingham. 17 March 1939.
https://avalon.law.yale.edu/wwii/blbk09.asp

Kristallnacht

[161] "The French Government"
Bonnet-Ribbentrop pact. 6 December 1938
https://avalon.law.yale.edu/wwii/ylbk028.asp

The Birmingham Speech

[162] Chamberlain: "Who can fail to feel"
Ibid 160

[163] "Both (Czech and German) sides gave expression"
Department of State Publication, Issue 7873
https://books.google.com/books?id=spUNAQAAMAAJ&pg=PA911#v=onepage&q&f=false

[164] "What further pressure"
http://www.universe-galaxies-stars.com/Joachim_von_Ribbentrop.html

[165] "It now appears"
The New York Times. 14 March 1939

Tigran Khalatyan

[166] "Does the Prime Minister say"
Debates in House of Commons. 14 March 1939
https://api.parliament.uk/historic-hansard/commons/1939/mar/14/czecho-slovakia

[167] Chamberlain: "In considering these events"
Debates in House of Commons. 15 March 1939
https://api.parliament.uk/historic-hansard/commons/1939/mar/15/czecho-slovakia-1

[168] Churchill: "It is not easy to imagine"
Ibid 68

[169] Chamberlain: "It was like the stupidity of the Opposition"
Ibid 91

[170] "The swift, smooth pace of the occupation"
"Surprize? Surprize?" Time Magazine. 27 March 1939

[171] Chamberlain: "I think it wrong to assume"
Debates in House of Commons. 16 March 1939
https://hansard.parliament.uk/Commons/1939-03-16/debates/9bf6fbd6-d378-4791-988f-c8de5444b551/OralAnwersToQuestions

Carpatho-Ukraine

[172] Hitler: "The world has sufficient space for settlements"
Ibid 61

[173] Hitler: "It only needs that in England"
Hitler's Enabler: Neville Chamberlain and the Origins of the Second World War. By John Ruggiero
https://books.google.com/books?id=KBt5CgAAQBAJ&pg=PA103#v=onepage&q&f=false

[174] "The German diplomatic and military"
The Sydney Morning Herald. 24 November 1938

[175] "England in the near future is not threatened by war"
Telegram of the representativ of the USSR in Great Britain M. Maisky to the People's Commissariat of Foreign Affairs of the USSR
November 30, 1938
http://www.hrono.info/dokum/193_dok/19381130may.php

[176] "What the position would be"
British Foreign Policy since 1870. By Will Podmore
https://books.google.com/books?id=ePjUrqrx8HkC&pg=PA94&lpg=PA94#v=onepage&q&f=false

[177] "The Nazis' Ukrainian blueprints"
"Liberation". Time Magazine. 23 January 1939

[178] "Chancellor Hitler in Virtual Ultimatum"
New York Times, 14 March 1939

[179] "On March 17 at 7:30pm"
Ibid 116

Chapter 10. Non-Aggression Treaty

[180] Hitler: "People were unpleasantly affected"
Ibid 62

[181] Stalin: "How is it that the non-aggressive countries"
Ibid 1

The 18th Congress of the Communist Party

[182] Stalin: "the present crisis"
Ibid 1

[183] Hitler: "at the turn of the century"
Ibid 62

[184] Trotsky: "We shall not pause"
"Problem of Ukraine" by Leon Trotsky, 22 April 1939

Tigran Khalatyan

https://www.marxists.org/archive/trotsky/1939/04/ukraine.html

The Polish Question

[185] Rydz-Smigly: "With the Germans"
Days of Adversity. The Warsaw Uprising 1944
By Evan McGilvray 2015
https://www.history.com/news/world-war-ii-begins-75-years-ago

[186] "between two flicks of the ash of his cigarette"
Appeasement: Chamberlain, Hitler, Churchill, and the Road to War.
By Tim Bouverie
https://books.google.com/books?id=qOLhDwAAQBAJ

[187] Beck: "Peace is a valuable and desirable thing"
Speech by M. Beck. 5 May 1939.
https://avalon.law.yale.edu/wwii/blbk15.asp

The Leningrad Conference

[188] Chamberlain: "I must confess"
Ibid 91

[189] "he (Kennedy) could tell Chamberlain"
Mission to Moscow. By Joseph E. Davies. 1941

The Whaling Conference

[190] Chamberlain: "The only question"
Ibid 91

[191] "Did Hesse really think"
Ibid 102

[192] Chamberlain: "The communications"
Ibid 91

The Molotov-Ribbentrop Pact

[193] Hitler "Everything that I have in mind"
Ibid 102

[194] Stalin: "The American falsifiers"
Falsifiers of History. By Soviet Information Bureau, Joseph Stalin. 1948. https://archive.org/details/FalsificatorsOfHistory

Tigran Khalatyan

PICTURE CREDITS

Elbe Day, 25 April 1945
By Pfc. William E. Poulson - U.S. National Archives and Records Administration, Pictures of World War II, image #121 (111-SC-205228).
https://catalog.archives.gov/id/531276, Public Domain, https://commons.wikimedia.org/w/index.php?curid=765680

"Let's sit by the sea and wait for the weather!"
Russian Propaganda Poster. Moscow. 28 February 1904.
https://ru.wikipedia.org/wiki/%D0%A4%D0%B0%D0%B9%D0%BB:Sit_by_the_sea_and_wait_for_the_weather_1904.jpg

Russian Czar Nicholas II and British King George V, 1913
https://en.wikipedia.org/wiki/File:Tsar_Nicholas_II_%26_King_George_V.JPG

"Comrade Lenin cleans the earth of evil"
https://ru.wikipedia.org/wiki/%D0%A4%D0%B0%D0%B9%D0%BB:Lenin_1920_plakat.jpg

Unemployed men lined up for free food
U.S. National Archives and Records Administration, Public Domain,
https://commons.wikimedia.org/w/index.php?curid=17057587

Adolf Hitler, Fuhrer of Germany, 1937
https://commons.wikimedia.org/wiki/File:Hitler_portrait_crop.jpg
License: Bundesarchiv, Bild 183-H1216-0500-002 / CC-BY-SA [CC BY-SA 3.0 de (https://creativecommons.org/licenses/by-sa/3.0/de/deed.en)], via Wikimedia Commons

"Bloody Saturday"
U.S. National Archives and Records Administration
https://en.wikipedia.org/wiki/Bloody_Saturday_(photograph)

The True Origins of World War II

Leaders of Europe meet to satisfy Hitler's demands
By Bundesarchiv, Bild 183-R69173 /
CC-BY-SA 3.0, CC BY-SA 3.0 de,
https://commons.wikimedia.org/w/index.php?curid=5368502

A cartoon on the Soviet-German Non-aggression treaty
http://spartacus-educational.com/RUSnazipact.htm

Tigran Khalatyan

Tigran Hobbies presents
World War II Playing Cards

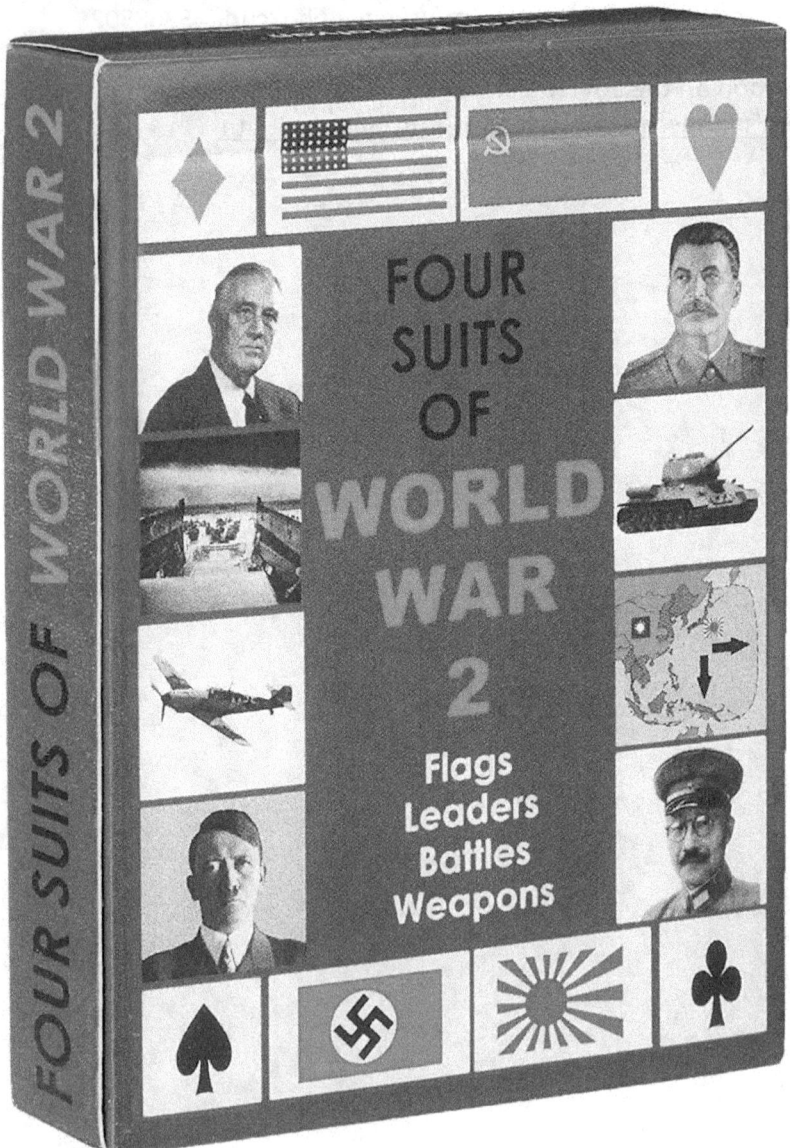

www.ingramcontent.com/pod-product-compliance
Lightning Source LLC
Chambersburg PA
CBHW051350290426
44108CB00015B/1959